WHO'S THE

Slow Learner!

A Chronicle of
INCLUSION & EXCLUSION

SANDRA ASSIMOTOS MCELWEE

outskirtspress
DENVER, COLORADO

Dedication

This book is dedicated to my amazing husband Rick. You were my balance in all the times I became unbalanced. You are my rock every time I want to crumble. You are on every page of this book as you allowed me to disappear to write, and endured the piles of papers as I reviewed old IEPs and communication notebooks. You never discouraged me from this endeavor or any other I have dreamed up. The best father Sean could have, patient beyond imagination as you coach him and his friends in multiple sports. I Love you.

In Memory of
Shelley Green
Jonathan Riggs

Acknowledgements

To the Gurus of Inclusive Education, who taught me in many conferences, Dr. Richard A. Villa, Jacqueline S. Thousand, Ph.D, Dr. Mary Falvey, Richard Rosenberg, Ph.D, Norman Kunc and Paula Gardner, Ed.D, and many more; thank you for your brilliant presentations. Your hearts and tenacity to keep moving forward with all of the resistance to change that you encounter while executing systems change is admirable.

I want to thank Julie Warnick and Joyce Taylor for their steadfast support beginning at Sean's birth and continuing on to even today. Your mentorship in the Inclusion journey has been invaluable. Juda Carter your professional consultation made all the difference for Sean and myself, and gave us the basis for knowing what was truly right and wrong and that the key is in how the IEP goals are written. From the bottom of my heart I thank Sean's first grade teacher who went above and beyond to modify materials and support Sean. You didn't just make it up as you went, you truly researched and provided the right tools and ideas to help him learn in *his* way. Thank you to the kindergarten, first, and second grade teachers who had no support from the principal or the district—you pioneered with us and hung in there as we figured out everything together. To the elementary school principal and psychologist that transformed our elementary school into a model inclusive school, you were instrumental in changing the lives of so many children with and without disabilities. Their parents enjoyed stress-free IEPs due to supports already in place—thanks to you for doing the right thing for them all. To all of the elementary school teachers that Sean had, you

DEFINE the word *educator* and you all should be teaching and mentoring other teachers in the true meaning of the word *teacher*. To the fifth grade teacher—you got to know Sean better than most—your sense of humor and calling to be a teacher is a gift to all your students and their parents. To the classroom assistants, the third Independence Facilitator in Intermediate school and Sean's aide in high school—you ladies were the glue to bring all of the preparation together. Sean loved you all, and I appreciate the stealth code you used in his communication notebook to let me know when things weren't quite right. To the district inclusion specialist and inclusion facilitator – your imagination and support made the journey easier. I know how hard it was to sit and watch while your hands were tied while Sean was being discriminated against. To the high school case carrier that believed in Sean and advocated for him; thank you for always doing your best to provide opportunities for growth. Thanks go to the high school Special Day Class teacher who allowed Sean to join her class one period a day for work experience. And to the Varsity Baseball Coach who embraced Sean as a team assistant; I pray you advocate for your son and make sure he has at least as many experiences as Sean has enjoyed. To the high school principal, I am sorry you got caught in the cross-fire.

I even appreciate the educators who discriminated against Sean and spent more time and creative energy trouble-shooting how to exclude him, instead of how to include him. If it wasn't for you there would have been no story.

To the women in my Bible study who encouraged me, and laughed at the stories of Sean's creativity let me know this could have some entertainment value, I thank God for you all.

To my PTA Ladies, love the laughs we have shared, and your encouragment and acceptance was a model to both the teachers and not only your children, but all the children you touched with your volunteerism and love.

Megan Fries, you are an amazing young woman who growing up with Sean probably knows him better than most. Your assistance in editing and recommendations on this book were priceless. Thank you for being a lifelong friend to our family.

Kellie Perez and the Down Syndrome Association of Orange County, thank you for providing Sean many opportunities for volunteering and giving him the platform to shine. His self esteem has grown because of you.

Sensei Wayne and your staff of Sensei's grew Sean's sense of responsibility and self-confidence with your weekly Karate lessons, and you gave him the means to defend himself in the world, which has given us the security to allow him more freedom and independence in the community to know he can defend himself.

Kelly McKinnon without your dedication and guidance in social skills, even after Sean graduated from your class, Sean would not be the well balanced young man he is today.

To the multiple speech and language therapists that Sean had over the years, thank you for not giving up on his challenging diagnosis. Today he is understandable to most people because of your hard work and diligence. Special thanks goes to Kathleen McFarlin, Maarten Voodg, Gary Fitzpatrick, Derrick Pinnecker, Terrie Gero-Smead, Terry Brown, Amy Kendall, Todd Rolph, Briana Kather, Megan Schley, Ashley Jones, Ayden Loeffler, A.J. Borland, and Kyle Olinger, and our awesome neighbors; Bill, Pam, and Katie Schley, Rod, Michelle, Cameron and Cassie Turner, Scott, Donna and Brooke Kather, Bruce, Janine, Ethan, McKayla and McKensie Oliver.

Gratitude beyond words go to our friends, most with children with disabilities, who supported us through the trials and tribulations. You also supported me through this project. There is no way we could have ever survived without the weekly "bleacher therapy" hashing out the most recent unbelievable comments and behaviors of adults with the title "educator." Supporting each other, sharing strategies and discovering services we never knew existed while our children performed amazing feats of athleticism are times I will never forget.

To my good friend and co-advocate Kristi Golden, you endured many of the same battles at a different school. You're diplomacy amazes me and I am glad our sons are best friends.

Contents

Foreword xv

Introduction xix

    IF You Are Married .... *xxii*

    For Teachers .... *xxiii*

Sean's Education Began at 14 Days Old 1

    Having a Score Limits Opportunities to Soar 2

Preschool 6

    Back to California 12

    Little Lambs 12

    Community Advisory Committee 13

Kindergarten the First Time Around 15

    The Running Boy 17

    Neighborhood Elementary School 19

Kindergarten the Second Time Around 21

    On Behavior and Communication 26

    Assistive Technology 30

    Teaching about Down Syndrome 31

    Assess This 35

    Inclusion Is a Right—And a Philosophy of Human Existence! .. 36

    Encouraging the Educators 39

    Haircuts from Hell 40

    Giant Stuffed Winnie the Pooh 41

First Grade 44

    This Land Is Your Land 46

Teaching about Sean 47

Communication Is Key 50

Attempting Change 51

Spelling with a Sense of Humor 52

Reading with a Purpose 53

District Day Care 54

Second Grade 56

Second Grade (continued) 61

Reading, Writing, and Arithmetic 62

Day Care Again 64

Giving Back 65

Third Grade 68

Sharing Resources 72

Triennial Assessment 73

Cursive, I Presume 74

The Daily Checklist 75

After-School Activities 79

Cub Scouts 79

New Principal 79

Fourth Grade 81

School Talent Show 85

Appreciating the Angels 87

Tutors 94

Tenth-Birthday Survivor Party 94

Fifth Grade 96

Puberty 101

Orchestra 103

School Site Council 104

Science 105

Discovery 106

Sixth Grade 108

Triennial Assessment 110

Band 115

Big Anxiety 117

Students Vs. Teachers Softball Game 117

More Appreciation 118

Fast-Forward 4 Years 120

Intermediate School Saga 122

The Tour 123

Hiring Help 128

Behavior Equals Communication 129

Positive Behavior Management Plan 131

Open House 137

The Transition Meeting 139

Seventh Grade 141

From Heaven to Hell 142

Complete Lack of Cooperation Earns Compliance Complaint 149

You Can't Dance 157

Recovering Behaviorally 158

Ditching Eighth Grade 159

Buddy Sitters 160

Freshman Year 162

The Basketball, the Bagel, and the Bus Driver 165

Trailing Sean through His Day 168

Special Ed—Not So Special 172

Snack and Lunch Entertainment 173

The First Football Game 175

The Disco Dance 175

First High School IEP Meeting 177

More Issues 178

A Case of Mistaken Identity 180

The Disability Discount 181

A Huge Shock 182

Golf Team 183

Electives 185

The Dream Team 188

Photography 190

Football Assistant 190

On Safety 192

What the Law Says 194

Preparing for Sophomore Year IEP........................... 196

Summer.. 199

Sophomore Year 200

Drama about Drama 203

Drama Continues 216

Sean's Part in the Play... 220

Prima Drama's Revenge 220

Baseball Assistant.. 221

School Site Council—Insider Information 223

Social Skills Class.. 225

The R-Word 225

Winter Formal... 226

ASB Commissioner of Athletics Election 228

Giving Back... 230

Newsworthy!... 231

That Poor Disabled Boy 235

Principal Selection Committee 237

Junior Year 241

You Aren't Smart Enough to Be Elected.................... 250

Spread the Word.. 251

To Run or Not to Run... 256

Not Sean's Safety 261

Civil Rights Complaint.. 262

Resolutions 264

Real Independence Includes Transportation.............. 269

Proud AND Pissed... 270

Bleacher Therapy... 272

Senior Year 275

Ball Boy.. 277

Glee Fan Club... 280

Scrooge 281

Retalia-Shunned.. 282

Graduation Speech 287
Diploma or Certificate of Completion? 290
Graduation—Not the End, but the Beginning 291
Grad Night Accommodations 292
Social Life 294
When Inclusion Becomes Exclusion 294
Cool Club 296
Afterward 301
Hindsight Is 20/20 303
Positive vs. Punitive 305
Hope for the Future 306
Will You Carry the Torch? 307

Foreword

As parents of a son with Down syndrome, Stephen (4 years older than Sean), we read this book with great interest. *So Who's the Slow Learner?* is a chronicle of a mother's journey to bring out the best in her child with special needs, while surviving and thriving herself. Sandra reveals the joys, sorrows, rewards, failures, and the daily challenges of raising and educating a challenging child.

From infancy through adolescence, Sandra explains, often in graphic detail, how she used a mother's determination to advocate for the best available resources to help her son navigate a not-always-friendly educational system.

By reading this book and often identifying with the author, you will also learn how to use educational and occupational resources in your community that best fit the special needs of your child. Of course, every child is not like the star of this book, nor can every parent do what this mother did. Glean from this story what fits your child and your family. As you read, some pages will make you smile; others will prompt anger and sadness. Our hope is that this very personal account will encourage you to be a wiser and more informed advocate for your child.

William Sears, MD, and Martha Sears, RN
Authors of *The Successful Child: What Parents Can Do to Help Kids Turn Out Well*

Foreword

Sandra McElwee is a true testament to my favorite quote by Martin Luther King, Jr.: "Cowardice asks the question, is it safe? Expediency asks, is it polite? Vanity asks, is it popular? But conscience asks the question, is it right? And there comes a time when one must take a position that is neither safe, nor polite, nor popular—but one must take it because it's right." When a mother gives birth to a baby, there is much cause for celebration, for great anticipation, for sheer exaltation. Instead, mothers of children with Down syndrome are often presented with sheer dread, fear of the disappointments and hurdles ahead. Why? Because most, if not all, of the professionals—the doctors, nurses, genetic counselors, ultrasound technicians, etc.—never had the chance in their life to get to be friends with a guy like Sean. Sean was, and continues to be, vital to our human race. He has, and must continue, to teach us how to value and respect diversity. As a species, we are bland, monotonous, insipid, banal, and lifeless without him. Our humanity is continued to be denied the vibrancy, texture, and opportunities afforded it because of disability bigotry; because so much of society is afraid and ignorant. Whenever we have the conversation about inclusion we always hark back to civil rights issues.

Another favorite quote helps elucidate this conundrum: "Nothing in the world is more dangerous than sincere ignorance and conscientious stupidity." People of various cultural and racial backgrounds are unfamiliar and therefore feared. Even still, racial, ethnic, and gender diversity, no matter how unfamiliar, is now protected by law and little, if any, segregation is legally abided or supported. The only marginalized segment of our population in this country for which segregation is not only permitted but encouraged is that of individuals with disabilities.

Sandra McElwee chose to take a path for Sean that was neither safe, nor polite, nor popular, but was right. Moreover, when Sandra took the right path, Sean benefitted from an inclusive education that most likely led him to tolerate and succeed in spite of the period of time in which he was segregated. Although his environment made him more disabled during his time in his segregated day class, he managed to overcome those obstacles, against all odds; to rise up from the ashes of exclusion like the powerful phoenix that he is, and look forward to a future of integration with a quality of life befitting any valued, respected, worthy human being on earth.

Jan S. Weiner, Ph.D.

Introduction

Only God can turn a mess into a message, a test into a testimony, a trial into a triumph, and victim into a victory. God is Good All the Time!—Rick Warren

I was once asked why I write, and my answer was, "To educate and inspire." God gave me a son who is an inspiration. Sean was born with Down syndrome and has been a blessing from day one. He has a great sense of humor and loves people, especially girls. In this book, I chronicle his education experience, which is mostly cataloging the reactions he engenders as he finds his place in this world. Since birth, Sean has had a magnetic personality and draws amazing people toward him, and like a magnet, he is also a force to be reckoned with. He repels people who are narrow and prejudiced. Sean is very strong willed and determined, which serves him well when he is working to achieve a goal. He is also impulsive. He inherited his father's fantastic sense of humor, good looks, and athletic ability, and from me, his determination, drive, and outgoing personality . . . and inability to accept "No" as the answer to any question.

My goals for writing this book are to chronicle my son's educational experiences, and the education I subsequently received in the process. This is not a "How-to" book, but a "How we did it" book. This compilation of stories contrasts the good and the bad, the funny and the sad, the great character and poor character of the educators Sean encountered in his years of public schooling. I have interspersed stories of Sean's life experiences—they are mostly chronological—but some cover the span of many years. My hope is that parents will understand the challenges, learn the educational rights their children have, and recognize that ability does not dictate whether a student can be fully included in regular education classes or not.

I have included Sean's IEP (Individualized Education Plan) goals for each school year. I did this to demonstrate that Sean was not on track with his regular education peers, but he did make progress and learned much more than he would have had the opportunity to learn in a special education classroom. I have only listed the crux of the goal. Each goal is actually written beginning with the area of need being met, a baseline goal, then measurable goals gradually increasing over three assessment periods. The goals always end with language like, "with 80 percent accuracy in two of three trials as measured by observation and data collection." Most of the goals after seventh grade were poorly written and don't deserve to take up more paper on this earth.

Sean once told me he wanted to be a teacher. I responded, "You already are a teacher." Sean teaches people patience, tolerance, careful listening, creativity, and compassion. As for those who don't want to learn from him, he teaches me about their character if they openly reject his presence with bigoted words and actions. I particularly appreciate that lesson so I don't have to waste my time on them.

The idea for this book began when Sean was in seventh grade, and the IEP team at his intermediate school was displaying some extremely slow learning and bad behavior when they were working overtime to exclude him from regular education. I realized I had a lot more material from all of Sean's life—and many situations where I was the slow learner in relation to Sean!

At first, I really hesitated, because some of these stories could be construed as negative, and some of the character flaws of the educators could really be depressing. But there *is* humor in every situation, and there is hope, and there is an opportunity for the educators to learn what *not* to do from this documentary of human flaws. Also, parents can learn to be aware of the hidden meaning of subtle, and not so subtle, phrases made by *the professionals* and know to ask more clarifying questions to make sure they fully understand the implications of recommendations made by educators.

Another lesson I hope readers take away is that we do not need to be offended when people say and do cruel and ignorant things. Rather, we can take those situations to teach them the error of their ways and hope to open their minds in kind response. Don't deflate. Educate! It can be so easy to crumble when conflict occurs, but remember, everything you do is for the benefit of your child. Most of the educators are only temporary figures as your child moves through the educational system. But these educators will have the experience of working with you which can positively impact their interactions with other students with diverse learning needs in the future. We have a great opportunity to leave the world a better place!

I once asked a district-level special education administrator why I didn't experience the negative situations that many parents were telling me they were experiencing (this was before seventh grade). She responded, "When somebody has a concern about Sean, you listen and work *WITH* them to solve the issue at hand. Most other parents take offense to everything and feel like they have to *defend* their children's poor choices instead of working *with* everybody to create a different outcome."

We, as parents, can make things harder for our kids when we micromanage every aspect of our child's education and don't agree with every little action of the educators. This can be so annoying to the point people make rules to exclude our children because of *us*. When there is something you feel needs to be changed, there are ways of doing it. Thankfully, the parents who walked this path before us advocated effectively and now we have the Americans with Disabilities Act (ADA) and the Individuals with Disabilities Education Act (IDEA). Even the United States Department of Education's Office of Civil Rights provides the legal basis to support us and our children. But even when we have the law behind us, do not expect that educators and others will *know* the law. We may have to respectfully educate them on the law. But if they continue to ignore us, then there are ways to respond with Compliance Complaints and Civil Rights Complaints.

One big lesson I have learned is you can legislate rights, but you can't legislate attitudes. While it is our children's right to be included in a regular education class, if the educator is so fearful and set against including our children, then I have learned it is better to not force the issue with that particular teacher. The outrageous behavior some educators exhibited toward Sean were not worth the mental anguish that he experienced being in their presence.

Also, do not get overwhelmed by reading this book. I have the great ability to quickly overwhelm, and I want you to know, Sean is my only child, I have a ton of energy, and an incredible husband that is on the same page as I am on everything. I know when you are on your own, or you don't share the same philosophies with your spouse, everything becomes harder. You aren't just battling the *system,* but the battles can start at home—and home should always be a place of refuge and comfort, not strife and contention.

Every obstacle can be viewed as an opportunity or a stumbling block—and I see this as an opportunity to learn and be aware of some outdated or prejudicial ideas that people may still have. And I pray you never encounter any of the negatives, but can savor the positives and recognize when all is awesome . . . How sweet it is!

IF You Are Married

It is critical that both parents be on the same page in philosophy and beliefs. It is very easy for the educators to *divide and conquer* when it comes to educational decisions, and be very careful you don't *divide* to the point of a permanent marital divide. They particularly will use this tactic when a divorce is already present. Remember Hillary Clinton's famous line, "It takes a village"? Well, it certainly does. Seek support from parents who have traveled this path. Discuss what your plans are before IEP meetings and know that decisions do not have to be made on the spot. It is acceptable to schedule another meeting and allow yourself time to discuss matters in private and research answers outside of the meetings. Make huge attempts to not disagree in front of the educators (or your children). This chink in the marital armor is all some need to move their agenda forward. Nurture your relationships. Untended fires soon become a pile of ashes.

For Teachers

This is Sean's story; a story of how his inclusion was done right, and how his exclusion was done wrong—not a "how to" book. This is from my perspective, and as an educator, you may not agree with many of my observations and opinions.

One thing you need to know about people with Down syndrome. They may not be able to tell you what they are feeling and thinking. But please know that they *CAN* tell what *YOU* are thinking and feeling. And they will react to your feelings in kind if you are kind, and with unbelievable acting out if they know you don't want them or accept them. There's a sixth sense on who is an angel and who is an avoider implanted in the twenty-first chromosome. People with Down syndrome also have incredible memories and won't forget what negative things have happened to them and will remember something that happened in the past and react as though it happened just this moment and you won't know why they, all of a sudden, are angry or upset. You may think it's because of something that just happened when, really, it happened a month ago. They remembered it, and had the same emotional response as they did when it actually happened.

The question is—will you *ENDURE* having a student with a disability in your class? OR, will you *EMBRACE* the opportunity to grow and learn? What you learn about teaching a student with a disability will help you teach all of your students. All of your students will benefit by learning acceptance, respect, and to value and be unafraid of people with disabilities. Your students are the future teachers, coworkers, managers, physicians, parents, and, hopefully, friends of people with disabilities. Simply being in class with children who are differently abled may inspire their future more than you can know. Will you step up to the challenge of inclusion? Will you step out of the box and grow and allow *ALL* of your students the benefits of inclusion?

To the teachers who got it right: You are the wind beneath my wings. As my inspiration, you gave me the strength to keep going when the going got tough later on. I wish all children could have teachers as amazing as you are. You accepted Sean even though he acted unacceptable many times. And I truly appreciate how you worked with me in problem solving and didn't discount any suggestions that I had.

Sean's Education Began at 14 Days Old

Passionate hearts committed to a shared vision can accomplish the impossible.
—Byrd Baggett

On the day Sean was born, the hospital social worker gave us a phone number to the local Down Syndrome Association. I didn't know why I should call them, but I did, and what a blessing. I was assigned an amazing mentor parent. She had a daughter with Down syndrome who was 2 and had adopted an infant son who also had Down syndrome.

Since Sean had been 9 pounds 3 ounces and stuck in my birth canal for 3 hours I had earned a C-section. Actually I begged for one after 3 hours of pushing. Sean also had ingested meconium, and was born with pneumonia because of his long visit in the birth canal. He was stuck in the NICU on IV antibiotics for the first 10 days of his life. When we sprang him from the hospital, I was ready to get out, but was still unable to drive due to the C-section.

At the ripe young age of 14 days old, my mentor drove Sean and me to *The Infant Group Program* in Laguna Beach, California. The program was perfect for us—a Mommy-and-Me-style program where you went station to station to a physical therapist, a speech therapist, and an occupational therapist. The program empowered parents and taught us how to teach our children—so we could perform the exercises at home every day, all day, so our children could learn and develop faster. Performing the therapy exercises improved muscle strength, and most of our kids walked earlier than children in other therapy programs that performed therapy weekly and didn't include teaching the parents the various exercises. The speech therapist worked on feeding and oral motor, a precursor to speech. The sessions began with Circle Time, singing and signing songs. By the time they were 1 year old, most of our kids knew the signs to all the songs. Sean loved Circle Time.

After the therapy stations were all visited, the babies took a break and some sweet grandmothers from the Assistance League would feed and play with them while we had a 1-hour group discussion time. This time was led by a licensed clinical psychologist. During the discussion time, they provided us with information on our children's rights and what we would be encountering as we transitioned into the school district at age 3. When Sean was only 3 months old, they hosted a speaker who educated us on inclusive education, which was a recently won right in Special Education Law. Learning early what to expect was key to being prepared for the transition at age 3.

Having a Score Limits Opportunities to Soar

Never say Never and Never accept Never from anybody else. — Me

When Sean was just a tiny baby I was warned by my mentor to never allow any IQ testing. I was curious as to why not, and her response was, "What's your IQ?" Well, I have no idea. And most of us don't unless we're Mensa material.

So, I asked for clarification. "Good point. But what's the reason for *not* having Sean's IQ tested?"

She told me that in our school district the score would be an albatross around Sean's neck his entire school career. She mockingly said, "Why bother teaching him to read? His IQ is sooo low. Why does he need to know addition? He *can't* learn that because his IQ is so low." She explained it would greatly limit his ability to be exposed to curriculum that he *could possibly* learn and simply limit his opportunities.

Sean's sense of humor was developing. At the Early Intervention Program, he would frequently choose the wrong answer just to be funny (and to get more attention). He would get this smirk on his face and just do the wrong thing on purpose. Today, he's the funniest person I know, but to channel that sense of humor to work for you and not against you is a huge challenge . . . but more on this later.

When Sean transitioned from his Early Intervention Program to the school district preschool program, he was assessed by the therapists who had worked with him for the previous 2 years and 10 months. He trusted and loved these therapists and performed for them wonderfully. His assessment scores were extremely accurate.

His age equivalent development was scored:

Gross Motor: 2.9 years
Fine Motor: 1.11 years
Cognition: 2.10 years
Receptive Language: 2.10 years
Expressive Language: 1.5 years

Back in the day, the *old* labels included, "Trainable Mentally Retarded" and "Educable Mentally Retarded." They came up with these labels based on the IQ score—could the child be *trained* to perform rote tasks, or could the child benefit from *some* education?

The school district wanted to perform their own assessments of Sean. I wanted to know *why*, since they had a very reliable, detailed report from the Early Intervention Program staff. But they wanted to see where to *appropriately place* him in their *segregated school.*

We were about to move to Washington State for a yearlong project Sean's father was being assigned to. I had been advised to go there with an IEP in hand, because without it, we risked a potential 60-day delay in starting his services. So I played along with the school district's assessment desires and brought Sean to the segregated school site to be assessed.

The woman doing the assessing was assuring me she knew "Down's kids" well. I was already on the side of People First Language and her referring to Sean as a "Down's kid" turned me off immediately. People First Language aims to avoid subconscious dehumanization when discussing people with disabilities. The basic idea is to name the person first, and the condition second. The disability is not the identity of the person being referred to. For this woman to describe Sean in a pool of *all* "Down's kids," she was showing her prejudice that she already had low expectations without seeing him as an individual with his own strengths.

To perform the assessment she took Sean into this relatively small room, with a little table and shelves and shelves and shelves of toys. SO MANY TOYS SO LITTLE TIME! Sean was thrilled to be in there! And then he saw it. The apple of his eye. The thrill of his heart. A HUGE Purple Dinosaur! BARNEY!!!!!! The Barney doll was on the third shelf, a little high for Sean to reach, so being the acute problem solver that he is, he began to climb the shelf! Oh, what an animal he must have looked like; so unruly, so uncontrollable, so single-minded. *All* he wanted was BARNEY! His assessment was supposed to last 1 hour. Forty minutes later, she emerged, exasperated and satisfied. Yes, this boy was severely retarded.

I then asked for a tour of all the preschool classes in the district— the ones on the *regular campus*. We were only going to be gone a year so I wanted to gather information for when we returned. The district representative gave me a tour of the segregated school site and told me, "This is the best placement for Sean." The class where Sean would be placed contained children who didn't walk yet. I observed a teacher working with the children on a huge air mattress, turning on a very loud motorized pump that blew the mattress up. (The students were sitting "on" the mattress and the point was to stay balanced and sitting instead of falling over as the air filled the mattress.) As the mattress filled she yelled over the sound of the pump, "Uuuup." Then she let the air out, and the mattress deflated, and she said in a normal tone of voice, "Doowwwnnn." Sean would not have been impressed with this ride after 2 years of Disney Annual Passes. I thanked her for her opinion but said I needed to see the other sites too. One class was specifically for students with speech delays. That class seemed the best to me since speech was Sean's greatest challenge. They also used sign language in this class, and I had been signing with Sean since he was born. Sean knew well over 100 signs and was able to communicate best with sign, since his articulation was pretty unintelligible. We scheduled the IEP.

Sean's father, Rick, and I went to the IEP meeting. The *professionals* told us we were making a mistake on choosing the class that focused on speech. Then they tried to attach a label to his IEP.

A little on labels—you actually need a label for the school district to qualify for additional special education funding from the federal government. *But* the actual label doesn't come with more or less funds; they come with the same amount of funds.

With Sean's lack of cooperation on the testing, he was certain to have tested in the "trainable mentally retarded" area—if we had approved an IQ test.

There is also a *qualification* titled *Other Health Impaired* and that was the box I asked them to check off. My justification was that they didn't *know* he was mentally retarded since he had not had an IQ test, so selecting *Other Health Impaired*—then filling in the blank with "Down syndrome," was the most appropriate categorization for him. Then the administrator looked at me in all seriousness and said, "You are in denial. You have to face the fact that Sean is mentally retarded." I wanted to jump across the table. It took all of my powers of self-control to not yell, "We're moving, so thank God I don't have to deal with you!" They wanted to limit Sean from the beginning. We wanted to give him opportunities—we knew that Sean would show them all.

Preschool

A truly happy person is one who can enjoy the scenery on a detour.—Unknown

As Sean was turning 3 Rick was transferred to a 1-year project in Eastern Washington State. Specifically the Tri-Cities area, to manage a project at Hanford Nuclear Reservation—established in 1943 as part of the Manhattan Project, the first full-scale plutonium production reactor in the world—plutonium manufactured at this site was used in the first nuclear bomb detonated over Nagasaki, Japan, and today, Hanford is the most contaminated nuclear site in the U.S. . . . the focus of the nation's largest environmental cleanup and is full of scientists.

As we met the locals, we realized there were two types of locals. There were people who were there for projects at Hanover, and there were farmers. The farmers were there to stay; EVERYBODY else was on temporary projects, and here's how the first meeting would go. "Hi, it's nice to meet you. How long will you be here for?" When my answer was 1 year, the 5-year people were polite, but not interested in investing time to get to know somebody who would be here and gone too soon! I tried with, "We live near Disneyland, and have a guest room." But even that bribery didn't work. So, I was extremely lonely and didn't realize how precious my support network in OC was till then.

Coincidentally, we rented a house two doors down from a family who had a 6-year-old son with Down syndrome. But as we got to know them better, we realized he also had autism and was nonverbal. I became friends with his mother, and we babysat for each other occasionally.

When we moved into our house we ordered a second phone line, subscribed to a dial-up Internet service, and joined the Internet explosion! It was late 1996, and I had heard about this Down syndrome Internet discussion listserv where there were a lot of parents with kids with Down syndrome sharing info and supporting one another.

Thank God for that dial-up, slow connection and all. It was my connection to the support I so desperately needed! I am still connected to the core group of parents on that listserv today and also subscribed to "splinter" e-mail and Facebook groups that developed for specific topics.

This year was my "Paul" year. My year of exile . . . And I didn't realize it until later, years later . . . but the prison of loneliness was the time I needed to write, create, and think. And research inclusive education to prepare for our return to California.

Sean attended the local district preschool. The town had a population of 36,000 people, and this preschool of 3 to 5 year olds had 120 students—and 105 of them were diagnosed with autism. Many of their parents were nuclear scientists, their kids all rode the bus, and I never met their parents. They didn't send a little bus either. It was the regular-sized yellow school bus. I believed since I was a stay-at-home mom, I should drive my child to school. That way I could talk to the teachers every day, and if any behavior issues arose, help them troubleshoot and solve them immediately before any bad habits started. Sean, on the other hand, saw the bus as a Disney ride.

It was no problem taking him *to* school—but leaving—wow, that became a fight! He would see the other kids getting on the bus, and he would point and cry, "Buh! Buh!" over and over . . . and after a few days, he started to throw himself on the ground, crying and screaming, "Buh, buh, buh." So, I decided I would drive him TO school and let him take the bus home! It was the beginning of my picking my battles and knowing what to fight and what not to fight. It was a long school day—8 A.M. till 1, then an hour on the bus. He wasn't home till 2! He was usually exhausted and took a nap too. I had a lot of time to surf—the Internet, that is.

The listserv was my daily bread. I logged on as soon as I got home from taking Sean to school. On slow days, it was like my friends had abandoned me. On busy days, there could be as many as 50 posts to read! And answer! And it was slow going . . . that dial-up . . . *wow, back in the olden days, it used to take 10 minutes to log on to the Internet.* Kind of like how my mom walked 10 miles in the snow to school . . . barefoot . . . right? I spent the entire year immersing myself into inclusive education, education law, experiences others shared, all to prepare myself for the return to California.

Sean's speech was way behind his cognition. The words were in there, he just couldn't make them come out. He had been diagnosed with apraxia of speech, and he was born deaf in his right ear and had also been given the diagnosis of auditory processing disorder. In Washington, the state-funded services were more generous than in California. With these two diagnoses, Sean qualified for DAILY 30-minute speech therapy with a private therapist paid for by the state! The therapist was great. She couldn't get 30 minutes of attention out of Sean to do one thing so she changed it up a lot and made it into a game. His articulation was getting better, and my *translation skills* were also improving . . . But we had a long way to go.

As I did when Sean was younger, I just decided on what to make for dinner without consulting Sean. I didn't consider he might have a preference for what he wanted to eat. He started throwing the food back at me. At first, I thought he was just being a brat. But finally, I realized he was trying to tell me, "I don't want to eat *THAT!*"

I realized this the day he kept going to the cabinet and pulling out the box of Rice Krispies cereal. I thought, *Oh, you want some cereal.* I put some Cheerios in a cup for him. He ate his Cheerios, then went back to the cabinet and pulled out the Rice Krispies box again. So, I gave him some more Cheerios in a cup to eat. He ate them, but then went back to the cabinet and once again pulled out the Rice Krispies. He was so exasperated at what a slow learner I was that he mustered up all he had to get the word out, pointed to the box, and emphatically yelled, "TEET!"

Ohhh! "You want Rice Krispies Treats!" DUH! So I dropped everything and rewarded that hard fought word by making him a pan of Rice Krispies Treats.

While Sean attended the district's special education preschool, I sought out a typical preschool. I found a Montessori school located at a Catholic church and decided to enroll him there 2 days a week. He would attend the special ed program Monday, Wednesday, and Friday, and Montessori on Tuesday and Thursday. I waited a couple of weeks, then went in to observe Sean in the Montessori preschool. (I was hiding behind a bookshelf, with a few books removed to peek through so he didn't see me.)

The two schools had very different philosophies. The special ed school let the kids pull out all the toys, trash the room, then, at the end of the day, spend 30 minutes or more putting it back together again. Montessori School required the students take a carpet square, lay it on the floor, then take one toy at a time and play with that one toy on the carpet square, and then return the toy to its rightful place before selecting another toy. These two practices were incredibly contradictory.

I observed Sean take a carpet square, play with a toy, then another boy decided he wanted to play with that toy and Sean let him. Sean then went to the paint easel. I was absolutely thrilled to see all the steps he followed:

1. He found the apron and put it on
2. He selected a paintbrush
3. He selected 2 containers with 2 colors of paints
4. He put the paints on the shelf of the easel
5. He began to paint!

I wanted to cheer from behind the bookcase! Those were a lot of steps, and the only way he had learned it was by being there, observing, and following the directions! But out of the corner of my eye ran a teacher to stop Sean. "No! No! There's no paper, Sean!" I was too far away to see that minor detail. Nobody had placed paper on the easel, and he was just painting the white surface. And in Montessori, if you make a mess, you clean it up. So, Sean had to get a bucket of water and a sponge and clean the paint off of the easel. *Then* the teacher put paper on it, but by then, he was *done* with that activity.

As he returned to the carpet square area, the other teacher chastised him. "Sean, didn't you have this toy out? You need to put it up."

I signaled the teacher and asked, "Umm . . . Excuse me, but if another kid wants to play with the toy, does Sean have to put the toy away, then let the other kid get it from the shelf? Sean didn't forget it. Another kid played with it after him . . ."

And then snack time came. Another amazing moment. Each student was given a cookie and a glass of juice. Then they prayed. Sean actually sat there with his little hands clasped and waited to eat that cookie till "Amen" was spoken.

He stayed in the school for another month, but each day that I picked him up, they peppered me with stories of his inability to perform the tasks *perfectly*. Sean became frustrated and started throwing himself on the floor and crying, and then he wouldn't go into the class one day. Not only was it confusing to have two sets of rules, the Montessori teachers were losing patience with him, and he felt their disapproval. They were stringent and not very nice and 3 year olds should never be exposed to mean people. I was so excited by all he was learning there, but they just never gave him positive reinforcement, just plenty of negative feedback. And I was paying for this? I decided he needed to experience success at school, so he continued the year at the special education preschool 5 days a week.

Sean's physical therapy, occupational therapy, and speech therapy were provided at the special education preschool. If I had pulled him out for a full-inclusion preschool, he would have lost those services. At that time, school districts didn't provide preschool classes for typical students, so there was little opportunity for inclusion in public schools for preschool. The school did have a "reverse mainstreaming" program, where typical children were in the classes most of each day in addition to the special education students. Through the reverse mainstreaming program, Sean was having the opportunity to model appropriate behavior.

Sean learned to recognize his name and the names of his classmates. At the beginning of class, the students put up their lunch boxes, hung up their coats, and then went to a table where each student's name tag consisted of a photo on one side of a laminated strip of construction paper and their written name was on the other side. The name side was up, and the students would turn over each name tag. Then when they found their photo, they would insert it into a plastic sleeve on the wall—this was their daily roll call. By the end of the year, Sean could find his name, without turning it over and looking at the picture. I came to volunteer in class one day and the teacher told me that Sean could read all the student's names. She tested him and asked him to hand her Tom's name, and he picked up Tom's name tag and handed it to her, photo side down. She kept going until he had handed her all eight students' name tags. Sean was 3 years old and sight reading already.

One weekend we attended a local festival. There was this children's singing and dancing group performing and Sean went nuts. He communicated by pointing at them and saying. *"DAT!"* Then he pointed at himself and said, *"ME DO!"* No question he was letting us know that he wanted to join this group.

I called the director of the children's group and explained that Sean was 3, had Down syndrome, was deaf in one ear, could barely talk, and could not carry a tune. Before I could finish my pitiful description she stopped me. "None of that matters. I have many special children in the Sunshine Generation. Bring him to rehearsal." Sean rehearsed every week and performed about once a month with the Sunshine Generation, kind of singing and definitely dancing—he had all the moves down! After every performance, people sought us out and commented on how Sean had touched their hearts. He inspired many. His purpose was found—to inspire and encourage.

Back to California

Look at life through the windshield, not the rearview mirror.—Byrd Baggett

We moved back to California the following fall. Sean started in the "speech-based" preschool class we had selected before we left. His school day was quite a bit shorter than it was in Washington. Sean went from 8:30 till 11:30, Monday through Friday. So I decided to put him a private preschool program on Tuesday and Thursday afternoons. He would arrive there in time for lunch and stay till 5. He would take a nap there, have a snack, and play. We had the best of both worlds.

Little Lambs

Nobody cares if you can't dance well. Just get up and dance.—Unknown

After leaving the Sunshine Generation, Sean still wanted to perform, so I put him in the children's choir at our church, The Little Lambs, who would perform usually for 30 minutes, and about 20 minutes into the performance, he would sit down on the risers, but still sing his heart out . . . mispronouncing every word and completely off-key. (They just kept the microphones away from him.)

The Christmas show was coming, and Sean was chosen to play one of the Three Kings. There was a dress rehearsal, but somehow the Angel in the cast never rehearsed with her wings on.

The performance culminated during church. In front of 3,000 people, the Little Lambs Choir began their songs, Sean and the cast members were dressed and ready for their cue. Joseph and Mary holding the Baby Jesus sat behind the manger, and the Angel presided next to them. Then the Kings made their grand entrance with their gifts. And then Sean noticed it. The Angel had on wings! He was enthralled and couldn't stop staring at her wings, the expression on his face was priceless . . . and then he had to touch them, to see what they felt like! The congregation was rolling on the floor laughing at his wonder at those wings!

After their performance was done, they quickly removed their costumes to reveal their choir shirts underneath and joined the rest of the choir for the next song. But Sean decided he was still a King. Instead of going to his place on the riser, he joined the choir director, standing by her side, and imitating her every arm movement as she directed the choir! Once again, the congregation became Holy Rollers with laughter!

Community Advisory Committee

Never doubt that a small group of thoughtful, committed citizens can change the world; indeed, it's the only thing that ever has. —Margaret Mead.

I began attending the Community Advisory Committee for the Special Education Local Plan Area (CAC—SELPA) meetings when Sean was in preschool. This was a committee of parents, special education administrators, and teachers from collaborating school districts in our area. It didn't take me much time to realize this committee was a *do-nothing* committee. I had been attending school board meetings as well and discovered that the school board didn't even know the CAC existed, or its purpose. The main purpose of this committee is to edit the Local Plan for Special Education to bring the districts into accordance with the state laws as they changed. This was due every 3 years. We also revised the bylaws that would be included as a part of the Local Plan for Special Education. So until the third year when the Local Plan review was due, it was simply the special ed directors reporting on what was happening in their districts.

I found being a member of this committee beneficial because I had access to our district's special education director at every meeting and could get a feel for her thoughts and beliefs on inclusion. I would like to say I built a relationship with her, but I did not. But I built an awareness with her. She was aware of my beliefs and that we intended on including Sean in elementary school. I also was able to meet parents whose children were at other schools in each of the three districts, and the ones who were in our district we were able to collaborate with for many years to come.

As the chairperson for the Parent Education Committee, I convinced the CAC that we needed to create a parent survey for all three school districts' parents to learn what parent education programs they wanted. It took 4 years to get a parent education program on the calendar. We also developed a parent handbook to help guide parents of children with special needs, and we identified the topics parents wanted to learn about for a parent education series.

The Parent Education Committee had no budget, but the districts gave us printing and mailing services, rooms to hold the sessions in, and refreshments for the attendees. I had to find seven speakers who would present for *free*—and I found six! I also discovered Norman Kunc was going to be in the area on one of our set dates, and I petitioned for a stipend to pay his fee, and it was granted.

The titles for the parent education sessions included: Building Teamwork and Trust, Positive Behavior Strategies, Exploring Inclusion Together, Facilitating Friendships, My Child Is Moving Up, Now What? (Transition) Help! My Child Is Struggling, What Do I Do? (Designed for parents whose children may not have a diagnosis.) Making Curriculum Work (modifying curriculum). We had banner attendance, and the evaluations of the programs were extremely positive.

The series was a success. Although I had delegated a member of the Community Advisory Committee to be in charge of each of the sessions I burned out. From the beginning of creating the surveys to the end of the speaker series took 5 years. I later dropped off the committee because it was back to being a *do-nothing* committee and I needed to put my energy elsewhere. But by being involved, the director of special education knew I knew the laws and was not afraid to use them. This was important for future battles we would face.

Kindergarten the First Time Around

We have to change the way people think before we can change the way they act. Altering perceptions is like breaking a stone with drops of water. It can be done, if you're willing to take the time. — Paul Daugherty

Sean's preschool teacher in the speech-based preschool decided to teach kindergarten the following year so she was Sean's special education kindergarten teacher too. Because I volunteered frequently in her class and she had Sean for 2 years we became close. She was a great woman who had a *tough love* attitude that made all the difference in the world with Sean. She didn't put up with his teasing, but then she also didn't *punish* him for being himself. She had an uncanny way of stopping a behavior before it became a habit. Sean tried kicking his shoes off as an avoidance technique when he was asked to hold a crayon and draw or color anything. She asked my permission first, and I agreed to allow her to use clear packing tape and taped his shoes to his pants (loosely so there was no circulation cut off). She only had to do it twice, and then he stopped trying that trick. He tried again in regular education kindergarten, and I sent him to school with his shoes taped onto his pants the next day, and he stopped immediately.

We had made the decision that Sean would be repeating kindergarten at our neighborhood school in a regular education class. I shared with the teacher that Sean would need an aide, and that it needed to be written on his IEP. She confided in me about a week before the IEP that the district director of special education was not allowing her to include an aide—she even said, "The director told me if he can't keep up with the regular education students he doesn't deserve to be in a regular education class."

Riiggghhhttt . . .

I wrote a letter insisting that the director of special education be present at Sean's IEP, and if she was not available that day, we would reschedule. She attended, and when it came time for the aide, she explained that the district had a policy against one-on-one aides for students with disabilities, but they could provide a *classroom assistant* who would be available to help all the students in the class. I agreed that would be acceptable, and she simply wrote it into the IEP! No questions, no further discussion! Sean's teacher was so angry. The director was throwing her under the bus, setting her up for a big argument with me. My big lesson that day was to always have the person who makes the decisions at Sean's IEPs. For future meetings, the director of special education sent one of her staff members, a special education administrator, and we never had to do any back and forth with the school staff . . . till much later.

As the IEP meeting was winding down, the school psychologist, Mrs. Sunshine, felt compelled to try to talk me out of this foreign idea of *inclusion*. "Are you sure this is what you want to do? Do you think he will learn as much in a regular class? What if he doesn't want to come in from recess? Do you think the other students will accept him?"

Thank God for that boring year in Washington—I had all the answers. "This is definitely what I want. Sean will learn more than he would in a special ed class—simply because he'll be exposed to more. And there are a lot of studies showing the benefits for the regular education students. If he refuses to come in from recess, the aide can deal with him so the teacher isn't taken away from the other students. The other students will see Sean as a classmate." Remember this conversation for a future chapter.

The Running Boy

Do what you can, with what you have, where you are.—Teddy Roosevelt

When Sean finally walked at 22 months, it only took a few weeks for him to start running . . . Running away, running toward traffic, running through shoppers' legs at the mall—who thought, he was so *cute*. I frantically chased him, unable to fit through the shoppers' legs myself and panicking as he got further and further away from me. Nobody ever stopped him for me!

He ran out of class at school. We lost him once in the Chicago O'Hare airport between flights! He ran away any time he could.

I finally asked the psychologist from his Early Intervention Program how to get him to stop running. She said, "Don't chase him." Hmmm . . . tempting, but I would probably be in big trouble if I stood by as he ran in front of a car in the grocery store parking lot and was killed or maimed beyond recognition! She then suggested we go to a *safe* place and when he ran, not chase him.

Well, that took a lot of thinking to come up with a *safe* place. I'm a pretty slow runner, and when he got enough of a head start on me, there's no catching him!

One day I realized that the stores in our mall don't open till 11 A.M. on Sundays, BUT you can go into the mall center and walk. So, one Sunday, when Sean was 4, I drove over, and let my husband out in the middle of the mall (if Sean was going to run and I couldn't catch him then he'd be there to stop him before he got completely away).

Sean and I went to the far end of the mall and walked inside.

We only took about 5 steps before he took off—and I ducked into the doorway of one of the closed stores and hid. I could see him through the glass display window, but he couldn't see me. He ran and ran, then started looking back with an expression that took me by surprise—he was laughing, smiling, and had his "I got you!" mischievous look on his face! The little stinker thought this was a fun game, and I realized he was getting an endorphin rush from being chased.

He finally realized that not only was I not chasing him—I was nowhere to be seen! He stopped, turned around and around, then sat down and cried . . . and I let him cry for about 2 minutes. (That's a long time to hide in a doorway letting your child cry—but I was pretty sick of chasing him all the time.)

I finally emerged from the doorway and said, "Sean, you were lost. I couldn't find you. Stay with me and you won't be lost again." We walked to almost the middle of the mall, and he took off again. I ducked inside a doorway once more, he dropped to the ground, cried, and I once again explained that he needed to stay with me so he wouldn't be lost.

I thought we would have to visit the mall for a few more Sundays before he learned this lesson. But it was easier than that! The next day we were in a fabric store, and he was staying with me the entire way . . . *following ME!* It was the most pleasant shopping experience I had had in years! I turned a corner and for a minute was out of his sight and he immediately began to cry! WHOO-HOO! HE finally CARED that I wasn't there!

Now, I'd love to say he never ran again—but EVERY time he encountered a new situation—a new teacher, aide, babysitter, etc., he would *test* them and run. If they *DID NOT* chase him, then he didn't do it again, but if they did, then he would play the game. Then the hard part was teaching them not to chase him.

At school we asked them not to chase him when he would run out of class. And he ran out of class a lot in kindergarten and first grade. The protocol was when he would bolt out of the room, the aide would go to the window to see which direction he was going. The little stinker would get outside and stand waiting for them to come after him, and when the door didn't open he would go back into the room and sit back in his seat like nothing ever happened.

I have to remind everybody that it takes two to play the game. If you simply don't play, the fun is gone and the game ends.

Neighborhood Elementary School

The true realist is the person who sees things both as they are, and as they can be. In every situation there is the possibility of improvement; in every life the hidden capacity for something better. — Lester B. Pearson

To prepare for regular education kindergarten at our neighborhood school, I called the principal in April the year before Sean would be attending and asked for a meeting. He wanted to know why I was requesting a meeting. So I explained that I had created a video and written a letter that I would like him to have the kindergarten teachers pass around so one of them could decide if she wanted to be Sean's teacher the next year.

He was not sure about inclusion; he had never done this before. He told me about the different things he had heard about doing "inclusion." "What if he has a behavior issue? What if he doesn't want to come in from the playground? The teacher can't be strapped with one child and neglect the other students."

I sympathized with him. "I realize this is new to your school, but it's not a new concept. Also, Sean will have an aide, and she can be the one to deal with him if there's a behavior issue, so the teacher doesn't have to be distracted from the other students."

He told me to just stop in, and, of course, he wasn't in the office when I did. I learned from other parents that he was 3 years away from retirement and that was discouraging. I was afraid he might be way too old to change his ways . . . I HAD to have a teacher that *wanted* Sean since it was apparent I was not going to have a principal that would support inclusion. I had a copy of the National Down Syndrome Society's Study on Inclusive Education and the number-one success factor in inclusion was the teacher's willingness to have the student with Down syndrome in their class.

The reason I made the video (that included an interview with his current kindergarten teacher AND her complete honesty in what kind of accommodations he would need) was to alleviate any potential fear. Fear of the unknown is the biggest detractor. I had also included cute photos and a video of Sean performing and being cute.

The next evening the perfect teacher called! She almost made me cry she was so wonderful and so accepting. "I believe all children should be educated together! I would be honored to have your son in my class. I will do the best I can to educate him." Wow, she got it!!

Kindergarten the Second Time Around

We must have the freedom to dream, the courage to risk, the faith to believe, and the will to succeed.—Byrd Baggett

In special education, the IEP goals were not so individualized. They were pretty standard for what the entire class was working on. For inclusion, we helped to write the goals each year specific to Sean's needs, and sometimes used language that facilitated Sean's inclusion. Our school district had guidelines for each grade that listed the standards for each area of learning for each grade. We requested these guidelines each year and used them as a basis for Sean's IEP goals.

Sean's Kindergarten IEP Goals:

Hold scissors correctly and make snips in paper.

Attempt to draw a person, including head, legs, eyes, arms, mouth (stick figure, OK).

Exhibit a tripod grasp on a writing utensil.

Button and unbutton.

Imitate a horizontal line and circle.

Initiate wiping chin (when drooling).

Complete a standing long jump.

Catch a ball.

Follow verbal directions—i.e., put the item beside, above, below, etc.

Point to the correct picture representing the pronouns *he, it* and *they*.

Demonstrate understanding of sequence and closure (first/last).

Will follow verbal/visual directions of two to three tasks; i.e., get lunch out and line up, get your backpack and jacket, then sit down.

Repeat a number of animal sounds in sequence.

Appropriately respond to *"wh"* questions involving *"why"* questions using pictures or object cues.

Match letters by placing the letters on top of matched letters.

Make the sound and show the gesture of the zoo phonics letters.

Point when asked to seven colors.

Match uppercase letter to lowercase letters.

Point to common safety symbols showing correct corresponding meaning.

Model appropriate peer behavior during free time in the classroom setting.

Reduce the frequency of disrupting other students who are trying to work, listen, etc., to no more than four times per day.

Participate in an activity for 10 minutes engaging cooperatively.

Use one word to solve problems, e.g., no, don't, please, mine.

Respond to teacher request with one to two reminders from an adult.

Share something weekly during "share" time.

Transition between activities with the help of a "peer buddy."

Join in play and play cooperatively with one or two children for 15 minutes with appropriate behavior.

Work with an adult by doing an activity for 5 minutes with minimal prompting from the adult to stay on task and finish.

Choose a free-time activity and participate.

Relate a picture to a story.

At random identify numbers to 20.

Participate in basic scientific investigation, recording changes, processes of sequence picture prompts.

Move from front to back of a book in sequence.

Know that print is read from left to right.

Sequence three story events.

Correctly ID days of the week and date on a calendar with the assistance of one to two cues.

The first day of kindergarten I was apprehensive. Were the other parents going to like Sean? Were the other kids going to like Sean? Was Sean going to act like he always does with new people? The other parents were wonderful and accepting. Half the class came to Sean's birthday party the following month. The moms stayed for the party, and I got to know them better. I almost cried when two of them thanked me for having Sean in their child's class. They saw the benefit—they saw their children changing in good ways.

I kept in communication with his teacher and classroom assistant; here is one of the first letters I wrote to them after volunteering in class and observing Sean one day:

September 25, 1999
Dear Teacher and Classroom Assistant,

I want to write you both to discuss some concerns I have about Sean's behavior that I observed on Friday.

You both are doing a good job with him, but I want to try to explain his behaviors that need to be controlled. He tests every new person he comes in contact with to find out his boundaries.

Sean has been involved in many activities in his short life, including multiple therapies, Sunday school, gymnastics, choir, soccer, baseball, Indian Guides, and recently, day care, and at one time, he attended the district preschool and a private preschool at the same time. In EVERY situation he has tested the instructors. So he isn't doing anything new in testing you both. And he isn't doing any new behaviors that we haven't dealt with in the past.

Sean's one consistent pattern is he will keep pushing and keep pushing until he finds the limits. That is why it is SO important that the limits be set immediately. He will only escalate, and the behaviors he is able to get away with in one situation will carry over to other situations. I can tell you many stories about him "getting away" with inappropriate behaviors and how it took 3 or 4 months to get him BACK to the way he should have behaved on the first day. I truly don't want this to be the case in any school classroom situation. He has started crawling under the dining table at home, which leads me to believe this has been happening a lot at school.

I need to know about all of his behaviors so I can help you both in the techniques that work the best with Sean.

The examples I observed on Friday were:

During cutting, he didn't want to finish, so he kicked his shoes off. This is a great avoidance technique that he uses to divert attention to getting his shoes back on and takes the attention from what he is supposed to be doing—cutting—And he succeeds in avoiding cutting. In this situation, it doesn't matter if his shoes are on to sit and cut, so ignore the shoes till he is done, then he has to retrieve them and put them on (still needs a little help with shoes) before he can do anything else. If the other children are leaving for the next activity and he is late because of putting his shoes on, he won't want to try this again. I will send him with his shoes taped on for a few days; this worked very well last year in stopping this behavior.

After he removed his shoes and didn't get any attention for that, he left the table and wanted to be chased. Unless he is running toward the street, NEVER chase Sean. This is a game that I pray never starts again. He used to ALWAYS bolt and thought it was hysterical to see me chase him. He still thinks it is funny to be chased. It is better to yell to him to "STOP," and if that doesn't work, then yell "SIT DOWN." I am saying "yell" because he is really fast and you will not be close enough to say it quietly.

I started to go after Sean when he left the table, but I saw the "I'm going to run" look on his face and decided to leave him at the end of the table for a few minutes. Many times he will return to where he is supposed to be, but in this case, he stayed at the end of the table. I walked down to him and said, "Sean, you have a choice. You may finish your work or take a time-out. What do you want—work or time-out?" He said, "Work." And he went back to his seat.

Remember that negative attention is just as important to Sean as positive, so if he gets positive for good behavior, then he will continue the good behavior. Time-outs work great, but if the very act of removing him gives him the attention he wants, then that won't work. The best tack is to establish a "time-out" chair or area in advance, showing him that's where he will go when he breaks a rule, and then when he does break a rule just say, "You need a time-out," and have him go there. After a while, just threatening a time-out if he doesn't stop the behavior will work miracles.

Never discipline him with a smile on your face. Body language is clearer to him than the spoken word, due to his visual communications being stronger than his auditory communications.

I am sending a notebook that I would greatly appreciate his aide writing in each day that Sean does something inappropriate. That way, I can communicate a way to deal with the behavior that will stop it immediately. Also, I would love it if one thing you did as a class was written so I can ask Sean about it specifically at home. For example, "learned a new song." Something short—I'm not looking for a novel each day.

Also, his aide needs to be granted the authority to discipline Sean. He knows right now that she doesn't have the authority and is taking advantage of it. I can tell you that she is going to have a huge fight on her hands, and he will still push at this point since she hasn't been able to discipline him yet. When she works with the occupational therapist on Mondays, she can also help with some behavior management techniques . . . Sean really tested her when they first started last year. She understands the need to be firm and consistent with Sean. My hope is his aide really likes being Sean's aide and wants to follow him into first grade too!

We are a team, and I am here to support and help both of you. PLEASE feel free to call me at any time. I wish I could be there more to help.

Thank you both so much. Sean is participating great, and he really likes the class and both of you. He will have a lot of success this year and is showing a lot of interest in reading, not listening to books but trying to read the words himself. I am very excited about this!

Thank you,

Sandra McElwee

On Behavior and Communication

Communication is the lifeblood of trust. — Byrd Baggett

Communication is key. If you don't know what behaviors are occurring, then you can't help them troubleshoot a solution. I've heard stories of schools that tell the parents everything is going great, and that their child is participating and behaving, then 2 months into the school year, after no behavior interventions have occurred, the school personnel tell the parents, "This isn't working, we can't handle your child." They completely blindside the parents into a placement change. The sooner you address a new behavior, troubleshooting to understand why the behavior is occurring, the easier it is to alleviate. The longer it goes on, a child forms a bad habit, and we all know how hard it is to stop a bad habit.

Things can get out of hand and take awhile to get back on track. It is also important to realize that facial expressions and tone of voice are lost in when you are writing, so be sure to include praises in any written communication, or the educators might misinterpret letters as criticism instead of offers of help to them. At the beginning of the year set the tone that since you can't talk every day you will be writing and they have your full support.

Because I was volunteering in the kindergarten class, I was able to see for myself how Sean was behaving. I realized quickly that the classroom assistant had been instructed to let the teacher discipline Sean, and he figured out quickly that he didn't need to listen to the classroom assistant. I empowered the school, the teacher, and the classroom assistant to correct Sean, and he gained more respect for her quickly and did respond to her more appropriately.

Because I served on the Community Advisory Committee and volunteered with my husband in the Little League Challenger Baseball program, I was lucky to create a network of friends who had kids with a variety of disabilities. My friends whose children had autism were invaluable with teaching me positive behavior supports. Positive behavior support is a set of research-based strategies used to decrease problem behavior by teaching new skills and making changes in a person's environment. They suggested we reward Sean more frequently for the desired behavior, hourly, or even every 5 to 10 minutes depending on the appropriate behavior we were working toward. This way, he sees more rewards more frequently and experiences more success. We gave the teachers sticker books, and they created charts that stayed on his desk and would give him a rubber stamp or a sticker as a visual cue he was behaving appropriately. That provided a constant reminder of the rewards in front of him.

Another suggestion was to change the wording to positives instead of negatives. Instead of saying, "Don't touch others," say, "Keep your hands to yourself." Instead of "Don't throw rocks or don't run out of the room," use language that is positive and directive, like, "Leave the rocks on the ground," or "stay in your seat," or "stay in the room."

His kindergarten teacher took photos of the appropriate behaviors we wanted him to do, and the classroom assistant would carry them with her in class and on the playground. Then when he needed a re-minder, the classroom assistant could just point to the photo, instead of saying anything verbally which might disturb the other kids, AND draw attention to Sean, who LOVES attention.

We included this typed letter in his communication notebook to his teacher and classroom assistants. We left it stapled in for the entire school year for substitutes:

First of all, Sean is deaf in his right ear. He has some loss in his left ear that comes and goes. If there is a lot of background noise or you are on his right side, he probably won't hear you at all. So, you need to tap him on the shoulder to get his attention before even trying to tell him something.

Sean loves other kids. He will want to play with everybody. If somebody doesn't want to play with Sean or can't understand what he is saying, please ask the kids to just tell Sean they can't understand his words. He will try again, or even show them what he is talking about. Within a couple of weeks, they will be able to understand him.

When you change from one activity to another, Sean will need some warning. Especially if it is moving from recess to the classroom. If you can give him a countdown, for example:

"Sean, next we are going to go inside and watch a movie." "We are going to watch the movie in 5 minutes." "Sean, in 3 min-utes we are going to watch a movie." "In 1 minute we will watch the movie." "It's time to go watch the movie!" (You can do this all in an actual 2-minute period. He doesn't really have a concept of how long 5 minutes is.)

Also, in transitions it is easier if you give Sean a job. Have him be in charge of carrying a clipboard, be the line leader, pick up the ball, any job, just something he has responsibility for. If he is balking, send a couple of cute girls to take his hand and say, "Come on, Sean." That one works a lot of the time.

Sean will test each and every person working with him until he has figured out what he can and can't get away with. When you are telling him to stop something, DO NOT SMILE. Look like you mean it; body language means more to him than the spoken word does. When Sean is doing what he is supposed to be, just give him a quick praise for appropriate behavior. When he is doing something he isn't supposed to be doing, don't give it TOO much attention . . . for Sean, negative attention is just as good as positive attention.

Sean will respond to the kids better than to adults, so don't be afraid to ask one of his peers to give him directions or grab his hand and have him go with you.

We are always talking about making good choices. Sean can be given a "choice" of what you want him to do or a time-out (or something else he won't want), and nine times out of 10, he will make the "good choice."

Sean will also "act" like he doesn't know what you are asking of him. As long as he can hear you, he can understand you. It is OK to ask him, "Do you understand?" Sean will look at you and smile and do exactly what you just told him not to do.

DO NOT LET SEAN GET AWAY WITH ANYTHING! If you cut him some slack on the first few days, then it will take you 2 to 3 weeks to get him back in line. If you start with consistency on day 1, he will have more respect for you and better behavior right away. Appropriate consequences would be a time-out (in a chair in the corner or outside the door) or losing a privilege. It has to be something that happens now though. Don't say, "Tomorrow you can't do this" because tomorrow he won't remember why.

Sean will avoid going to the restroom as long as possible. Be sure he is told to go periodically. He is still learning to stand up and go, so it's OK if he wants to sit down.

Sean has a bad habit of chewing his fingers. It is an oral motor stimulating action. Please, please, please, stay on this. One thing to tell him is "Happy hands" and he will clasp his hands together and take them out of his mouth. (You can tell him this if he is touching other kids or stuff he isn't supposed to as well.)

Last but far from least, Sean has a problem metabolizing sugar. If he has more than 15 grams of sugar in a serving, he will have diarrhea pretty quickly . . . and can't usually make it to the restroom. Watch him with snacks and at class parties. Salty stuff, chips, etc., are fine, fruit in small portions is fine, not too much, though . . . When there is cake or cookies present and no label to say what the sugar content is, then err by giving him half or a quarter of a serving. (He doesn't care that it is less, he only cares that he does get what everybody else has.) JUICE and JUICE BOXES are the worst things for him to have.

Thank you very much. If you have any questions or need some immediate advice or need me to talk to Sean about behaving, feel free to call me any time on my cell phone at ____.

Assistive Technology

You have to be able to imagine lives that are not yours.—Wendell Berry

Sean was born with a hearing loss in his right ear. His left ear tested in normal ranges, but over 50 percent of the hearing was lost in his right ear. In situations where there was a lot of background noise, he simply couldn't hear one person talking. When we would be at the playground, if I was on his right side and calling to him, he didn't hear me at all.

In kindergarten, he wore a hearing aid, but between kindergarten and first grade, the ear was tested as completely deaf. Assistive technology is allowed for in the IEP process, and Sean qualified for an FM system. The way it worked is the teacher had a wireless microphone that captured her voice, and there were four speakers placed, one on each side of the room. When the teacher spoke, it didn't matter where in the room Sean was seated; he was able to hear her very well.

This was a benefit to all the students in the class as well. But the microphone took some getting used to for the teacher. Many times she would be outside the classroom talking with another teacher or a parent and forget to turn the microphone off. And a few times she forgot when she went to the bathroom! There were quite a few laughs at the faux pas surrounding the FM system.

Teaching about Down Syndrome

Darkness cannot drive out darkness; only light can do that. Hate cannot drive out hate; only love can do that. —Martin Luther King, Jr.

I felt that it was important to educate the children in Sean's classroom and their parents about Sean and Down syndrome.

Fear comes from the unknown, so to make sure people aren't afraid of those who have disabilities, to educate them alleviates the fear. When I was on the Down syndrome listserv, a sibling posted once advising us that we tell our children that they have Down syndrome. She relayed a story about her sister, who was 14 years old. A social worker came to her house to begin the planning for her transition. Her sister asked this woman, "Why are you asking me all these questions?" The social worker responded, "Because you have Down syndrome and we're planning for your transition to adulthood." Her sister was livid and stayed mad at her family for quite a while because they had not told her before and this stranger was the one who delivered the news to her.

I made sure that I told Sean that he had Down syndrome. I was adopted and can't tell you the first time my parents told me; it was always a *normal* part of my life just knowing that. I wanted Sean to know he had Down syndrome and for that to be a *normal* part of his life too. I couldn't imagine him being surprised by some stranger telling him when he was older, and acceptance of yourself is so critical in being a self-confident adult.

I would read him books about children with Down syndrome, then say, "You are just like him! You have Down syndrome too!" He began to recognize the facial characteristics of other children with Down syndrome. I didn't expect him to be so enthusiastic about recognizing other people with Down syndrome, and he caught me off guard one day. We were attending an event at the local Down syndrome association and Sean ran up to several children, pointed to them, and said in his inarticulate manner, "Thown Thyndome!" I was laughing inside. I knew what he was saying, but thankfully, nobody else could understand his words. Not every parent had told their children yet!

So, in regular education kindergarten, I grabbed the first opportunity I had to educate his classmates and teachers. This letter went home with each student:

Dear Parents of Mrs. _____'s Students,

The theme of this year's "Red Ribbon Week" is disability awareness. Since our son, Sean, is in your child's class and has a disability, it seemed appropriate to make the children aware of Down syndrome. We are sure many of your children have asked you questions about Sean, and that is great. We have two copies of a really good book titled, *Hi, I'm Ben! . . . And I've Got a Secret!* The teacher will be sending it home with two different students each day so you can read it to your child, then please send it back for another child to read tomorrow.

This book answers many questions that children have about Down syndrome. It stresses that children with Down syndrome are more like them than different. One big question that startles adults is, "Can I 'catch' it?" This is a very real concern that children have from age 4 to about 9 or 10. The best way to alleviate this fear is to explain that you have to be born with Down syndrome, just like they were born with brown or blond hair. They can't 'catch' Down syndrome just like they can't 'catch' blue eyes.

Please take a moment to read the first two pages that are directed to adults before you read this book to your child. Then at the end of the book, you might ask, "Do you know anybody that is like

Ben?" If your child says, "No," then it's fine to leave it there. But I am sure most of the children will pick up on the facial characteristics that Ben and Sean share. They will also relate to the speech teacher, as Sean's greatest challenge is his speech difficulty.

Please remind your children that they are all Sean's teachers. Sean will learn as much, probably more, from your children this year than he will from his teacher and his aide. So it is important that they show Sean good things to do, because he will also copy the not-so-good things!

Thank you so much. This year has been a dream for us and is a greater success than we imagined it could be!

Rick and Sandra McElwee
P.S. Please feel free to call us with any questions. We do not get offended by anything. We've heard it all.

I volunteered in the class quite a bit the first few months. The teacher was the sweetest angel of a woman who was truly living her life-calling teaching kindergarten. She loved all those kids and took her job of preparing them for first grade very seriously. There were many opportunities for class performances for every holiday. Each student was celebrated for a week and got to take home *Special Bear*, then their parents came to class on Friday of their special week and shared information about what the student liked to do at home. Sean thrived in the class.

The classroom assistant that was hired because of Sean's inclusion was a mom who needed a part-time job. There was no training provided for these positions. We were lucky that she was very open to listening to our suggestions. I have heard stories from other parents of classroom assistants who enlisted their own discipline systems and made some situations much worse due to no training on ways to react to students with special educational needs.

Sean's teacher gave him a job every day to hand out the snack bags to his fellow classmates. They were to stay seated, Sean would read their names off of their bags, and then they would come and take their bag from Sean and say, "Thank you." This empowered Sean and allowed him to learn each of his fellow classmates' names and he was pretty important to them—no snack till Sean called their name!

After Christmas, I was comfortable with the way everything was going so I went back to work. It was about 4 months before I could go back and volunteer in class again. When I did, I was so disappointed. Sean had been included in everything the class was doing up to Christmas. But what I didn't know was that after the Christmas break, they started learning to write their names. Sean couldn't hold a crayon, but he should have been able to participate in some way. I received notes home that he was throwing markers. Most likely that's because he didn't have the physical ability to hold a crayon or marker. I requested that his OT give them some ideas, and assumed they were working with him, but when I made it back to volunteer in class around May, I discovered that during writing time, the teacher had him leave the class and go outside and throw bean bags. I still don't know the educational benefit he derived from that. Consulting my Internet friends I asked what modifications they had used for these circumstances and the answers were quick to come.

I asked for an informal meeting before school one day. I brought in a cookie sheet and magnetic letters, and wanted to give them to the teacher and ask that Sean use that to learn how to spell his name while the other kids were writing their names. The principal scolded me and said, "How DARE you tell this experienced teacher of 30 years how to teach." I was blown away. It was also 6 weeks before school ended, and I chocked it up to needing to be more involved in the future. Lesson learned.

Over the summer, Sean attended a Montessori School (more nurturing and nowhere near as strict as the one that he had attended in Washington). He also had occupational therapy and gained the ability to hold a crayon and a pencil. When first grade started, he was ready to roll!

Assess This

Success is not how far you get. Success is how far you get from where you started. — Steve Prefontaine

Every 3 years, the school district is mandated to test students receiving special education services in order to identify if they still qualify for services. Sean was fully included in regular kindergarten, was 6 years old, but the school psychologist, Mr. Patrick, did not believe that was the right placement for Sean. And not only was he the *educated professional,* he was also the father of a girl who had Down syndrome who was 4 years older than Sean. The Evaluation Consent Form was sent home for me to sign. It listed each area they would be testing, including one titled, "Intellectual/Cognitive Development." I called my mentor and asked her which ones to allow and which ones to decline. She told me to write next to the psychoeducational assessment, "Do not administer an IQ test. Please administer a test that gives an ordinal skill reference, such as Brigance Diagnostic Inventory."

Sean did not know Mr. Patrick, so he pulled out all the tricks. He stalled, he purposely answered incorrectly, and he threw pens, papers, and other tools. He could not identify the pencil drawing of the woman ironing clothes—a scene he had never witnessed at home! He messed with this stranger to the max, laughing hysterically the entire time.

Our mentor had advised us to always ask for assessments and IEP goals 1 week in advance of the meeting so we could read them in the quiet privacy of our home. Many times there were tears, and we were able to recover from the shock of the assessments in privacy. We could also address the IEP goals if they were not challenging enough by requesting changes in advance. This kept our meetings relatively short and focused.

But this assessment was unbelievable. Mr. Patrick had completely ignored my note and had performed an assessment that did assign Sean an overall *Age Equivalent of 1 YEAR 11 MONTHS!* I was not only angry, I was certain he had broken the law by ignoring my instructions. At the IEP meeting, I explained that the Age Equivalent

Assessment needed to be destroyed immediately, and I did not want Sean's future teachers to think they were going to be teaching a *toddler* to read. They said they were unable to destroy it but were able to "seal" it and file it in an administrator's office. We agreed to this and have never seen the assessment since.

Another thing I later found out that the test that was given required around 100 questions that the parents were to answer on what the student was able to do at home. He did not ask us those questions and made assumptions on his own—also illegal.

During this IEP meeting, we discussed Sean's articulation with the school's speech therapist. She was suggesting Sean needed a palate expander and had some more suggestions for improved articulation. Sean was unable to articulate the "sh" sound—his name came out sounding like "John" instead of "Sean." When we asked the speech and language pathologist to add a goal so he could at least be able to pronounce his name—she emphatically stated, "It is inappropriate to teach him the SH sound!" She was working according to a hierarchy of sounds, and could not step outside the box and jump a few sounds ahead to SH. Rick took the time over the next few days and visually cued Sean with the "shhh" sign with his fingers to his lips. Sean had the sound, and his name, nailed within the week!

During this conversation I asked Mr. Patrick, "I've heard that once our kids start reading, their articulation while reading is clearer than spontaneously speaking. Is that true for your daughter?" He almost choked. He turned red and hemmed and hawed, then said, "I'm not sure." Turns out that his daughter was attending the segregated school and she could not read at all.

Inclusion Is a Right—And a Philosophy of Human Existence!

Life is ten percent what you make it and ninety percent how you take it.—Benjamin Franklin

I am a salesperson in the medical field and once at a conference I heard a speaker say, "Changing a hospital system is like moving a graveyard—you're not going to get any help from the inside." I can certainly liken changing a school system to changing a hospital system—as there is often no help from the inside! In my son's school system, there was some help from the inside, and that made a huge difference.

I also function according to a combination of the "It's easier to gain forgiveness than permission" principle and the Nike tag line, "Just Do It." Sean has been signed up for everything he was interested in. His right to participate is protected under the ADA and IDEA. I also believe the word "No" constitutes the need to find a different alternative way of achieving the objective.

Information on inclusion isn't a secret; it's readily available. It's over 20 years old! It's evidence-based! It's part of Special Education Law! So I don't believe for a minute that I am as ignorant as I've been accused of being over the years. Instead, I believe that educators who do not continue their education are negligent. I believe that parents who do not read everything available, attend seminars and presentations, and seek out mentors and advocates, are shortchanging their children. I completely understand being overwhelmed and empathize with the families who have several children. I encourage them to employ advocates, and there are organizations and people to support them and who will provide advice free of charge. Please, for the sake of your child, take it! Every parent needs a mentor—or two or three—who have gone before them in the same schools and district. A mentor can illuminate the path, warn of imminent pitfalls, make sure the people who will support are in place, and alert them of people who may sabotage their journey.

Most parents listen to the school district's recommendations for their children. By simply believing the "professionals," they select the easy way out. Of course, the professionals should have your child's best interest in mind, and across the country, many do. But unfortunately, in the school district where my son attended school, the status quo was of greater importance.

I also believe that taking the easy way out is an insult to the parents who came before us. Parents who fought for our children to be free from institutionalization, fought for our children to even be granted a free education, and then fought for an appropriate education, not just a glorified babysitting program. If we do not appreciate what price those parents paid, many with their own funds, their own sleepless nights, and their own tears, then we are ungrateful and undeserving.

According to the *Educational Challenges Inclusion Study, conducted by Gloria Wolpert, Ed.D., for the National Down Syndrome Society, 1996*, most parents reported that the match of teacher personality to the child was crucial to having a successful year and is a primary predictive factor of success. Many parents reported having problems with teacher attitude, while only two parents reported the teachers as not being competent to handle their child. One parent summed it up by saying, "Inclusion is no problem. The teachers who don't give it a chance are the problem."

In our experience, we found the teacher *WANTING* to teach Sean to be the number-one factor in the success of inclusion for Sean. The number-two factor was that the principal supports the philosophy and implementation of inclusion. We were extremely fortunate to encounter two principals with this support, although one had less effect than the other one. And unfortunately for Sean, we encountered three others who were not supportive, one, of whom, actually sabotaged Sean and set him and his staff up for huge failure (more on that in future chapters). But the teachers made all the difference. The ones who wanted Sean in their classes made a huge difference in his life and the lives of the other students in their classes. The ones who didn't want him made Sean's life, and our family's life, a living hell.

Robert Jackson, Ph.D., examined 40 years of evidence comparing segregated educational practices with inclusive practices and found that children with an intellectual impairment benefit from inclusion academically and socially. While the advantage over segregation was sometimes nonexistent or small, in the larger samples and meta-analysis, significant benefits were found for inclusion, with children who were segregated losing percentile ranks in comparison to their peers. No review could be found comparing segregation and inclusion that came out in favor of segregation in over 40 years of research.

During Sean's inclusive kindergarten year, our district started the arduous task of educating the educators on inclusive education. I was invited to attend a presentation to hear Richard Villa, Ed.D., president of Bayridge Consortium, Inc., an international consultant in school restructuring and educational reform. His presentation was to all principals, psychologists, selected general education teachers, selected special education teachers, selected parents, and district administrators of instruction and pupil services.

The 1½-hour presentation was on the philosophy of inclusion and how it benefits all students—with and without disabilities. I was thrilled. I thought I was seeing change occur, and Sean would be the beneficiary of this change.

Richard Villa passed out flyers for a 2½-day seminar that was being held at California State University in San Marcos in July titled, "The Inclusion Institute." I registered, along with my five friends whose children were being fully included at other elementary schools in our district, and we attended the extremely educational program. We were privileged to learn from the gurus of inclusion.

Encouraging the Educators

It is fine to be zealous, provided the purpose is good.—Galatians 4:18, NIV

Sean's kindergarten teacher was a pioneer in his elementary school. She was professional, compassionate, and embodied the definition of acceptance. I decided to send a letter to our district's superintendent and the school board praising his teacher, classroom assistant, the district administrator who supported them, and even though the principal was truly not on board with this whole idea of inclusion, I praised him as well. The last paragraph of the letter read, "The success of Sean's program was evident in the fact that he met and exceeded the majority of his IEP goals. We had hoped that Sean would make some friends in his class; he has made many friends who have played with him, invited him to their homes to play, attended his birthday party, and invited him to their birthday parties and even joined our family on outings. Several parents have told us they are glad their children are in class with Sean. One even said she believed the other children have benefitted by Sean's presence in her son's class."

The letter went into their permanent personnel files and word got around that we were grateful. The first-grade teacher stepped up to welcome Sean in the coming year, and we were on the road to continuing his inclusive education.

Haircuts from Hell

No pressure; no diamonds. — Bear Grylls

Due to sensory issues, haircuts were traumatic experiences for me—oh, and for Sean too. We were lucky to have a children's hair salon close by who specialized in the quick haircut. Not cheap, but quick. Rick or I had to smock up ourselves, then hold Sean on our laps and hold his hands down while they quickly trimmed up his locks. In kindergarten, Sean made a good friend named Jeffrey. He loved Jeffrey, and Jeff's mother even invited Sean to come and play at their house. They lived close by, and she became a good friend of mine too. As the school year was ending, Jeff got a summer buzz cut, and Sean was enthralled with it. He came home from school saying, "Hair like Jehwee's." At first, I had no idea what he was talking about and called Jeff's mother and asked if Jeff had changed his hair.

The most awful haircut experiences had included the electronic clippers. We would warn the hairdressers if they even pulled them out that they were losing their tip. And here was a haircut that only involved electronic clippers! But, oh, the peer pressure. Sean wanted that haircut—bad. After a month of him begging every day "hair like Jehwee," I told him I would take him, but he had to sit in the chair by himself, and if he even tried one time to bat the hairstylist's hand away, the cut would stop immediately. I also told him I would take him to McDonald's and let him play in the balls and tunnels if he would sit still.

He wanted it—bad. He was struggling to sit still. He didn't take his eyes off the mirror. He made faces, but he sat still, and he clasped his hands in his lap, struggling to not take a swipe at the stylist. And he got it—the buzz cut! Afterward, he couldn't stop rubbing his head and pointed and told everybody, "Hair like Jehwee." From that day forward, Sean was great for haircuts, and by the time he was 10, we could give him the money, he would walk in, give his name to let them know he was there, pay and tip the stylist, and I would read a magazine in the waiting area! Positive Peer Pressure—Success!

Giant Stuffed Winnie the Pooh

Some mistakes are too much fun to only make once. — Brad Paisley

We had annual passes to Disneyland and frequently went for 3 or 4 hours at a time. On an excursion to Disneyland before first grade started, Sean had eyed a giant stuffed Winnie the Pooh Bear and pointed and said, "Dat! Pooh! I want dat!" (translation: dat means that)

Sean had a really bad habit of chewing his fingers. We had tried the nasty-tasting polish you can get in the Walmart pharmacy, but it only slowed him down a little. We had tried verbally prompting him to "keep your fingers dry." He did . . . while we were looking, then the minute we turned out backs, both hands were back in his mouth. The calluses on his fingers were substantial, and he made this awful noise while gnawing. So I hatched an idea and made him a deal. "If you can keep your fingers dry for 30 days" (supposedly you break a habit in 30 days), "then I will bring you back and we'll get that Pooh Bear." When we got home, I made a calendar on the computer and included a Pooh Bear on it, printed it out, and we started crossing the days off.

It was a hard habit to break. Sean would sit on his hands when he was watching TV to keep them out of his mouth. He went to bed and put them under his pillow. He wanted that Pooh Bear badly, and this motivation was working! After we brushed his teeth at night just before bed, I would take the calendar, "X" out another day, and show him how close he was to getting the Pooh.

Finally, the 30 days were up. When I crossed off the last day, I told Sean we would go to Disneyland the next day and get his Giant Pooh Bear. He woke up so excited. The calluses had almost disappeared on his thumbs. I was so thrilled my plan had worked. I thought I was the most brilliant mother who ever walked the earth.

We went to Disneyland just to get the Giant Stuffed Winnie the Pooh, and then get a picture with *THE* Winnie-The-Pooh. Sean clutched his Pooh Bear as we walked to Critter Country seeking out the giant Tubby Little Cubby All Stuffed With Fluff. Sean posed with both Pooh Bears, I snapped the picture, and we headed home. I buckled him into his car seat, and he was still hugging that stuffed bear as I was exiting the parking lot. As I looked in the rearview mirror to change lanes on the freeway, I caught a glimpse of Sean and Pooh—and Sean's fingers, *all 10 of them,* IN HIS MOUTH *SILENTLY CHEWING* to his heart's content! My heart sank. I had just spent $60, which I thought was a trade-off for one private speech therapy session (that's how I justified it to Sean's dad), and it had not worked. The habit had not been broken. I was not a brilliant mother, just a manipulated mother. In Sean's mind, he believed he had earned the Pooh for not chewing for a month—I guess I forgot to tell him he could never chew his fingers *ever again.* I should not have left that important information out. And now, he was chewing silently, so I didn't have to hear the indescribably annoying termite-gnawing sound of his fingers being chewed into calluses.

The finger chewing never stopped. At age 18, he still does it (silently, of course). A speech therapist explained to me why he does it. She described the feeling of low tone in the mouth, the same fuzzy feeling like when your foot goes to sleep. You want to stomp and give it some pressure to feel something. Thus, chewing gives that pressure. It is defined as a proprioceptive oral motor sensory input issue. Later, after an assistive technology evaluation, the school provided him with chewy tubing and other appropriate things to chew. The district administrator who attended Sean's IEPs pointed out to me that many people need oral input to focus, and she showed me the end of her pencil where she had chewed it significantly. So, this isn't so weird after all. Chewing gum, once he learned not to swallow it, was a better option. Then he got braces, and couldn't chew gum. You would think that it would hurt to chew your fingers with braces on—but that didn't slow him down either.

First Grade

People who say it cannot be done should not interrupt those who are doing it!—George Bernard Shaw

First-Grade IEP Goals:

Vertical jump 5 inches.

Catch an 8-inch ball.

Speak in three-word sentences.

Use appropriate voice level.

Turn pages in a book.

Give the correct letter sound for all of the 26 letters.

Recognize all 26 uppercase letters and 16 lowercase letters.

Model appropriate peer relationships.

Attend for 12 minutes in a small group setting.

Correctly identify a square and a rectangle.

Identify a circle as a circle and not a 0.

Point to the colors red and blue; give the names of all the nine basic colors.

Rote count to 20; recognize the numbers visually in numerical sequential order.

Write the numbers 1 to 20.

Copy vertical, horizontal, diagonal, and curve lines.

I had to insist on a classroom assistant for first grade, *and* that there be one for all day, not just in the morning. The district would not provide a full-time aide, but did provide two part-time aides. The great assistant from kindergarten came along, and in the afternoon, the other assistant was a wonderful woman that had been a classroom assistant from Sean's preschool class! The classroom assistants helped everybody, and everybody helped Sean; this is the way inclusion is supposed to work! The people who visited Sean's class could not immediately pick him out or tell that he was "different." Sean was doing everything the other kids were doing, at his own pace.

The first-grade teacher had a daughter 2 years older than Sean who also had Down syndrome! But sadly, her daughter was not included. I never understood how she could do so much for Sean and not include her daughter. I know she taught her daughter at home, and she was very smart, but I never asked her why she made that decision—but deep down I *knew*. She didn't want to fight the entity that was paying her. And she would have been ahead of us, and she would have been the pioneer.

Sean had occupational therapy two times a week now. The bus would take him there after school, and either Rick or I would leave work early to pick him up from the therapy center. He was making progress in writing.

As we experienced in the past, Sean challenged his new teacher— he would take off and run out of class for no apparent reason. The campus grass had been removed for replanting, and there were rocks everywhere. Sean loved to throw rocks and could't resist the temptation to pick them up and randomly throw them. This was a big concern for the school because he was endangering other students. But his teacher was great at communicating with me and letting me help her with his behavior. She understood that nobody knew Sean better than I. She also listened when I told her not to run after Sean, and that he would come back to class if he got no attention for running out. His aide would watch out the window and see him stop, turn, and look, then all dejected, walk back into class when his trick didn't work.

He would do the big stop, drop, and flop whenever they were walking to the playground, an assembly, or another activity. We collaborated and realized that everybody was walking too fast for him and he was feeling like he was being left behind. His first-grade teacher figured this out, and also figured out when Sean led the line, he set the pace and was empowered as the line leader. He became the example for everyone, and that behavior quickly disappeared.

After kindergarten and collaborating with my five friends whose children were also being fully included, we realized that there was no training for the classroom assistants. We all requested at our individual IEP meetings the prior year that there be a basic training to be held before the first day of school, including positive behavior support techniques, how to know when to assist, when to bring in a peer tutor, and when to discipline and how. It also included fine-motor techniques to assist in cutting and writing, "hand over hand," and knowing how to tell if a pencil is being held properly. With each of us requesting this separately and putting it in writing on our IEPs, we were successful in having this training provided for the first time in our district.

This Land Is Your Land

God's gifts put man's best dreams to shame.—Elizabeth Barrett Browning

Choir was a class period in first grade that Sean loved. Toward the end of the school year, the entire first-grade class performed patriotic songs for the parents, and I was one proud mama as my son was placed front and center waving his tiny American flag, along with the other students, and singing at the top of his lungs, "This land is your land, this land is my land." Yes, Sean, it is your land too.

In future years, budget cuts affected the arts programs at Sean's elementary school. But the PTA came up with the funds for an after-school choir program. The great thing about Sean being in the on-site after-school daycare program was that he could participate in the after-school activities. He wanted to be in the choir—yes, he still had much difficulty in articulating the words, no, he couldn't carry a tune, but he didn't care, and neither did the awesome man who directed the choir. Mr. R. welcomed Sean into the choir with open arms. I never heard one word from him that was negative about Sean. He always praised Sean and went on and on about how great the other students were with Sean, how they loved to help him, and how they truly accepted him as a friend. Sean was in every production, all the way through sixth grade, right up front, singing at the top of his lungs, and sometimes sitting down on stage when he got tired. Mr. R. didn't care, and neither did anybody else.

Teaching about Sean

Extraordinary people visualize not what is possible or probable, but rather what is impossible. And by visualizing the impossible, they begin to see it as possible.—Cherie Carter Scott

I showed the first-grade teacher the book *Hi, I'm Ben! and I've Got a Secret,* and she had the idea to create a book about Sean and title it, *My Name Is Sean and I Have Something to Share.* Using a computer, we scanned in photos of Sean with captions that explained different things about him that were the same and different. One page said, "I like to throw rocks, but I need my friends to help remind me to leave the rocks on the ground." That helped to address the rock-throwing issue that we were having this year. (You can see a replica of the book at https://mynameissean.shutterfly.com.)

She went to all four first-grade classes and read this book to them. Sean was an instant celebrity.

After an extremely successful school year, I nominated Sean's first-grade teacher for the Educator of the Year Award from the Down Syndrome Association of Orange County. SHE WON!

Dear DSAOC:

I am writing to nominate my son's first-grade teacher for the Educator of the Year Award. There are so many things I want to tell you about her I don't know where to begin. Last year when our school's principal asked the first-grade teachers to volunteer to be Sean's teacher next year, she stepped right up to the plate. Truly believing that all children should be educated together regardless of their abilities, she started her homework during Sean's kindergarten year. She spent her break time in Sean's kindergarten class observing and learning about his "uniqueness." She attended his IEP last year and participated in goals and problem solving in advance of any possible problems that could serve as barriers to Sean's learning.

When school began this year, she made sure Sean was an equal and participating class member and fully involved the other students in his education. Sean challenged her behaviorally, and she had unlimited patience and incredible consistency in dealing with his behaviors (which have virtually disappeared under her guidance and positive behavior support system). As Sean recognized sight words, she made sure that during class he was the student called on to read the words he recognized, giving him a great sense of accomplishment. She started a "reading buddy" program where the other students read with Sean and helped him when he was reading a new word or sentence.

When I take Sean to school, the children are lining up, asking if they can be Sean's reading buddy that day. He loves having the other children help him, and although he does have two wonderful classroom assistants, they are just that, CLASSROOM assistants (one in the morning, one in the afternoon).

Sean's first-grade teacher has done an incredible job of truly including Sean and directing the assistants in helping all the children in the classroom. I constantly hear the comment from classroom visitors that they didn't know which student was the inclusion student while visiting Sean's classroom because he was right in with the other students participating and didn't stand out as different in any way.

His first-grade teacher has also taken a book that I wrote about Sean to every first-grade classroom and read it to all of the students. She did this on her own initiative and answered the students' questions about Down syndrome . . . relieving any fears that the children had that they could "catch" it. She is truly providing positive awareness at his elementary school.

Not only has she had a profound and positive impact on Sean's education and sense of belonging, but she has also mentored several other teachers, both in our school district and also in our neighboring district. She has opened her classroom to these teachers and their classroom assistants to come and observe her class. She has visited their classrooms and helped them with adapting materials and behavior issues.

In October, Sean's IEP team attended a district-sponsored inclusion in-service taught by Paula Gardner of California State University, Sacramento. She shared some of the materials that she had adapted for Sean, and Ms. Gardener was so impressed she asked her to present her materials to the annual conference on disabilities PAC/RIM in Hawaii in March. At this presentation, there was a standing room only crowd, from all over the world. The educators and parents were standing in the hallway trying to hear her presentation and see the materials she was sharing. The educators there wanted more, and she is now corresponding with them via e-mail. Also, the Maui School District's director of special education inquired as to her availability to come to his district and provide training for his teachers who have fully included students! Now she is influencing parents and teachers from all over the world, not just South Orange County, California!

She continues to have brilliant ideas, and even phoned me over the President's Day weekend with some ideas she had on helping Sean learn his colors. She was on holiday, and she called me. This sort of dedication is so impressive to me and proves to me that this is a teacher who truly believes in her heart that my son can learn and that there are endless ways to help him learn.

The school year is not yet over. Sean has achieved most of IEP goals and far surpassed many of them. I wish that every fully included student could have as incredible of an experience that Sean has had. Sean is learning to *love to learn* under her guidance. He is experiencing success. He has made many new friends this year. She is also already working with next year's teacher to make the transition easy and successful.

The educational base and social base that she has provided to my son is priceless, and I truly pray that you will choose her as Educator of the Year for PROUD, as I cannot express enough to her how grateful I am for her generosity, acceptance, and diligent creativity.

Sandra McElwee

The award was presented to her during class one day. The principal had some kind words to say, the local paper took photos, and the photographer had tears in his eyes. When someone gets it so right it is critical to honor them. Never let a great person go unappreciated. It also inspired the teachers in the grades ahead to be more inclined to volunteer to teach Sean.

Communication Is Key

If it is important to you, you will find a way. If not, you'll find an excuse.
—Jim Rohn

In special education preschool and kindergarten, I dropped off and picked Sean up every day. I saw the teachers and the aides, and they could fill me in on anything I needed to know about behavior they had seen in Sean, or what they had worked on that day so I could talk to him about it. His articulation was pretty bad, so if he tried to explain something that happened in school and I didn't have the knowledge in advance to be able to decipher what he might be telling me, I was completely lost.

We continued the communication notebook that we had started in kindergarten. This notebook was just a small spiral-bound notebook where each day his teacher or aide could jot a few notes about what they did that day and any cute stories about Sean or behaviors I needed to talk to him about. Most of the time the notations were short and sweet . . . Later, when he was having some big behavioral challenges, the notes could go on for pages and pages describing his entire day. Another benefit was I could document when his IEP was not being followed. The communication notebook was provided for in his IEP, and I wouldn't leave home without it.

Attempting Change

Cowardice asks the question, is it safe? Expediency asks, is it polite? Vanity asks, is it popular? But conscience asks the question, is it right? And there comes a time when one must take a position that is neither safe, nor polite, nor popular—but one must take it because it's right. —Martin Luther King, Jr.

The special education director for our school district was a master's level teacher at local universities, and she taught inclusion to future special educators. We began to see some additional education on inclusion being provided to the teachers and principals in our district. In first grade, there was also a 2-day program led by Paula Gardner from California State University in Sacramento who taught IEP teams how to develop a person-centered plan. Ten IEP teams of students who were fully included were invited to participate. Eight were from elementary schools, one from an intermediate school, and one from high school. Each team consisted of the parents, the principal, the current teacher, the classroom assistant, the school psychologist, the speech therapist, and other members of the team. The one high school student was the one whose parents had to sue the district for their daughter to be included 10 years earlier. She was also present since starting in high school the students need to be involved in planning at their IEPs. It appeared that our district was making progress.

A few years later, the district tried to close the segregated school site. Unfortunately, enough parents who believed that separate was safer for their children prevailed in not allowing the school to close. Sadly, the biggest cost for special education is the Little Yellow Bus. At the time, it cost our school district $5 per mile per child to provide transportation to special classes and schools. Inclusion is a huge savings when you go to your neighborhood school and don't need to ride the bus, sometimes 1 hour one way to get there. I never knew why the additional education stopped, but as far as I was aware of, these were the only two attempts of a districtwide effort to educate and prepare their staff for included students.

A great exercise we did during this IEP team inclusion in-service was called, "Best Hopes—Worst Fears." Each person on the IEP team was to voice what they were most afraid of and their biggest hopes. That was a very enlightening exercise, and I wish I had remembered to ask at the beginning of each IEP meeting in the future what the educator's best hopes and worst fears were. I voiced that my biggest fear was being blindsided—going along thinking everything was working, then finding out there were major problems and nobody mentioning them until it is too late, and I did mention that at future IEP meetings.

Spelling with a Sense of Humor

Laugh often and loud.—Robin Thomas

After school, we would work on Sean's spelling words (which were also his Dolch list "sight words" for reading) by using flash cards to read them, and then spell them. We did it before and after dinner, then again before bed. Thank goodness one of his accommodations was to only learn five words, when his peers could have as many as 20.

Rick had wanted to "help" Sean build a tolerance to being teased (which he never needed) with a sense of humor, so he had started telling Sean, "You're a goofball." And Sean would then say, "No, *you're* a gooseball." (Yep, no "f" in the sound deck yet.)

One evening when he was in first grade after his spelling homework, we headed up to his bath. As I was putting him in the tub, he said, "Mom, you're a gooseball." So I asked, "How do you spell *goofball*?" He looked up, thought for a moment, then spelled, "M-O-M." I still laugh out loud all these years later when I think of this.

Reading with a Purpose

Discovery consists of looking at the same thing as everyone else and thinking something different.—Roger von Oech

We moved into a new house during first grade. To help Sean read, we had put labels on all of the furniture, on the door (ex., "door"), on everything so he could learn to sight-read each of the items. I didn't realize how well he was reading till I was in the shower one morning. As I turned the water off and grabbed the towel, I smelled it. The unmistakable odor of microwave popcorn being popped—and I anticipated the next odor to be the unmistakable odor of *burnt* microwave popcorn. It was a winter day, and too cold to open the windows to air out the house—so I threw on my robe and ran downstairs to stop the popcorn before the inevitable burning was to occur. As I entered the kitchen, Sean was sitting on the counter (the microwave was over the stove) removing a perfectly popped bag of popcorn out of the microwave. A kitchen chair was pulled up that helped him climb up onto the counter. I stopped, amazed, because I could never get the microwave to make such a perfectly popped bag of popcorn.

I asked Sean, "What number did you push?" He looked at me like I was crazy and pointed to the control panel of the microwave and said, "Popcorn."

Duh! We had lived there about a month, and I didn't know there was a popcorn button on the microwave! *I* was the slow learner. And Sean was using his newly acquired reading ability.

District Day Care

Morality is simply the attitude we adopt towards people whom we personally dislike. — Oscar Wilde

Two weeks before the summer school session began the after-school daycare program called my cell phone to tell me that Sean could NOT attend their summer program! He had been enrolled 2 months earlier, and at this point there was no time to find another summer program for him! Of course, they called me on a Friday—at 4:30 P.M. from the school district's office. I was at work, sitting in my car with a new sales trainee who was listening to the conversation.

"What do you mean he can't be in the summer daycare program?"

"Sean sometimes runs away from the staff, and we go on field trips to amusement parks. We don't have enough staff to watch him."

"Doesn't the after-school program receive federal funds?"

"Yes."

"Then any program that receives federal funds must provide the necessary supports and accommodations to include students with disabilities."

"But we have a paragraph in our handbook that we can decline enrollment to students with disabilities after we have assessed them. During spring break when we went on a field trip to SeaWorld, Sean ran away to the shark tank. Our summer program has two field trips a week, so we have assessed that Sean does not qualify for our summer program."

"Where in the handbook is that written? That is discrimination. Can't you provide an aide for him for the summer? He's going to be in summer school all of July, we're going to be on vacation for 1 week of August, and there's only 2 other weeks in August that he will be there—he would only need an aide for 4 days, if you count the 2 days a week of field trips for those 2 weeks."

"I'm sorry; we cannot accommodate him. Good-bye."

I was in shock. I immediately called the director of special education, and she said she would look into it for me. When I got home,

I jumped on the Internet and posted this issue to my Internet Listserv . . . WOW, within minutes, I had the Web site to file a civil rights discrimination complaint. I had information on how all programs that receive federal funds must accommodate any persons with a disability, including providing an aide, if necessary!

By Monday morning, I had filed my complaint, including a request that they mandate changing the language that they can "assess" students with disabilities in the program's handbook!

There was a positive change made from the complaint. The handbooks printed in the future stated that they do not discriminate against any disability and will provide the appropriate supports, including aides, for students with disabilities! Sean did participate that summer, they did provide him with an aide, and he never ran from them at one outing. He enjoyed every day. We found out about a local church that had a summer day camp that was inclusive and would take students with special needs all the way through their senior year! So we utilized them for summer day care from then on.

Private programs are not held to the same standards as programs in public schools that receive federal funding. Anytime a program that receives federal funding tries to deny access to a student with a disability on the basis of their disability—including behaviors that are manifested because of their disability, they must provide the necessary supplementary aides and services to allow for inclusion of that student with a disability.

Sean never went to summer school again till high school. And we never blessed the summer after-school program with Sean's presence ever again either.

Second Grade

Never seek to become a person of success. Seek to become a person of value. Then the success will come. —Albert Einstein

Second-Grade IEP Goals:

Produce the "f" sound in the initial position of words.

Product the "sh" sound in the final position of words.

Produce final "ps" and "ts" clusters in words.

Produce initial "h" phoneme in words without a whisper.

Use a slow rate of speech in carrier phrases such as "I want the ___."

Identify four–six morpheme sentences involving the prepositions "in" and "on" and regular plurals when presented with pictures or object displays and given directions such as, "Show me the spoon is in the bowl."

Use sentences involving the prepositions "in" and "on" and regular plurals without a model. Use the sentence "The boy is ___ing."

Sean will recognize the colors blue, green, red, and yellow from different sources.

Sean will be able to recognize his phone number and communicate it orally.

Sean will recognize and communicate his street address orally.

Sean will begin to type his name using the IntelliTools keyboard on an independent basis.

Sean will begin to learn keyboarding skills using a typing tutorial program appropriate for his age.

Sean will be able to play language arts and math games available in the classroom on his level using the mouse and/or IntelliTools keyboard.

Sean will use the Handwriting Without Tears program at least two–three times per week and up to five times a week to develop printing skills.

Sean will be able to approximate writing 10–15 letters.

Sean will use magnetic letters or letter cards to spell eight simple words that follow a CVC pattern when given Zoo phonics prompts from the teacher.

Sean will match all lowercase letters to the uppercase letters.

Sean will organize and sort his sight words by the beginning consonant sound.

Sean will increase his sight word reading vocabulary by 20 words from the Dolch word list.

Sean will be able to look at pictures in a story and make two–three predictions about the story that are appropriate to the illustrations when asked.

Sean will be able to answer two–three *"why"* questions orally from a story using the text and situations.

Sean will be able to track the appropriate line or words with his finger when echo reading or following along in a story.

Sean will recognize a penny, nickel, dime, and quarter and be able to add pennies up to 10 cents.

Sean will demonstrate appropriate peer relationships in a group or 1 to 1 setting in the classroom, on the playground, and on an independent basis.

Sean will be able to go to the bathroom independently and fasten his clothing properly, wash and dry his hands after wiping himself in a hygienic manner. He will have appropriate behavior in the bathroom.

Every morning around 6 A.M., Sean would crawl into bed with me and we would talk before getting up and starting the day. I asked him how he liked his new teacher, Mrs. D. His speech still not so perfect, he would respond and say, "No, Mrs. W." (Mrs. W was the special education teacher he had during summer school.) I was really wondering why he didn't know his new teacher's name and thought he was just taking more time to learn it.

About 3 weeks into second grade, I ran into the special education teacher, Mrs. W. She said, "Sean is reading so great in my class!" I almost dropped my teeth. I asked her why he was in her class—he was supposed to be in Mrs. D's class. She responded, "Oh, she sends him to me for reading and math."

I immediately called an IEP and in that meeting discovered Sean's daily schedule:

8 A.M. report to Mrs. D's class for 15 minutes (Pledge of Allegiance, morning announcements)

8:15–10:15 report to Mrs. W's class for reading and math (not on his IEP)

10:15 snack/recess with Mrs. D's class

10:30 speech therapy

11:00 adapted PE

11:30 back to Mrs. D's class for 1 hour

12:30 lunch/recess

1:15–2:30 Mrs. D's class

No wonder he didn't know who his teacher was! During this meeting, we decided to remove adapted PE from his IEP—he didn't need it by then anymore anyway.

Mrs. D. revealed during the meeting that she didn't feel adequate to teach Sean; she thought she had to be *special*. I had to encourage her that she WAS special and that she was capable. And after that, the only time Sean left her class was for speech therapy. She did a great job, and he learned a lot that year.

As I look back at the IEP notes from that meeting, I have to chuckle. There is a note that says, "Mr. and Mrs. McElwee have a 'purist view' of full inclusion." The schedule Sean had before we altered it was more of a model of "mainstreaming."

Many people confuse the terms *mainstreaming* and *inclusion*. Taken from the Wisconsin Education Council's Web site, here are the definitions:

Mainstreaming

Generally, mainstreaming has been used to refer to the selective placement of special education students in one or more "regular" education classes. Proponents of mainstreaming generally assume that a student must "earn" his or her opportunity to be placed in regular classes by demonstrating an ability to "keep up" with the work assigned by the regular classroom teacher. This concept is closely likened to traditional forms of special education service delivery.

Inclusion

Inclusion is a term which expresses commitment to educate each child, to the maximum extent appropriate, in the school and classroom he or she would otherwise attend. It involves bringing the support services to the child (rather than moving the child to the services) and requires only that the child will benefit from being in the class (rather than having to keep up with the other students). Proponents of inclusion generally favor newer forms of education service delivery.

Full Inclusion

Full inclusion means that all students, regardless of handicapping condition or severity, will be in a regular classroom/program full time. All services must be taken to the child in that setting.

The benefits of inclusion are not just for the student with special educational needs. They also benefit the regular education students. I was frequently told Sean wouldn't be able to function because, "there's 20 other kids" or 32 from fourth grade and up. But this is a blessing—Sean had 20 other teachers! And the blessing to the regular education students? When you teach something to someone else, you have the information cemented in your brain. The students who worked closely with Sean in the early elementary grades later tested into the Gifted and Talented Education Programs (GATE). Did they achieve because they were smart to begin with? Or did they excel because teaching Sean gave them the foundations they needed?

Many families and teachers have the common misperception that students with disabilities cannot receive an inclusive education because their skills are not "close" enough to those of students without disabilities, or they can't keep up with the pace. Students with disabilities, however, do not need to keep up with students without disabilities to be educated in inclusive classrooms; they do not need to engage in the curriculum in the same way that students without disabilities do; and they do not need to practice the same skills that students without disabilities practice. Learners need not fulfill any prerequisites to participate in inclusive education.

Today, it still astounds me when people, mainly parents of kids with disabilities, ask, "Did he do the entire general education curriculum? Did he keep up with the regular education kids? Was he at grade level?" The information on inclusion isn't hidden, it's not secret, and it's not new! No, he did his own material, with the same information that the other kids are learning. He didn't write three paragraphs, but he could answer the questions by circling the correct answer or short fill-ins. He learned vocabulary words like *redundant* and *afflict,* and he uses them appropriately all the time.

Sean learned the same material that the other students did, but in different ways. He had customized worksheets where he could match answers, or circle the correct answer when he was unable to write well, but could read the information, or have it read to him by the classroom assistant or a peer. There are many creative ways to help students with disabilities access the curriculum, and once the teachers learn how, it benefits all of the students in the class. He also didn't learn every fact in every subject that the other students did. But he did learn enough of the facts to be able to understand that water boils at 212 degrees, that we elect our presidents, and that Congress and the Senate make our laws.

I requested that Mrs. W collaborate with Mrs. D in modifying Sean's curriculum, something I had learned at the Inclusion Institute seminar the summer before. Sean benefitted from their successful collaboration. He also started with a tutor the summer before second grade. This tutor had been a classroom assistant in an inclusive classroom and was extremely interested in improving the educational outcomes of students with Down syndrome. She had around 40 students that she tutored and having her service compliment Sean's learning at school truly thrust his reading abilities forward.

Second Grade (continued)

Mrs. D had a very positive way of dealing with behavior and Sean had a real problem in second grade with keeping his hands off of other people's desks. The teacher came up with the idea of making Sean responsible to make sure everybody else kept their hands off other people's desks. When he was empowered by being put in charge of the situation for everybody he responded the most positively.

On the playground, Sean was mastering the game of Hand Ball. There were four Hand Ball courts set up, and the students waited in line to play two at a time. They used the same type of balls that were used for Dodge Ball when I was in school. Sean became obsessed with the game and played on our garage door every day after school to improve his skills. He became a real contender, but truly hated to leave recess and the Hand Ball game. His teacher set it up so he would be the one to carry the class Hand Ball back from recess. He thought it would be funny to chuck the ball into the bushes on the way back from class a few days in a row. After the classroom assistant retrieved the ball a couple of times, they wrote in his communication notebook what was happening. I advised they just leave the ball in the bushes and keep going to class. The next day, predictably, Sean tossed the ball into the shrubs. They didn't skip a beat and said, "Bye-bye, Hand Ball" and kept walking to class. The classroom assistant retrieved the ball later when Sean was in class, and the next day, there was no ball for the class to play with. Sean never did that again.

Reading, Writing, and Arithmetic
To make headway, improve your head—B .C. Forbes

Sean's first-grade teacher had begun teaching him to read when it wasn't even on his IEP. We were thrilled to keep the pace moving.

Using the Dolch Sight Word List and focusing on learning to spell, read, and write words from the Dolch lists, Sean had a great visual ability to recognize the words.

Dolch sight words are a list comprised of 220 words that must be learned in order to master the English language. These words include 50–75 percent of the most common words in the English language, such as "the, it, are, so," and so on. Sean's second-grade teacher built daily routines that gave Sean opportunities to practice reading, speaking, and writing these words, instilling confidence and excitement for reading.

Sean still had a number of fine-motor issues. He was still seeing an OT after school, and the OT came to school each month to work with the classroom assistant and his teacher. We identified the program *Handwriting Without Tears* and used it with Sean. He traced many letters for a long time. The low tone in his hands made it difficult to write for very long periods of time. It wasn't until he was in high school that I met a mom who had held a *Walk in My Shoes Disability Awareness Day*. She had stations set up, each one allowing the students' hands-on learning, simulating the way things felt for people with disabilities. The articulation simulation included giant marshmallows stuffed in the students' mouths, and then they had to give another student instructions verbally to simulate poor articulation and how frustrating it is for people to not understand you. There were wheelchair races. But the one that turned on my lightbulb was the pencil placed inside a giant straw, and you had to grasp it so tightly that after simply writing my name my hand hurt badly. Then I understood why Sean hated writing. Later in high school he had a device that was like a small typewriter to type his spelling assignments on. Where was the iPad? Not developed till late in his senior year. The iPad would have made Sean's educational experience so much better, and I believe he can still learn a lot on one now. Beg, borrow, do a fundraiser, but somehow get an iPad. School for your child will be a much more enriched experience by using one. And please don't be so *entitled* that you force the school to buy one for your child to use. You may wait ages, and you can't use it at home in most cases, so bite the bullet, get a used one, but somehow get one.

I am ashamed to admit that I told the second-grade teacher that it didn't matter if Sean memorized his "math facts." She insisted we try. He not only memorized the ones she taught him, but was able to verbally answer equations that we asked him—verbally with no visual cues. He also learned "Touch Math." Touch Math was a system where there were dots on each point of the numbers. One dot on the number 1, two dots on the number 2, etc. Then you touched the dots to count while adding from 0 to 9. I use this program quite a bit still today to add up columns of numbers. The beauty of inclusion is the students with special educational needs are exposed to more than in a special education setting. Sean learned so much that was not on his IEP and became a real lover of learning.

Sean loved school. He would wake up in the morning singing, "Oh Say Can You SEEEE" and knew all the words (could read them also) to the "Star Spangled Banner," because he was the student assigned to hold the pointer and point to the words on the poster of the song on the wall every morning at the beginning of class. Sean was Fully Included.

Day Care Again

Our lives begin to end the day we become silent about things that matter.
—Martin Luther King, Jr.

Sean continued to have problems in the after-school day care program, particularly on Fridays. The director of the program was still angry that she *had* to include Sean over the previous summer. She was looking for reasons to remove him from the program. In order to be able to keep my job, I HAD to have the program be successful for Sean—it was convenient, he was there with his friends, and it was CHEAP!

On Fridays, they had "movie day," and ALL of the kids had to sit quietly and watch a movie—even if they had no interest in the movie and even if they had been sitting in class all day and wanted to play—like Sean who had no interest in sitting any longer.

Our local United Cerebral Palsy Association had a great program titled "Inclusion Connection" that intervened when children with any disability were having a problem with their day care setting. This program was funded by a grant and by donations. I contacted them, and they sent a wonderful woman who talked with the director of the day care program. She came for three different 2-hour observations, assessed how the program was currently working, and created a *plan* for Sean! She then trained all of the staff on how to implement *the plan*, and also was successful in convincing them that the students should have choices of activities every day. She convinced them that allowing a physical activity choice on Fridays would solve all the behavior problems they were having.

She observed that when you tell Sean what "to" do, he understands better than telling him what "not" to do. For instance, if he's running, instead of saying "don't run," say "walk." Because of Sean's hearing impairment, he would only hear the word "RUN" and not the word "don't." That one bit of information made a huge difference for Sean, and I also shared this information with his teachers and future caregivers. She also observed that during movies, he had a hard time hearing so he needed to be moved closer to the front of the speakers, unless it's a movie he has no interest in, then at the back is better. She also stressed the importance of giving Sean a warning when changing activities. She said if he has a chance to "finish" what he is doing and transition to the next activity he would do better. From this, there was an incredible improvement to his behavior! Sometimes it takes an outside person to point out the simplest things to make a huge difference.

Giving Back

Anybody can be great because anybody can serve. You don't have to make your subject and verb agree to serve. You don't need a college degree to serve. You only need a heart full of grace and soul generated by love. — Dr. Martin Luther King, Jr.

I was involved in many aspects of the PTA. I feel it's critical to give back, especially when you have a student that is *taking* more than most. Having the spirit of giving provides a feeling of being on the same team with the school administrators. In my case, I'm a sarcastic joker, and by being around me in other settings than just IEPs, people understood my personality and knew when I was kidding and when I was serious. The bonds I created with the moms of the PTA and the principal were strong. And these women were my eyes on campus! If anything seemed askew, they knew they could call me any time. For example, one of my PTA friends was on campus volunteering and noticed Sean and his aide eating alone *AFTER* lunch for a couple of days in a row. My PTA friend called and asked, "Is there a reason why Sean would be eating lunch with his aide after lunch is over?" I thanked her profusely, and then I popped by the school the next day after Sean's lunch period was over. I signed in at the office (PTA duty, you get access to the campus for volunteering, but you have to sign in!), then I casually strolled by the lunch tables . . . and there, 15 minutes after everybody else had gone back to class, was Sean and classroom assistant having a relaxing lunch together!

I asked her, "Why is Sean eating now?"

She said, "Oh, he has just been playing at lunch and not taking time to eat, so I'm letting him eat before he goes back to class."

Oh boy, did he have her wrapped around his little finger! I said, "No, if he chooses not to eat, then he can just be hungry. He has to go to class."

I knew from other situations over the previous years where she let Sean manipulate her that she was not going to listen to me with my simple request so I had to call an IEP meeting.

During the meeting, I explained that he was not going to starve. He went to day care one hour after lunch ended where he could eat his lunch . . . or maybe after a few days of being hungry he would decide to stop playing and eat. The classroom assistant was so angry. She pounded her fist on the table and said, "I *HAVE* to put my foot down! He *HAS* to eat!"

I wanted to laugh, but instead, I calmly replied, "I'm his mother. If I say it's OK to let him starve, it's OK. I will bet you big money that within 3 days he will stop playing to eat." And he did. While I called her "mom away from mom," I truly appreciated that she had Sean's best interests at heart.

Second grade ended as a huge success. Sean's teacher came into her own and was a great inclusive educator. Sean made a lot of friends and achieved almost all of his IEP goals. He still didn't know his colors, but he was reading, adding, and subtracting, and writing simple words. I suggested that his future third-grade teacher attend the Inclusion Institute in San Marcos the upcoming summer and provided him with the information on registration. We also instituted one new item into our IEP meetings. From the seminars I had attended we wanted to keep Sean at the focus of the IEP meeting, and since he wasn't present in the meetings, we created a Long-Term Goal sheet that stated our long-term goals for Sean and included photos that demonstrated those goals. His long-term goals remained the same year after year, but the photos reflected current situations. We gave everyone present a copy, so we would all remember where we were going, and who we were talking about, keeping the meeting focused on Sean.

Sean McElwee's Long-Term Goals

Contributing Member of the Community

Articulate Speech

Appropriate Behavior in Any Situation

Third Grade

We could learn a lot from crayons . . . Some are sharp, some are pretty and some are dull. Some have weird names, and all are different colors, but they all have to live in the same box.—Robert Fulghum

Third-Grade IEP Goals:

Long jump 36 inches.

Target kick accurately.

Count up to 15 objects.

Use Touch Math to complete simple addition and subtraction problems.

Practice writing numbers legible.

Begin using a calculator.

Produce the "L," "V," and "Ch," sounds in isolation.

Produce the initial and final "V," the medial "L," and middle "F," and initial "Ch."

When presented with pictures, use the target structures, "he," "she," "they."

Sean will attend to a lesson after the teacher has given the chosen listening cue two–three times.

Sean will identify four–six appropriate classroom behaviors and four–six inappropriate classroom behaviors.

Sean will follow classroom rules with one–two reminders from a teacher or aide.

Sean will be able to state three–four basic facts from each social studies unit.

Sean will name the days of the week and identify "yesterday" and "tomorrow" by pointing to a calendar.

Sean will recognize his phone number and communicate it orally.

Sean will recognize his city as well as communicate it orally as in "Where do you live?"

Sean will recognize and communicate his street address orally.

Sean will be able to echo read in the third-grade literature series.

Sean will be able to locate the page number and point to some sight words from the story.

Sean will participate in reading groups with his peers with modifications, such as buddy reading.

Sean will increase his sight word vocabulary from the Dolch word list and the literature selections by four–five words per week.

Sean will be able to read 10–15 words that follow the CVC pattern when presented in a repeating pattern.

Sean will be able to dictate five–six simple sentences and copy them using peer, aide, or teacher guidance. He will then read back what was written.

Sean will follow the class writing projects with modifications, such as peer help, aide help, shortened assignments, be able to copy a model, and dictate his answers or have simplified steps.

Sean will accurately copy all uppercase and lowercase letters of the alphabet.

Sean will recognize the colors blue, green, red, and yellow from different sources.

Sean will button and unbutton three buttons on a shirt.

Sean will demonstrate improved lip closure and reduced drooling.

Kindergarten didn't require a lot of modifications to the materials for Sean to be fully included in participating with what the class was doing. The first-grade teacher went way above and beyond in modifying materials and created real learning success with her materials. The second-grade teacher collaborated with the special day class teacher and Sean's tutor for modifications, but it was becoming evident that as the curriculum was increasing in difficulty that it was going to be impossible for the teachers to keep up with modifying materials to Sean's ability level.

Conspiring with my five friends whose children were fully included in five different schools, we decided to add to our IEPs that the inclusion specialist would modify materials for the teachers. The inclusion specialist—the same person as the district administrator—had been integral in troubleshooting reactions to Sean's behaviors. She helped to identify the antecedents (what the triggers were) and appropriate reactions so the behaviors didn't escalate. She had collaborated in ideas for adaptations. But she was one person and around 20 students were now being fully included within the school district. We added this language to the IEP, "Inclusion specialist to adapt general education curriculum for general education teacher to Sean's ability level." We also worded some of the IEP goals to read, "Utilizing materials modified by the inclusion specialist, Sean will complete social studies worksheets on the Orange County unit." Five of us added this language to our IEPs.

Because the inclusion specialist had other duties, the district hired a woman who had worked in special education in the school district, and she collaborated with our teachers, modified and adapted materials for Sean and the other fully included students, and was an awesome addition to our IEP teams. The pressure was off of the teachers to fully include special education students. They had classroom assistants, modified materials, and peers who helped Sean. We were incredibly blessed.

Sean's first male teacher was this third-grade teacher. He had the same two classroom assistants, and that made a huge difference every year because they knew his tricks, and he knew they did so he was trying new tricks, but let the old ones that didn't work go. They had worked with him on appropriate bathroom skills. One even made it fun to wash his hands, making "big bubbles," and then shooting a basket with his paper towel.

Spelling tests changed in third grade. Now, instead of the teacher just reading the word and the students writing down the correctly spelled word, the teacher would read a sentence that included the spelling word, then the students had to write the entire sentence that was read aloud.

I didn't know that the spelling tests were different. About 3 weeks into school Sean's aide wrote in his communication notebook that he was having a hard time during the spelling tests. While the other students were learning 20 spelling words each week, Sean's modification was to learn 5 words. The teachers in the past would place "his" words about one every three or four words so he had time to write his one word while the other students were writing more (they would visually cue him when it was "his" word to to write down).

The easiest way for me to problem solve was to observe, so that following Friday, I went to see what was going on. The upper grades had "pods"—little rooms that joined four classrooms, and had windows into each classroom for observation—and I was able to enter the pod from another classroom so Sean didn't know I was there. The teacher cracked the door open a little so I could hear.

The spelling test began. The teacher read a sentence, repeated it a few times watching to see when everybody stopped writing. Then he said, "Underline 'shark'." And repeated this process twenty times asking them to underline the spelling word in each sentence. Sean just sat looking bewildered and didn't participate.

After the test, the teacher came into the pod and I asked him if the sentences were prewritten or if he made them up. Turned out they were in his teacher's book, and he just read them off during the test. So together, we came up with an accommodation for Sean, where he could participate, be successful, and learn.

Each Monday, Sean's aide would send home the entire list of spelling words, with the five that Sean was to learn to spell underlined. The aide also would type the sentences from the spelling test.

Then at home, Sean would practice following along while I read the sentences aloud, and then Sean would underline the spelling word. This was practice for his test on Fridays.

He was so proud of himself that Friday when he took the spelling test. He was able to participate with the class when the teacher said, "Underline the spelling word _____." He was able to read along in the sentence, identify, and underline the word. Being able to participate with the same information, with his materials modified, allowed him to feel included in the test.

Sean finally learned his colors in third grade too. But he didn't learn them in class, he learned them playing Hand Ball. His first-grade teacher suggested since he was so interested in that sport that we purchase several hand balls in a variety of colors for him. One of our neighbor's daughters would come over every day after school and play Hand Ball with him up against our garage. She would say, "Sean, let's play with the blue ball next." And he had to go into the group of balls and pick out the correct color. Making his lessons meaningful to him was a true key to successful learning.

Sharing Resources

There are two ways of spreading light: to be the candle or the mirror that reflects it.—Edith Wharton

During third grade, Sean didn't really need an aide during lunch or recess. He knew the rules and was following them. If he made a bad choice, all of his classmates were there and ready to help him remember the rules. I received a phone call one day from one of the special day class teachers who asked me if she could borrow Sean's aide during lunch. I told her she was welcome to borrow the aide. Sean's aide was great with the special education class's students. His aide even invited some of Sean's friends over to sit with the special education students, and they were more included during lunch, and Sean's friends invited them to play after they had finished eating. It was a win-win for everybody.

Triennial Assessment
Greatness isn't defined by what you've achieved but by what you've overcome to be able to achieve. —Michael Oher

Sean had his triennial assessment toward the end of third grade. He had finally learned his colors, so that was part of his test. As the school psychologist pointed to objects that were different colors and asked, "What color is the car?" Sean got his mischievous smirk on his face and would intentionally name a wrong color! Blue became pink, orange became purple—he thought this was hysterical. The psychologist, Mrs. Sunshine, was the same one who had been at Sean's special education preschool and kindergarten. She had been transferred to our school in first grade, and Mr. Patrick (who tested Sean at a 1 year 11 month development level) had been transferred somewhere else. She didn't try to perform Sean's assessments all at once; she broke it up into shorter sessions to keep his attention. At another testing time when they went back to colors, "What color is the car?" Sean's response, "Don't you know that?" She told me later that she couldn't keep a straight face. They moved on to the next part. She had been working with Sean for a couple of years, and she knew that he knew his colors, and she knew that he was teasing her.

People think they are testing Sean, but really, he is testing them. He's like the Velociraptor in *Jurassic Park* pushing and pushing on the fence, always looking for the weak spot, ready to break through.

Most of the tests that are given are timed. If you don't answer all of the questions or identify all of the pictures by a certain time, the rest of the questions are counted as "not knowing." So answering slowly, because your mental processing is slow or your speech is slow—or having to wait for somebody to understand you, and repeating things two or three times, OR worse, not understanding you and "guessing" what you said was different than what you actually said—are all recipes for disaster and have the impetus to garner you a score that is less than you actually deserve.

So as Sean's school days passed, setting goals and objectives on his IEPs and measuring his progress based on whether he achieved them, with the appropriate modifications and accommodations, were the most reliable forms of measuring his advancements.

Cursive, I Presume

A right delayed is a right denied. — Martin Luther King

Things were progressing so nicely in third grade. I was very relaxed and trusted completely that Sean's needs were being met. In order to be prepared for IEP to plan for third grade I had asked for the third-grade standards, so we could write IEP goals for each area. The staff looked a little chagrined: the IEP could have been 100 pages long if we actually did that. They suggested that we just write the goals for things that Sean really needed to focus on, and everything else would simply be taught since he was fully included anyway. That sounded logical to me.

Sean's birthday is in October, and most IEPs in our school district are held near the student's birthday. We changed that standard and were holding Sean's IEPs around April. That way, we could identify the teacher for the following year, invite that teacher to the IEP meeting, review the current year, and plan for the following year.

We frequently had small IEP meetings in between about different things—OK, usually behavior problem solving, but you *can* hold an IEP every day if you need to (or if you really want them to hate you).

In April of Sean's third-grade year, we were writing Sean's goals for fourth grade. I asked when they started teaching cursive writing. While Sean still had fine-motor issues, he *was* writing. I had heard from my Internet group that cursive is actually easier for kids with fine-motor issues to write, because they don't have to pick up the pencil between each letter, and there is more writing success than with printing.

The school IEP team all looked at each other wide-eyed. After a moment, his teacher confessed, "Cursive is in third grade. But I don't teach it. Instead, I trade off with another teacher. I take her class to PE, and she takes my class and teaches them cursive. I've just been taking Sean with her class to PE too since I thought he'd rather play than write."

Well, he was probably right, but I was angry that Sean had not even had the chance to *SEE* cursive being written. That was going to impair his reading of his classmates' handwriting, and he also needed to at least be able to sign his name one day. They calmed me down by explaining that cursive is used so little anymore because there are so many variations that it is difficult for everyone to read and computers and typing are taking over anyway. I decided to let it go, but made sure I was more aware of everything that was supposed to be taught for the remaining elementary years. The district administrator/inclusion specialist provided me each year after this with the standards for each grade level so I could see what content was taught each year and select areas to focus on for Sean's IEP goals.

The Daily Checklist
Vision. Without it a strategy is but a dream. — *Unknown*

Having behavior support from the school psychologist was a huge key to success with Sean's education. She was able to observe him and see what triggers and motivators were effective with him. She also pointed out that he needed frequent and visual positive feedback on how he was doing. To help him with transitions, he needed to know what was next in the day so he could be mentally prepared for the next thing.

She created the daily checklist, and in the beginning it would be taped to his desk, and every 5 to 15 minutes somebody (teacher or classroom assistant) would put a Happy Face on it if he was positively participating. In the beginning, they left it blank if he didn't do what he was supposed to and later added a sad face if he made a bad choice. Later, he was scored on a scale as to how well he chose to participate.

During elementary school, there were some things that happened every day, then others that changed, so they preprinted the things that were consistent, and then wrote in each day what was going to happen that day. They would read it to him when he was unable to read it. Knowing what was next reduced his transition behaviors immensely.

June 13, 2003

Sean /

Glasses ☑ 🙂

~~**Book**~~ ☐ ○

Flag Arrived after flag salute ☑ ○

Attendance ☑ 🙂

Sharing ☑ 🙂

Spelling * ☑ ○

* Sean wouldn't work with me on this but responded ☐ ○ well to tables and did the spelling words.

_____ ☐ ○

Recess - ☑ 🙂 but wouldn't stop bouncing ball in hallway.

Math ☑ 🙂

Beach Blanket ☑ 🙂

~~Lunch~~ bathroom/meds ☑ 🙂

Lunch ☑ 🙂

Desk Cleaning ☑ 🙂

TLC ☑ 🙂

Mrs. Walter came into class for a while to work with Sean. He went to her class for a short time.

3s these two: $1/day reward, $5 days in a row, $5 bonus on Friday

Each 3 pays 5 minutes of X-Box or GameCube time

Date_____	Positive Participation	Finish Work/ on Task	Focus/ Compliance	Hands to Self	Kind Words
9:00–10:00					
10:00–11:00					
11:00–12:00					
12:00–1:00					
1:00–2:00					
2:00–3:00					
3:00–4:00					

Codes: 1/needs improvement   2/satisfactory   2/exemplary
Sean must give this to his parents on a DAILY basis for video game time and money rewards

The motivators evolved over the years. In fifth grade, his teacher made *McMoney* and he earned play money that had his picture on it. He brought it home, and he paid for TV time and video game time. He was obsessed with his video games, so this kept him from having unlimited time to play them. We added real money at times when we had a trip coming up to give him spending money for the trip.

Sophomore and junior year the checklist looked like this:

Codes: 1/Needs improvement   2/Satisfactory   3/Exemplary
Teachers are to fill in a code # for each period.
Sean is to give this sheet to his parents on a DAILY basis for positive rewards as decided upon with his parents.

Date ___ TUESDAY	Materials/ on time	Cell phone to aide	Positive participation	Finish work/ on task	Focus/ compliance	No hands to mouth
Per #2						
Per #3						
Snack		allowed				
Per #4						
Per #5						
Lunch		allowed				
Per #6						
Per #7						

Turn cell phone on after school.

And as a senior, the checklist included a column for Sean to also grade how he thought his behavior was during each class too for self-monitoring. There was a column that stated if he didn't give the checklist to the teacher to fill out, then he would not be allowed to go off campus for lunch. He sometimes chose to not give the check-list to the teacher when his senioritis was in full symptom, and there were times he threw it away before coming home. But we still had the communication notebook, so I had the full story—until he threw that away too one day.

After-School Activities
Play with abandon.—Robin Thomas

There were many after-school activities, and since Sean was already at the after-school day care, I signed him up for most of them. A tennis instructor came 2 years in a row and taught the basics of tennis to the students who signed up for his after-school program.

One parent decided to bring a Jazzercise instructor to the school to teach an after-school Jazzercise class. There was a fee for this program, and about 20 girls signed up . . . and Sean. He thought it was a dance class, loved learning the steps, and loved being the only boy. They had a final recital and performed a few of their routines for the parents, and Sean was right there in step with them!

Cub Scouts
"Why not" is a slogan for an interesting life.—Mason Cooley

Cub Scout troops formed at the elementary school during third grade. Sean's Den Mother would later be his fifth-grade teacher. He loved the troop meetings that were held after school and earning his belt loops, and especially standing on stage to be awarded his belt loops. Going on hikes in our local hills, participating in the car and boat derbies with Rick's help, Sean had opportunities to build relationships with his friends outside of school. He lost interest after a couple of years, and we didn't continue to Boy Scouts when intermediate school rolled around. Many boys with Down syndrome have even earned their Eagle Scout rank.

New Principal
Every time we choose hope over despair, acceptance over intolerance, and optimism over negativity, we are doing our part to change the world.—Leeza Gibbons

At the end of Sean's second-grade year, the principal retired. I danced at his retirement party! While he didn't stand in our way, he certainly didn't contribute at all to Sean's success. He had been silently tolerant, unsupportive, and skating his way to retirement. The new principal, Mrs. Easton, was a woman who was extremely fit. She taught Pilates classes on the side. She was beautiful, strong, and very interested in this inclusion model that Sean was pioneering at our school. There were two special day classes at our school first, second, and third grade were in one class, and fourth, fifth, and sixth were in the other. There were 12 students in each of those classes.

During third grade, Mrs. Sunshine apologized to me. Seems she had remembered trying to talk me out of inclusion at the end of Sean's kindergarten IEP when he was transitioning from special education kindergarten to regular education kindergarten. She told me that she had been wrong and was amazed at his progress and at the way his classmates adored him.

Mrs. Sunshine and Mrs. Easton teamed up to transition our elementary school into an inclusive school! They met with the parents of the students in the special day classes during their IEP meetings, inviting them to include their children in regular education classes for the following year. They arranged with the district to transfer the two special day classes to another school's campus for the students who were going to stay segregated in special education.

I had encouraged Sean's teachers the past couple of summers to attend the Inclusion Institute, and neither had attended. The second-grade teacher was in Paris during one that summer, and the third-grade teacher simply wasn't interested. I had received a very large bonus check from my company and decided to offer to pay for the fourth-grade teacher to attend. She accepted, and I was thrilled that Mrs. Easton and Mrs. Sunshine also attended! Sean's tutor was there, and it was a great 2½ days of learning and team building. With everyone educated, fourth grade was shaping up to be a banner year.

Fourth Grade

Alone, hearts are one of life's most fragile things, but together, their passion can accomplish the impossible. — Byrd Baggett

Fourth-Grade IEP Goals

Sean will add diphthongs and some regular vowel sounds to his phonics program.

Sean will be able to read CVC words and words with consonant blends at the beginning or end of the words (tr, dr, sl, bl, etc.).

Sean will be able to read words with the long vowel sounds CVVC and CVCV words.

Sean will increase his sight word vocabulary by 55 to 65 words from the Dolch word list or from the literature series.

Sean will be able to answer 2–3 *why, when,* and *who* questions orally using text and illustrations.

Sean will be able to circle the answer on a multiple choice test to demonstrate basic comprehension of a literature story, answering questions like main characters, sequence three events, identify two main events in a story.

Sean will use touch math to learn basic addition facts to 20.

Sean will complete 10 double-digit addition and 10 double-digit subtraction problems using touch math or manipulatives.

Sean will be able to point to pictures showing more and less.

Sean will be able to circle numbers that demonstrate the concept of more and less.

Sean will be able to count by 5s, 10s, and by rote to 100.

Sean will be able to point to all coins when named.

Sean will be able to name all coins and state their value.

Sean will spell eight out of 10 spelling words correctly on a weekly basis.

Sean will write a complete five-to-six-word sentence with one to two teacher prompts on a weekly basis.

Sean will be able to dictate a three-sentence story or paragraph to the teacher on a topic that follows topic or story, and will copy the paragraph from the teacher's example correctly.

Sean will be able to give his address and phone number orally when asked.

Sean will name the days of the week.

Sean will be able to point to the days of the week and name them on a calendar on a weekly basis.

Sean will be able to name the day of the week and identify yesterday and tomorrow by pointing to a calendar.

Sean will be able to tell time to the hour.

Sean will demonstrate an understanding of simple facts from fourth-grade social studies curriculum on Missions and California History.

Sean will participate in the fourth-grade science curriculum on physical and life sciences.

Sean will attend to a lesson when the teacher has given one listening cue.

Sean will work on a task for 5 minutes independently.

Sean will follow the classroom rules with one reminder from the teacher or classroom assistant.

Sean will go to activities such as PE, recess, lunch, and assemblies on an independent basis by demonstrating appropriate behavior and rule following for these behaviors.

Sean will use a tape recorder and record his sentences and stories in order to encourage speech.

Sean will use a slant board for writing activities.

Sean will increase his speech intelligibility and be able to produce in sentences "l" blends, initial "th" blends, and final "th."

Sean will increase his comprehension of linguistic concepts and be able to comprehend and carry out one- or two-step directions involving the concepts of "either or," "either one," "same," "first," "before," and "after."

Fourth grade was a turning point for our school. Mrs. Easton had met with each family whose students were previously in the segregated special education classes and invited them to have their child fully included in regular education classes! A few parents took her up on the offer (those that didn't transferred with the special education classes to a neighboring school). Sean had a new friend in his fourth-grade class. She shared the classroom aides. He now had somebody that he could mentor in class and that gave him more confidence and built his self-esteem greatly.

Fourth grade was a big year in several ways. From kindergarten till third grade there were only 20 students in each class. Starting in fourth grade, there were 32 students! This was the year they learned about California state history too. And California has a very colorful history! On field trips they visited missions and learned about the mission system. They spent a day on the tall ship *Pilgrim* and learned what it was like to be a swab on a ship.

Then the big trip—overnight to our capitol city—Sacramento. I went to chaperone the trip, but Sean stayed with three other boys in their own hotel room. The trip was two nonstop days, including a visit to the capitol and a tour of the train museum. Sutter's Fort gave a great feeling of what it was like in the early settlements of California. But the best part was going to the American River and panning for gold! There was a demonstration of how to pan for gold, and everybody was given a small vial in case they uncovered any gold to hold their flakes! All of the students talked about what they would purchase with their newfound fortunes. Sean panned and panned, and voilà! He actually acquired one tiny flake! I helped him put his flake into the vial, and he was done. He was then totally content to take the rocks from the shoreline and throw them into the water for the rest of the 30 minutes of gold panning . . . He was the only student to leave with a flake of gold.

Sean also learned how to play the recorder this year in his music class, and once again participated in the after-school choir and performed in the Christmas and End-of-School performances.

I started getting phone calls from friends who were trying to include their children in other schools in our district. I realized that Sean was enjoying a pocket of perfection in his school within a district that was not supporting inclusion overall. One of my five friends whose son had been fully included made the decision to transfer her son to a special education class at another school. They had a new principal too, but he was nothing like our new principal. He made the suggestion that her son discontinue inclusion on the campus. When school started in the fall the students and their parents were looking for "that boy with Down syndrome" and voiced their disappointment to the principal that he wasn't there anymore. That sent a message to that principal, he had made a mistake, but the damage had already been done. Inclusion died at that school, while it thrived at Sean's school.

One parent's observation caused me to think. She pointed out, "Every year, Sean gets the BEST teacher in that grade. How do you pull it off?"

"I simply have the principal ask the teachers to volunteer to have him. I guess he gets the best teachers because they are the ones who want the challenge, the ones who love teaching, and the ones who know they will become better teachers by educating Sean. You are right, he does get the best teachers, and the fact that they choose Sean is the proof!"

School Talent Show

To succeed in life, you need three things: a wishbone, a backbone, and a funny bone. — Reba McIntyre

In fourth grade, Sean decided he wanted to be in the school talent show. Here's how the conversation went as we were driving to Disneyland for the day:

"Mom."

"What?"

"Talent show" (pronounced "tawant sew").

"Talent show?"

"Yes."

"What about the talent show?"

"Me do it."

"What do you want to do in the talent show? Sing? Dance?"

"No, MAGIC!" (pronounced correctly!—with apraxia, the words sometimes come out right).

"Magic?"

"YES!"

"OK, we will go to the Disney Magic shop and see what they have before we leave."

A few hours later we were heading toward the exit of the Magic Kingdom, so we stopped by the Magic store and this great lady was working behind the counter. She truly had magical powers as she read my mind! I put my arm around Sean, gesturing with my eyes, and said, "Sean wants to do a magic act for his school's talent show . . . Do you have anything that *HE* can do?"

She was great. She said, "Well, if you are going to be on stage, you need something that everyone can see. I have two tricks that would be good. Here is a regular rope. Place it on the ground, and say, 'Sit,' then say, 'Stay,' then say, 'Roll over,' and pick it up and turn it over—it's kind of funny—THEN hold it out in front of you and say, 'lie down,' and it will stay straight out." (It had some sort of wire that allowed it to go straight out when held the right way.) "Then, roll it between your fingers and say, 'Play dead,' and it will flop down, just like a regular rope."

Then she also had the one scarf that you pull and out comes four different colored scarves.

The rope trick was great, but if nobody could understand the words, "sit down, roll over, lie down, and play dead," then it didn't make any sense . . . and it wouldn't be funny . . . Well, Sean had a plan.

I told him we were going to have to practice the words so everybody could understand him.

He said, "Becky help." (Of course, this is the girl he had a major crush on!) So, the beautiful assistant was added to the show. And here's how it went:

Becky came out first and announced, "Ladies and Gentlemen, I would like to introduce The Magical Sean McElwee the Magician!" Sean bowed and she continued, "Since the Magical Sean speaks Seanese, I will be translating for him."

Sean wore a black robe and a Merlin the Magician Hat complete with long gray hair attached to it. As Sean narrated the tricks, she then repeated into the microphone, as if to translate so everybody could understand him. He decided to take his bows even before applause occurred . . . The crowd roared with laughter and applause. Sean's act was a huge success! The parents were cracking up even after the show. His was one of the quickest acts and that made it a big favorite for the parents who sat through over 2 hours of *talent* from the elementary school students.

The best part for Sean? Becky had to come to our house for 2 weeks, two or three times a week, to rehearse and Sean was in heaven. After their performance, he still wanted her to come over and rehearse.

Appreciating the Angels

It doesn't matter what we have or what we accomplish in life. In the end what truly matters is who we have beside us. — Byrd Bagget

I nominated Sean's entire team for the Down Syndrome Association of Orange County's Educator of the Year Award. TEN incredible women—teacher, principal, school psychologist, BOTH classroom assistants, district inclusion specialist, her assistant that modified Sean's materials, the resource specialist, speech therapist, and Sean's private tutor. Even if they were not selected as the winners, the nominees were always invited to the Annual Women's luncheon where the winners would be honored. Well, turns out it was supposed to be *"a nominee."* I didn't know you couldn't nominate *"a team"!* But really, it took a team! They were willing to host two of Sean's team members for the luncheon, but I couldn't let that happen—they *all* needed to be recognized and rewarded for their dedication and hard work. So, I paid for the additional seven women, and my luncheon fee; $65 per person. It was a little bit of a financial sacrifice, but worth every penny. I wanted these women to be appreciated and feel appreciated. Their dedication and hard work truly paid off and benefitted not just Sean, but now all of the fully included students with disabilities at our school. They never knew that I paid for their lunches!

Here's their nomination letter:

As I slowly inch my car up the drop-off line, I am thinking about how much progress Sean has made in the last 5 years. It's Sean's turn. He unbuckles his seat belt, grabs his backpack, and slides open the van door. I call to him, "Bye, Sean. Make good choices today!" He calls back, "Bye, Mom." He closes the door and walks, independently, to his fourth-grade class. And I drive away. I feel normal. I feel so proud of him. I feel so thankful to the IEP team who listened to our goals of independence for Sean and made them their goals too.

After 5 years of inclusion, this year, Sean's IEP team has proven that it really does "take a village." The key to the team's success is cooperation, collaboration, and communication, and this team really doesn't have an "I" in it!

There is some controversy on who has the pivotal role in inclusive education. Is it the teacher or the principal? The teacher is the daily provider of instruction, but the attitude of the principal and her educational philosophy trickles down to the entire teaching staff. The principal is definitely a critical piece to the puzzle. Then there is the staff that provides the teacher with the critical support that make the inclusion experience a good one for everybody. So, I made the decision that I needed to not only nominate Sean's teacher, who is phenomenal, but the entire team that has made fourth grade Sean's most successful year academically and socially.

The teacher volunteered last year to teach Sean. She visited his third-grade class to familiarize herself with Sean and his abilities. The summer before the school year began she eagerly attended the 3-day Bayridge Consortium's Summer Inclusion Institute at California State University, San Marcos, in July 2003, to learn about inclusive education to prepare for not only Sean, but another student who was going to be included for the first time in her fourth-grade class. Sean has been challenged educationally, with all his materials being adapted to his ability level. He has been expected to behave appropriately and has risen to that expectation. I asked the other included student's mom to give me her impression of the teacher, and she said, "I like her kindness and patience. The positive nurturing environment she creates in the classroom benefits all the students. That starts from her and is reflected through the students in their interactions with my daughter."

The teacher collaborates beautifully with the entire IEP team. She directs the classroom assistants to help all the students in the class. She learns from Sean's private tutor, the inclusion specialist, and her assistant, taking all suggestions and putting them into practice with enthusiasm. I have experienced a great peace of mind knowing that Sean is learning more this year and is growing in his independence level.

The principal was transferred to our elementary school only 2 years ago, and she has been an incredible leader to the entire school. When the special day classes were moved to another campus last year, she invited the students to remain at our school and be fully included. She supported them in the inclusion process. There were 28 students with IEPs attending regular classrooms at Sean's elementary school the first year the school converted to an inclusive elementary school. When the school applied for the California State Distinguished Schools Award that year, the principal made sure to feature the Exceptional Child Committee of the PTA (I was the chairperson) and the fact that all students are supported in the least restrictive environment and are provided full access to the standards-based curriculum. Mrs. Easton also attended the Bayridge Consortium's Summer Inclusion Institute in San Marcos. When Sean was testing his teacher earlier in the school year, she was extremely helpful in talking to Sean about making good choices in school.

The principal is supporting and promoting differentiated instruction skills for the teaching staff that ultimately benefit every child in the school. She also encourages collaboration between all educators. Always a pleasure to talk to, always a positive outlook. The principal is a blessing to everyone at our elementary school. I also asked the parent of the other student included in Sean's class about her, and she said, "She is the first principal at this school who actually attended my daughter's IEP meetings. This shows me she is interested, dedicated, and involved in the education of all students here."

The school's PTA president said of the principal, "She gives our teachers, parents, and students her unconditional support. She ensures follow through and pays attention to every detail and task that is required of her and the teacher to ensure success for all students. Because of the principal and the teacher's efforts, every child has benefited from Sean's part in our school community."

There are two classroom assistants in Sean's class, one in the morning and one in the afternoon. The classroom assistants are there because of Sean and the other fully included student, but they are the CLASSROOM assistants; they help every child in the class and are masterfully directed by the teacher. The support they provide to the class is priceless. When I asked Sean's tutor about both of the classroom assistants, she said, "They are very hard workers and very dedicated."

The morning aide has been employed at the school for many years as a campus supervisor and as a classroom assistant in the school's former special day class. Sean relates well to her, and she has been a great asset to the classroom. The other parent said, "She has been one of my daughter's classroom assistants for the past 3 years, and made her transition to inclusion a smooth one. She is caring, nurturing, and helps my daughter as if she is one of her own kids."

The afternoon aide has been in Sean's classes since first grade. When she first started it was a coincidence that she had been an assistant in one of his special day preschool classes, so it was fun to have a familiar face. She is a staunch advocate for Sean. She won't let anybody get away with treating him unfairly, including me! It is a comfort to know there is somebody with him daily that cares so much about him.

Mrs. Sunshine was the first person to listen to my desire to include Sean when he was transitioning from special day class kindergarten to regular education kindergarten. Here we are 5 years later, and she is one of Sean's champions. Always prepared to provide a suggestion on a behavioral challenge and always a positive influence at the IEP meetings. Not only do the IEP meetings run smoothly because of her, but she helps me to remember items that I may have overlooked on the IEP each year.

Mrs. Sunshine's dedication and professionalism is not just

directed at Sean. The other included student in his class's mom said, "She is truly an advocate for my daughter. I always felt like she was 100 percent for what is best for her educational plan. She is so organized and knowledgeable in the system and her knowledge of the psychology of children. She puts the complete package together and ties it up with a cute little bow on top." She also rises to the challenge of coordinating the schedules of the IEP team members for the meetings. Now that's a tough job!

The school's resource specialist also attended the Bayridge Consortium's Summer Institute. She was eager to learn how to "push in" services as opposed to "pull out" in the resource room. She has been great collaborative support to the teacher throughout this year and provides support to Sean in the classroom without him being pulled out into another room. She has open communication with weekly notes, is very positive, and has been great at challenging both Sean and the other included student on their IEP goals.

The inclusion specialist wears many hats in the district's special education department. She is the district's expert on inclusion and is the glue that holds the programs together. She is also my "go-to" person when there has been a problem in the past, although I have not needed to call her at all this year. Always full of ideas, she trains the classroom assistants in shadowing techniques, provides support to the teachers, and is supporting 14 students that are fully included at the elementary level in the school district.

I always receive a call from her after she has visited Sean's classroom with her observations and opinions of his educational program and its efficacy. I am embarrassed to say she has been in his class much more than I this year, although that has been a wonderful break for me. Each call I have received this year has been so positive and encouraging. She has only had positive comments on her observations in the classroom or on the playground this year. She has had nothing but positive remarks about the fourth-grade teacher and how fantastic this school year is going. The parent of the other included child said, "She is great, her knowledge and expertise is impressive; she really wants our kids to be independent and make improvements. She always finds a solution to help my daughter move forward with her social and educational goals."

The assistant to the inclusion specialist plays an integral role in the inclusion process. As the curriculum became more challenging and time was lacking in the teacher's day, the district found it needed somebody to direct the classroom assistants and take the lead in modifying materials to the educational abilities of the students with special needs that were fully included. She meets with the teacher on a weekly basis and receives the lessons that will be taught for the following week and adapts those materials, or directs the classroom assistants on how to adapt the materials.

The speech therapist has been Sean's speech therapist since kindergarten. He has come a long way in both articulation and language. In kindergarten, he was barely intelligible, and now he can stand in front of his classroom and "share" during show-and-tell time, and the class knows what he is talking about. She collaborates with the teachers on ways to foster Sean's speech and, in the past, on cueing him to pronounce words correctly. She helps create meaningful goals for Sean each year, which can be carried over into the classroom.

Sean's private tutor tutors 30 students with Down syndrome and provides Sean with one-on-one learning on a weekly basis. It may seem odd that I am including her in this nomination, even though she isn't a district employee. But she is an integral part of Sean's educational team. The beauty of this team is everyone's ideas are respected and implemented. She has been to Sean's class twice to work with the teacher and classroom assistants. She has been so readily accepted and seen as an asset, not a threat.

I asked her about her impressions about the team, and she said, "I am very impressed they welcomed me into their class, listened to what I had to say, and implemented it. It is evident that the team effort benefits Sean, as evidenced by the great school year he is having." Now THAT is working as a team!

There are so many people involved at Sean's school that work with him each week: the science specialist, the music teacher—who is teaching the recorder this year, the computer teacher, the librarian, the PE teacher, the office staff, and the school health assistant. Even the custodians take an interest in Sean's development. But it does not end there. We also have the Cub Scout leader and chorus director and the after-school childcare team. It really does take a village!

While Sean walks to class in the mornings by himself he is never alone. I would be surprised if one of the 780 students at the school didn't know him. When I used to walk him to class EVERY person who passed him, student, parent, or teacher, would say, "Hi, Sean." *EVERY* one of them!

Inclusive education isn't easy, but when you have a team who is so dedicated to making the experience a success, the Dream is Alive! This team has created an environment that facilitates learning. They truly enhance the innate love of learning in every child. Sean's elementary school is a community that affirms and values the unique gifts and potential of each child. This is a model that every school should try to duplicate. His school exemplifies the characteristics and truly deserves the Down Syndrome Association of Orange County's Educator of the Year Award!

Sincerely,

Sandra McElwee

After the results were decided each time I nominated a teacher, or this year, a team, I would also write a letter to the school board members AND the superintendent of schools to let them know what a great team they had in both the district support people and the school staff. I provided each person mentioned in the letters a copy. I wanted them to know how much I appreciated all they did for Sean, and most of all, the spirit that they did it in. I was hearing stories from my friends at different schools that their children were not enjoying the same amount of success with the educators that Sean was having. Positive reinforcement works for everybody.

Tutors

When one teaches, two learn.—Robert Heinlein

Sean was really resisting doing homework at home, and I didn't want to battle him every night. So we hired a neighbor's daughter to come over and do his homework with him. She was in seventh grade when she began working with Sean, and he cooperated with her. I sent her with Sean to the tutor's house who specialized in children with Down syndrome's and she taught her some techniques for working with Sean. Today, she's a teacher in an inner-city school—and differentiates instruction for all levels of learners. She's a great teacher too!

Sean always responded to cute girls positively. Many of my friends adopted this model and paid neighborhood friends to do homework with their children. It made for a much-calmer household, and moms could cook dinner while the homework was being facilitated by a friend.

Tenth-Birthday Survivor Party

God gave us the gift of life; it is up to us to give ourselves the gift of living well.—Voltaire

We always celebrated Sean's birthday big. The party rule that 50 percent of the people you invite will not come never applied to Sean. We had 70 people at his first birthday, and every year it was a lot to entertain the masses. After he started school, we invited his whole class, then the kids in the neighborhood and his friends from his early intervention program. We ended up with around 40 kids each time. Trust me, that's a lot of goody bags.

We decided since 10 is the double-digit birthday that we would do something different. The television reality show *Survivor* was on the air, and we lived near a campground. We had a tent trailer and borrowed a couple of big tents and invited nine of Sean's guy friends and hosted the Survivor Birthday Campout. Each boy got their own Survivor Bandana, and I had several "challenges" for them to complete. We split the boys into two teams, each had won half of the challenges, and then we came to the food challenge.

I went into the trailer to prepare the Bats Blood (V-8 Juice) and the Petrified Miner's Brain (a brain Jell-O mold made with unflavored Jell-O and gummy worms inside it. The Bat's Blood wasn't such a big challenge. Some of the boys didn't finish it, but most did. With the Petrified Miner's Brain, I had used green food coloring, and they expected it to just be lime Jell-O . . . but there was no flavoring, and it was nasty tasting. One boy threw up his V-8 it gagged him so badly. Sean ate the whole thing—he was so used to eating nasty-tasting applesauce every day with his powdered vitamins in it, and so he won the challenge.

The boys still talked about that party when they were 18.

Fifth Grade

Flatter me, and I may not believe you. Criticize me, and I may not like you. Ignore me, and I may not forgive you. Encourage me, and I may not forget you. —*William Arthur Ward*

Fifth-Grade IEP Goals

When presented with a reading passage at 2.0 level, Sean will read the passage aloud with 75 percent accuracy.

When presented with a reading passage at K to 1 grade level, Sean will answer comprehension questions.

Sean will demonstrate his ability to compose a five-to-six-word sentence with correct grammar, close to accurate spelling and proper punctuation.

Sean will pass a weekly spelling test of increasingly more difficult words (1.5 to 1.7) grade level.

Sean will recognize, name, and know the value of the following coins: penny, nickel, dime, quarter.

Sean will demonstrate his ability to use the touch points given on numbers 10–15 in order to add those numbers to 70.

Sean will tell time to the half hour.

Sean will listen to teacher-directed lessons for following directions and complete his worksheet with 50 percent accuracy and three teacher prompts.

Sean will demonstrate increased on-task behavior without teacher prompts for 15 minutes.

Social Studies/Science/Health—through exposure to the fifth-grade curriculum Sean will gain in knowledge from his mainstream experiences in the regular education class.

At the conclusion of each unit covered in class in social studies, science, and health, Sean will learn two new vocabulary words from the unit and be able to identify those words using picture clues.

Produce words ending with "r" blends, initial "j," initial "r," initial "th," "l" blends, and "ch" sounds in a directed conversation.

Produce words in sentences ending in "r," "r" blends, initial "j."

Sean will use target structures (object and possessive pronouns, third-person regular tense, regular and irregular past tense verbs) in a directed conversation with a peer in the therapy setting.

Sean will increase his expressive language and question-asking skills for conversation and will be able to use the target forms (questions, future tense, and subject-verb agreement) and overall correct grammar skills in complete sentences during a directed conversation with a peer in the therapy setting.

Sean will increase his comprehension of linguistic concepts and will be able to carry out one- and two-step directions involving the concepts of "some," "before," and "after."

As I look back at the communication notebooks from kindergarten through fourth grade, there were many notes about Sean's behavior. Mostly the reason for his behaviors was avoidance of something that was hard to do, or attention seeking, or simply boredom. Sean spit, hit, and called his teachers and classroom assistants "stupid" (pretty good clusters in this word for him to articulate). He crawled under his desk, ran out of the room, told the teaching staff, "No," and threw balls into shrubs. All unacceptable behaviors, but the entire 5 years they collaborated with me and the school psychologist and inclusion specialist and her assistant to figure out the cause and eliminate the effect (the behavior). If it looked like a pattern was developing—where he was doing the same thing 3 days in a row—and their interventions didn't work, then we agreed to keep him home for a day to break the pattern. Sean hated missing school, and this almost always broke the unacceptable behavior pattern he was developing. The important thing was they never *disliked* Sean for his acting out. They were so patient and understanding, and each note home was factual; no negative opinions and *not one time* did anyone ever suggest he was placed in the wrong setting.

At the same time, there were many notes in the communication notebooks about how polite Sean was too. Manners and being polite are very important to our family. "Please, thank you" have been stressed with Sean since he was an infant, beginning with sign language. As I reviewed his communication notebooks while writing this book there were many notes telling me that they presented Sean with an assignment his response was, "No, thank you." There were smiley faces next to these notes.

For the fifth-grade talent show, Sean wanted to bring his dog and have him do dog tricks. The dog successfully sat and lay down, but refused to roll over. So Sean laid down on the stage and rolled over. More hysterical laughter.

I nominated the fifth-grade teacher for the Down Syndrome Association of Orange County's Educator of the Year Award. The nomination letter summarizes fifth grade:

> I would like to nominate my son's fifth-grade teacher for the Educator of the Year Award. She has been more than Sean's fifth-grade teacher. For the past 3 years, she led his Cub Scout troop. Sean had the privilege to get to know her through the Scouting activities, so the school year began well for him. Sean had been fully included since kindergarten at his elementary school, and the fifth-grade teacher took the initiative to attend the Inclusion Institute's Summer Program at California State University at San

Marcos to learn more about adapting curriculum and techniques for successful inclusion. She also worked closely with Sean's fourth-grade teacher to learn as much as she could about Sean's academic and behavioral abilities.

She saw potential in Sean that many did not, including me! She taught Sean multiplication! Then when Sean asked to learn fractions, like the rest of the class, she taught him fractions. He is very proud of his achievements in math.

Before Christmas, Sean was having a stellar year, both academically and behaviorally. Then his endocrinologist took him off of Synthroid in order to retest and confirm his hypothyroidism diagnosis. I didn't know that hypothyroidism caused emotional and behavioral difficulties, so I didn't attribute the next weeks of behaviors to the removal of the Synthroid. I wrongly attributed it to puberty.

Sean became depressed, he was sad for no reason. He became combative, angry, and argumentative. The schoolwork he previously had completed eagerly became a battle and an argument for every single sheet of paper. He began telling his teacher, "Don't want to, I don't have to, you can't make me" when she asked him to complete his work. He became angry, and this escalated from yelling to hitting. I could go on and on with the following weeks of behaviors, but the bottom line was Sean was awful, and his teacher didn't give up.

She has been phenomenal in communicating and troubleshooting this issue with me. Never once has she suggested that Sean be removed from her class. She persevered and advocated for his inclusion on every day, especially the ones where he was incredibly awful.

She assembled Sean's IEP team, and we discussed positive behavioral motivational plans. Not once during this meeting was it suggested for Sean to be sent to a special day class, and I truly expected this because his behavior had deteriorated so much. Instead, she came up with a "play money" plan where Sean would be "paid" for completing work, and have the option to choose

NOT to do his work, but then he would be the one who "pays." He comes home with his McMoney (which has his photo on it), and then he has to pay to play GameCube, watch TV, or any number of activities he enjoys. This ingenious idea also incorporated his IEP goals of learning money, addition, and subtraction! We have even implemented this at home so he is paid for making his bed, washing the dishes, and other chores he is learning.

This year began as the best ever for Sean academically and behaviorally and transitioned to the worse ever behaviorally. But now, thanks to his teacher's perseverance, commitment, and belief in Sean, he is back on track. When I thanked her for not giving up on him, she sent me a card. I am going to type the entire card's contents here, because this really says it all of what a dedicated teacher she is:

Dear Sandra,

Thank you for coming to the meeting yesterday. I want you to understand a few things. First, I really enjoy working with Sean. I learn from him, and he amazes me every day. Also, I really enjoy working with you! Your persistence to do what you in your heart know is needed is amazing. You remind me constantly what it means to be a Mom. I love how you can put your emotions aside and talk about your son and his needs. You are very strong. Sean has and will continue to make progress as a citizen and member of this world. I am proud to be his teacher.

Love and Prayers

Sean's Fifth-Grade Teacher

I am proud that she is Sean's teacher. I am nominating her for the Down Syndrome Association of Orange County's Educator of the Year Award. I certainly hope you will recognize her, as she earned this award and more this year.

Sincerely,

Sandra McElwee

She deservedly won the honor of Educator of the Year!

Sean's tutor (the one who specialized in tutoring children with Down syndrome) collaborated with his fifth-grade teacher until we made the decision to discontinue her services. Sean was doing great and progressing quickly in math—he had memorized his multiplication tables through the fives, and I asked her to add multiplication to her weekly repertoire. She refused, insisting that it was too soon and that Sean didn't know all of his math facts yet—and I overreacted. I accused her of limiting him and decided on the spot that we didn't need her services any more. I sorely regretted that decision after seventh grade when Sean's reading, writing, and math began to regress due to situations occurring at school.

Puberty

B is for Breasts of which ladies have two; once prized for the function, now for the view.—Robert Paul Smith

For somebody who had zero interest in breast-feeding as a baby, he had a ton of interest in breasts from the onset of puberty and on!

When Sean was in fourth grade, his aide was extremely well-endowed—and I'm certain she had back issues carrying those huge breasts around all day. She also wasn't very tall, and at the time, her breasts were at Sean's eye level. Toward the end of fourth grade she was lecturing Sean about yet another thing he had done wrong, and he had decided he'd heard enough. In an effort to quiet her, he took one hand and grabbed one breast and that stopped the lecture! Yes, he got in trouble, and we all decided it was purely a way to "turn off the lecture" and not a sexual act . . . but in fifth grade, it was a completely different story!

Sean was fully in the throes of puberty and one day reentering the class from recess he made a detour. Instead of going directly to his desk, he walked right up to the teacher who was standing at the front of the room waiting for everyone to be seated—and he grabbed BOTH of her breasts!

I was mortified when Mrs. Easton called to tell me *why* he was being suspended for the next day of school. But I didn't get the entire story till a year later.

Rick and I were at a school choir performance. And the fifth-grade teacher was sitting behind us. We were waiting for the production to begin and she asked, "Did I ever tell you the story of what happened that day?"

Rick and I said, "No, we were too embarrassed to ask."

She died laughing and started to tell us what happened. First, she began with the routine that she and Mrs. Easton had devised for when Sean inevitably would behave inappropriately. She would send Sean to the office with his aide. The aide would inform the principal of the infraction. The principal would send a substitute to manage the class. The teacher would go to the office, confer with the principal, then together, they would speak to Sean. On this particular day after he had grabbed her breasts, she thought she wasn't going to have to address Sean with the principal as the time passed and nobody had come to relieve her . . . but 15 minutes before the school day ended the substitute arrived.

While the principal was an amazing woman, she still was the teacher's boss, and the teacher found it tough to chastise Sean at all, especially in front of her boss.

So, the way it usually went was, they would ask Sean, "Do you know what you did wrong?" He would respond and was supposed to take responsibility. They would reiterate *why* the infraction was wrong, then tell him what his consequences were going to be.

At this point when she was telling us the story she was laughing so hard she could hardly talk. That caused us to laugh with her, and we didn't even know why! She continued the story telling us that she sat down with Sean—with Mrs. Easton observing—and asked, "Sean, do you know what you did wrong?" She said that Sean hung his head low, in shame, and with a low voice and octave she had never heard before, said long and drawn out, "Ni-ih-puls." (nipples). By now, the teacher was crying she was laughing so hard. She said it was all she could do to keep a straight face to Sean, and there's her boss sitting right there!

"Sean, you know those are my nip . . . You know you aren't supposed to touch other people's nip . . . Sean, don't do that again." Cracking up, she said she couldn't say, "Those are my nipples, you can't touch them" with a straight face!

She's been teaching fifth grade for several years and told us, "All the boys his age are thinking it; Sean was the only one brave enough to do it!"

She most deservedly won the Educator of the Year Award!

Later in the year as the planning IEP for sixth grade was wrapping up, the three sixth-grade teachers said, "Oh, and you won't have to worry about Sean groping any of us next year." I wanted to crawl under the table. They continued, "We're all flat chested." Thankfully he never did that again—with a teacher.

Orchestra

You need very patient people in your house when you have a violin.
— Kevin Eubanks

In fifth grade, all students have the opportunity to learn a string instrument. Sean selected the violin. Oh, the rehearsing at home was tortuous! But he learned to play "Hot Cross Buns," and a few other songs. At the end of the school year, the orchestra performed. As the students tuned their instruments on stage the parents entered and took their seats. Sean spied us in the audience and in true Sean form, stood up and danced around with his violin and bow. He got some laughs, and the music teacher didn't chastise him. The music teacher had a brilliant no-pressure offer for the students. If they wanted to play a solo, they were invited to do so. They had learned a repertoire of songs, and before the entire orchestra played the song, he said, "Does anybody want to play a solo of this song?" The first song, "Hot Cross Buns," Sean stood to perform a solo. I believe that is the only song he truly learned that year. He was very proud, and his music teacher was proud of him as well. Rick and I were thrilled.

School Site Council

L.E.A.D. = Learn, Educate, Appreciate, Develop. — Byrd Baggett

Being involved in PTA, having that access to the principal and learning what is going on around the school is invaluable. I learned about the school site council and put my name in the hat to be elected by the parents of the school.

The school site council is made up of parents and teachers who work with the principal to develop, review, and evaluate school improvement programs and budgets. Reports that are made during the school site council include demographics of the students, test scores, categorical funds that could be allocated for new academic programs, adding staff members, etc. In California, the school site council is responsible to prepare for the school's reaccreditation every 6 years.

One year after the elementary school had become an inclusive school and all students with special educational needs were fully included we received our school's test scores. As Mrs. Easton reported on the unprecedented jump in test scores, she said that she had no real reason to explain *why* the scores had jumped so significantly.

I knew why.

When she finished reading our school's new scores, I raised my hand and said, "The students' test scores have gone up because there is no more segregation here. The regular education students are helping the ones who have IEPs in their classes, and that is enforcing what they have learned. The students with IEPs are scoring higher because they are now being educated alongside their peers." Evidence shows this phenomenon over and over again in the documentation of what happens when schools are inclusive.

One 180-page study titled, *The Impact of Inclusion on Standardized*

Test Scores of Learning Supported Students, by Cynthia A. Johnson., Ed.D., at Walden University states, "A positive correlation was determined to exist between test scores of learning supported students and the percentage of time they were exposed to an educational placement with their non-disabled peers. The results of this study have provided implications for positive social change in that students with disabilities should be provided more opportunities to be included with their non-disabled peers in K–12 school environments; their inclusion has the potential to increase student achievement."

Science

What you leave behind is not what is engraved in stone monuments, but what is woven into the lives of others.—Pericles

I offered to present Down syndrome to the four fifth-grade science classes when they were learning about genetics, and the teachers took me up on the offer. I started off by taking a dry erase marker and made pairs of red and green lines on the white board. I would explain that the red lines were the half of the chromosomes that came from their mothers, and the green lines were the half of the chromosomes that came from their fathers. Then I would add one more line in another color and say, "And Sean has an extra chromosome, and that is added to the set numbered 21 . . . You all have two twenty-first chromosomes; Sean has three." I'd ask them to name what's good to have extra of . . . They would answer, "cake," "ice cream," "money," etc. Then I showed them a video of Sean playing basketball. In the first video he was 6 years old, and he tried and tried for 6 weeks to make a basket, but never did. Then I played a current video where he couldn't miss a basket. I explained how it takes him longer to learn, but once he does learn, he knows how to do what he's learned—really well.

Then I would ask the class, "What's your favorite subject?" Usually the unanimous answer was "RECESS!" (I didn't know that was a subject!) Then I would ask what their least favorite subject was—usually it was unanimously "MATH!" Then it would shock them when I said, "Sean's favorite subject is math!" They were so impressed with that. These students were Sean's same age peers. Most of them had been in school with him since kindergarten. This was the first time since first grade that more teaching about Sean and Down syndrome had been done. There were more students in the school who had Down syndrome and were fully included. There was no fear of Sean or the other students who had Down syndrome. The familiarity and daily exposure to different abilities had removed all possibility of trepidation.

Discovery

To an adolescent, there is nothing in the world more embarrassing than a parent. — Dave Barry

Just wait till the "hair down there" appears—that was a fun night—Sean was 12 and had been independent in the bathroom for a while so I was unaware that the "hair down there" had arrived. Sean was in his bathroom, supposedly preparing to take a shower when he started screaming, "MOM, QUICK! MOM, COME HERE!!!"

I ran upstairs to his bathroom completely expecting to see blood, and as I unlocked the bathroom door from the outside (love that little tool that allows you to unlock locked doors!), there he was standing with a washcloth in his hand. He said, "It won't come off!" He was trying to wash off "the hair."

Well, I had given him the video titled *Where Did I Come From* which is a cartoon narrated by Howie Mandel which is about changes in your body at puberty, making babies, etc. It was at the level of understanding that Sean was at—just enough information, but not so much he had instructions. Well, when they *penciled in* the cartoon hair in the movie, apparently Sean didn't relate that to actual hair.

Trying *SO HARD NOT TO LAUGH*, I said, "Oh, you're becoming a man. Just like the movie, you're growing hair. There will be more hair in your armpits, and maybe on your chest." Then thinking to myself, *But not if you take after Dad.*

From then on he watched his armpits, and lo and behold, the summer he was ALMOST 16—there it was—and he proudly said, "Mom, look!" As he took his shirt off and lifted his arms. "Armpit hair!" he exclaimed.

Ah, a proud moment.

Sixth Grade

The grass isn't greener on the other side. It's greener where you water and fertilize it. — *Lysa TerKeurst*

Sixth-Grade IEP Goals

Sean will demonstrate the ability to button two half-inch buttons with verbal cues.

Sean will have the choice to write or use a computer.

Sean will improve his reading comprehension skills to the 2.5 grade level.

Sean will demonstrate his ability to compose a five-to-six-word sentence with correct grammar, close to accurate spelling, and punctuation.

Sean will pass a weekly spelling test of increasingly more difficult words (1.5 to 1.7 grade level).

Sean will use the calculator to solve basic multiplication and division facts.

Sean will calculate the value of three coins (pennies, nickels, dimes, quarters).

At the conclusion of each unit in science, health, and social studies, Sean will orally discuss the pictures from the unit and be able to write a short sentence to describe what is happening.

Sean will cooperate during class instruction with one teacher prompt during a 60-minute class period and complete class work for three of five assignments.

Without prompts Sean will be able to self-monitor his speech and use a slow rate and developmentally appropriate phonemes in a structured activity.

Sean will be able to increase his expressive syntax/morphology skills and will be able to form complete and grammatically correct sentences and questions in a structured conversation, and with no more than one prompt/cue, will self-monitor and correct his errors.

Sean will increase his comprehension of the concept "after" and will be able to carry out two-step directions involving the concept of "after" (clap your hands after you say your name).

We had Sean's education nailed down by sixth grade: The district inclusion specialist's assistant had a new title, "inclusion facilitator." She was modifying Sean's materials. The current and past teachers could discuss with each other techniques that had worked in past years, and the school psychologist and the principal were on board with inclusion. There were no disagreements about anything. The FM system had been moved from class to class every year. For sixth grade, Sean would be changing classes and be in three different classrooms. The decision was made to keep the FM system in his homeroom class where he would spend most of his time.

In sixth grade, in order to prepare the students for intermediate school and make them comfortable with changing classes, the teachers broke up math, language arts, and science, and the students changed classes and teachers for those subjects. Since language arts was Sean's toughest subject, and they were changing classes, I asked that he go to the resource room for that period each day. He continued to make progress.

Both of Sean's aides took positions elsewhere in the district. They wanted to stay in elementary school and not continue to intermediate school. Sadly, we lost the one aide who had been with Sean since first grade, and her expertise in Sean's behavior and in motivating him was lost. The district did provide one aide for sixth grade that followed Sean to his academic classes, but was not there for the entire day. His independence was growing, and it was critical that he not become dependent on an aide. She bonded well with Sean and quickly learned his quirks and how to motivate him.

Sixth-grade students also had Buddy Classes with kindergarten classes and once a week they would go and spend some time with a kindergarten class, doing an art project with them or playing a game. Sean's class was paired with another class that had a new inclusion student who also had Down syndrome. Sean was this student's Big Buddy; talk about an esteem builder! All the years that Sean had been the one being helped and now he was able to help someone. This was a great program for all the sixth-graders, and they benefitted by learning patience and compassion and focusing on someone other than themselves.

Triennial Assessment

Courage is not simply one of the virtues, but the form of every virtue at the testing point. —C. S. Lewis

Sixth grade was a big preparation for intermediate school. It was time for Sean's triennial assessment. Triennial assessments are required to assess whether a student still qualifies for special educational services. The school psychologist observed Sean in class, reviewed his school records, interviewed his teachers, interviewed his friends, and utilized the Vineland Adaptive Behavior Scales.

Here are excerpts from the assessment report:

Education

Sean has attended his school since kindergarten, and he has participated in the regular education program since kindergarten. Full inclusion has been supported by an inclusion facilitator who has modified the regular education curriculum to ensure learning and participation at Sean's ability level and an instructional assistant assigned to the classroom teacher. The inclusion facilitator meets regularly with the teacher and instructional assistant to determine the need and level of Sean's modifications. Sean's parents are also actively involved and supportive of Sean's behavioral and academic program. In addition, the resource specialist is available on a consultation basis.

His sixth-grade teacher reports that Sean is an active participant in class. He is polite to adults and peers. He's very social and enjoys being a part of his peer group/class. Sean has good gross-motor skills and can be very competitive on the playground. Academically, math is a relative strength according to his classroom teacher. He understands concepts when provided with a breakdown of the steps. During reading Sean enjoys reading aloud, and discussing the pictures and meaning. He is given limited parts to read and gets help from peers and the instructional assistant when he encounters a challenging word. In general, Sean's ability to follow group instruction and work independently is inconsistent.

When Sean was asked about school he stated that he likes school and his friends. He is positive about himself and his "work." Sean states his favorite thing to do is play. He can state who his friends are and that he likes to work with his teacher and the classroom assistant. Overall, Sean presents as a happy person and seems to enjoy school.

Behavior observations

Sean was observed in different settings. On the playground, Sean was playing handball with peers. He is competitive and knows the rules. On this occasion, Sean seemed to be following the rules and playing like his peers. When called out by his peers, he was able to walk out and returned to standing in line awaiting another turn.

Sean was also observed during speech and language group,

which includes three other peers similar in age or grade. The group has just listened to a short story and was then required to answer "*WH*" questions. Sean seemed to have a limited understanding of the story as evidenced by his responses, but was also able to get several questions correct. When asked what would be a good title for the story, Sean gave a good response ("The Horse and the Snake"). Behaviorally, he was able to sit, attend to peers, and take turns. At times, he gave silly answers to get a laugh, but was very good when redirected to the speech rule (no silly behavior). The speech therapist mentioned that during the observation, Sean seemed a bit sillier, probably as a result of having this examiner observing the group.

Sean was also observed in the regular classroom on several occasions. Sean transitions well between periods. However, transitions in the sixth grade are very structured, and well supervised since the students' transitions to classes are in close proximity. The instructional assistant is available to help Sean whenever needed for 3.7 hours of Sean's day. So, there are hours in the day that Sean works within the classroom without assistance being readily available. Yet, on other occasions, the assistant sits next to Sean in order to complete specific worksheets or gain understanding of a concept. Generally, Sean needs directions simplified. Some of the time, peers direct him or Sean relies on visual cues to know what to do.

There have been situations when Sean demonstrates some maladaptive coping skills. This may surround an occasion or event that is "stress" provoking. For example, before science camp, Sean seemed "out of sorts." He left the classroom without permission; he hid from others and refused to do work. It was later determined that Sean was feeling "scared" or anxious about science camp. His understanding was that at science camp there were "big bears" since he heard from others that camp was in Big Bear.

Sean has recently been able, with help, to express his feelings more appropriately. When he does do something that is not appropriate he gets embarrassed and needs help on how to rejoin his peer group. In his mind, the others saw or know what he did, and he is apprehensive of how they will react. Peers are very important to him. He enjoys their attention, and it is important that Sean has opportunities to interact with peers in appropriate ways, such as in games and class projects. His behavior tends to get silly as a means to gain attention.

Adaptive Behavior

The Vineland Adaptive Behavior Scales, Second Edition (Vineland II) measures the adaptive skills of individuals from birth through adulthood. Adaptive behavior refers to an individual's typical performance of the day-to-day activities required for personal and social sufficiency. These scales reflect what an individual actually does, rather than what they are able to do. The Vineland II includes four domains: communication, daily living skills, socialization, and motor skills. Sean's mother and his teacher completed a Survey Interview Form.

Vineland II results suggest that Sean had some relative strength in his adaptive skills, especially in the area of socialization and motor skills according to his teacher and parents' observations. This reflects Sean's interactions with peers and adults at school. In his own community, Sean is able to visit his neighborhood friends independently. He rides a skateboard or razor scooter to friend's houses on his street or around the corner. Sean often has friends over as well. The teacher's rating of daily living skills reflects that Sean takes care of his own self-care needs at school. He eats lunch, uses the restroom, and cares for his backpack and things independently. Sean will also walk to the office after lunch recess to take his medication. Age equivalents: Receptive Language Age 11, Expressive Language Age 6.4, Written Age 7.9, Daily Living skills age 9.0.

Achievement

The RSP (resource) teacher administered the Woodcock Johnson III, Tests of Achievement (WKIII-ACH). Results indicate a notable gain in all areas, from 6 months to 1 year's growth. The most growth is noted in math; Sean demonstrated almost 1 year's growth in applied problems.

Language

The speech pathologist completed assessment in the areas of language and articulation. In spontaneous language, Sean uses good syntax in declarative sentences. He met his goal in the language area, except using *"why"* in question form. Sean is able to use *"what"* and *"how"* when asking questions but has difficulty asking *"why"* questions without confusing the verb. For example, "Why the cat's name is Bob?" Articulation goals were partially met, according to the test results. Although his articulation errors have decreased, Sean continues to make errors in spontaneous speech because his speaking rate increases. Sean also does not self-correct at this time. Sean's teacher and his instructional aide report that they can understand Sean's speech approximately 80–89 percent of the time, and that Sean will slow down when asked.

Summary and Recommendations

Sean is a 12-year-old sixth-grade student who was assessed due to a mandated triennial evaluation. His parents requested that cognitive testing not be administered. This evaluation was based on adaptive behavior scales completed by parent and teacher, as well as observation and testing results by the resource specialist and speech pathologist.

According to observations and the Vineland II, Sean is able to get along with others at school. He is able to participate in all grade-level assemblies and projects. His behavior is usually appropriate and benefits from being prepared about changes or upcoming events in his school schedule. Sean is independent at school in all self-care areas, and with assistance functions in the classroom academically. He also benefits from peers' assistance at times. When Sean is having a difficult time at school, he benefits from a break or from working with a peer. Sean thrives with peer attention. He will sometimes act silly in hopes of getting a laugh from peers that do not know him or want to abuse his friendship.

Sean continues to meet eligibility for special education services under the category of "Other Health Impaired" due to a diagnosis of Down syndrome. Educational services and placement recommendation shall be made by the IEP team which shall consider Sean's educational history, his classroom performance, examination of work samples, as well as scores on standardized instruments of achievement, and speech and language, and the clinical judgment of the examiners.

This assessment was the one that the intermediate school would be looking at. I felt it was a very good representation of Sean's skills and abilities and properly demonstrated his current developmental levels.

Band

Without music, life would be a mistake. —Friedrich Nietzsche

The first day of sixth grade Sean came home from school and said this year he wanted to play the trumpet. OH? He actually said "tumpet." I acted like I couldn't understand him. But he kept on, and then the next day he checked out a book at the school library on musical instruments and showed me a picture of a trumpet . . . I couldn't get out of this one.

Sean had issues even blowing out a candle; blowing bubbles had been a therapy exercise for years. I didn't think he could even make the sound come out of a trumpet. He had braces! How could he put a trumpet to his lips without making them bleed? I had to remind myself . . . don't limit him . . . don't limit him. Don't say "no," just let him figure it out for himself. So I called the local music store and I asked the owner if he had a trumpet teacher there that could work with Sean to see *if* he could even make a sound come out of the trumpet—and he did. The trumpet instructor called me the next day and said he would be happy to spend 30 minutes between students *FREE* to see if Sean could play a trumpet. WOW, this guy was an angel!

Sean was so excited. I was worried he would fail, and he refused to choose another instrument at all. He had decided the trumpet was his goal.

This instructor showed Sean how to purse his lips. He demonstrated on his own trumpet . . . Sean tried and tried. He tried for *TWENTY MINUTES*, and not one sound came out of that thing . . . but Sean refused to give up. I reminded him we were only going to be there 10 more minutes, and it wasn't looking good. Then he did it, one short burst of sound came out of the trumpet . . . and he was on his way! The trumpet teacher was such an awesome guy, I signed Sean up for 1 month of private lessons so he could be a jump ahead (the band teacher had 30 students and no assistants). The trumpet teacher taught Sean the notes, how to read them, and Sean was a part of the sixth-grade band! There were four trumpets in the band and during the concert later in the year they played a trumpet solo and Sean kept up with the other three perfectly.

Sean was never denied access to any extracurricular activity, either before, during, or after school at the elementary school.

At the end of the school year there was a final concert scheduled. The date had been set, and we were notified earlier in the year, but as the date neared, they changed the date and location of the concert. I didn't get the written notice. Sean came home from school and said, "Concert tonight." I corrected him, "Concert tomorrow night." He was flustered because I wasn't listening to him and repeated, "No. Concert *tonight*." I didn't listen to him. The following day I called the school to ask what time Sean was supposed to arrive at the concert that night, and Mrs. Easton got on the phone with me. She informed me that the concert had been the night before—just like Sean had told me—and the music teacher had been disappointed that he wasn't there. I was sick to my stomach. We missed the concert because *I* didn't listen to Sean.

Big Anxiety

Courage is not the absence of fear; it is the making of action in spite of fear.—M. Scott Peck

ALL of the students were experiencing some anxiety about transitioning to intermediate school the next year. And Sean was just like them. He would come home to tell me "Those kids are mean; they give *swirlies* and *trash* you!" Only in the movies. But the kids kept talking, and Sean kept listening and getting more nervous.

Sixth-grade science camp was just 2 weeks away. All of the kids, including Sean, were so excited to go to Big Bear and spend a week roughing it in cabins and having a great time. Then Sean started acting oddly in class. He seemed stressed out, and even walked out of class a few times for no apparent reason. One day when I came to pick him up from school, I found him sitting on the floor with Mrs. Easton who said, "Sean, tell Mom what you told me about how you feel about science camp." With tears and a trembling voice Sean said, "Horrible!"

I asked, "Why? Are you afraid?"

He said, "YES!" (finally, somebody understood!)

I asked, "What are you afraid of?"

He said, very emphatically, "BIG BEARS!" I had to hold the laughter in. He was so literal. Since they were going to camp in "Big Bear," he thought there must be big bears there! After explaining that the bears were hibernating and he wouldn't see any, he completely relaxed. It was great intuition on the principal's part to clue into the source of his anxiety.

Students Vs. Teachers Softball Game

We do not meet people by accident. They are meant to cross our path for a reason.—Unknown

A school tradition was an end-of-the-year softball game between the sixth-grade students and the teachers. Sean had played Challenger Baseball since he was 5 years old, and he tried out for the sixth-grade team and made it! There were 18 students out of 150 that made the team. The eighteen students were split into two groups of nine. Each group of nine played one inning against the teachers. The Down Syndrome Association found out that Sean was on the team and called our local paper. A reporter covered the game and did a story about Sean being the first fully included student with a disability to be promoted from the school. Sean played well the day of the game. Positioned at first base he tagged a couple of teachers out! He batted and made it to first but was tagged out on second base. The whole school came out to watch the game, and it was a fun experience, but also sad for me as the school year and entire school experience with the wonderful staff was winding down.

More Appreciation

People will forget what you said . . . they will forget what you did, but people will NEVER FORGET how you made them feel.—Maya Angelou

In the last weeks of sixth grade I wanted to honor Sean's team again—all of them. I enlisted the help of the PTA, and they let me have 20 minutes during the final meeting of the year. I invited the district director of special education, school board members, the superintendent, every teacher and aide he ever had, the principal, school psychologist, the inclusion specialist, the inclusion facilitator who modified his materials, etc. I created a 5-minute DVD of photos of Sean from when he began at the school to the present. I included the clip of him dancing on stage during the violin concert and listed which teachers were nominated and won the DSAOC Educator of the Year Awards. At the end of the video was Sean in a cap and gown standing in front of the school's new *California Distinguished School* sign saying very clearly, "Thank You for Believing in Me" and throwing his cap in the air. Not a dry eye in the house. Sean was there, and he read their names off the envelopes out loud and gave them each a personalized thank-you note and a copy of the DVD. Those people meant so much to us, and still do.

At the reception after sixth-grade promotion, parent after parent after parent came up to me and told me how their child was a better, more tolerant, more accepting person because Sean had been included with him or her all through elementary school . . . and how this had positively affected their family because their child was more patient with younger siblings too. I had trouble holding back the tears.

The principal told me that every year parents scheduled meetings with her and made a case for why their child should be in Sean's class. She said when she first came to the school she expected the parents to be asking that their child *not* be in Sean's class, and one of the reasons she decided to convert the school to an inclusive setting was all the parents who asked that their child be included with Sean. The purpose for inclusion was fully realized, both in Sean's educational accomplishments and in the acceptance of him by his typical peers' transformation.

Sean's homeroom sixth-grade teacher sent home this thank-you note after the PTA meeting:

Dear Sandra,

Thank you so much for the CD of Sean's elementary experiences. What a perfect gift to remember Sean. The presentation was lovely, and we all cherished the night. As school comes to a close I've been thinking a lot about Sean. I was nervous last September to teach him because I did not know a lot about Down syndrome. But, once I got to know Sean, I realized what a special young man he really is! He has such a love for life. He is gifted academically and in all sports. Sean loves to please and makes friends easily. I know it's not been an easy road for you and Rick, but you have worked so hard to bring out his best.

I truly wish Sean the best of luck in intermediate school. I know he will go far in life because of his talents. Thank you for choosing me as his teacher. I've learned so much from Sean. He is a young man who I will never forget!

Tears. Happy tears. And she chose Sean and to say he was gifted academically . . . well, anyway, the sports part was true. We were the gifted ones with her and the others at the school who taught and supported Sean.

Fast-Forward 4 Years

Experience is not what happens to you—it's what you do with what happens to you.
—Rick Warren, From The Purpose Driven Life

Sean's elementary school is where we go for public elections to vote. I had just punched my ballot, and as I was leaving the multipurpose room, I ran into Mrs. Sunshine. She asked me to come into her office. She wanted to tell me a story.

Since Sean had left the campus the district had transferred a few special education preschool classes to their campus. She told me there was a mom whose daughter had Down syndrome who lived in the school's attendance area and was in one of the preschool classes. At the IEP to discuss transition for her daughter from preschool to kindergarten, the mother was explaining how she wanted to see *EVERY* special education kindergarten in the school district before she decided her placement. And here's the conversation that ensued:

Mrs. Easton: "You don't have to send her to a special education kindergarten class. She can attend regular classes here at our school."

Mom: "But will she learn as much here as she would in special education?"

Mrs. Sunshine: "She'll learn more, because she'll be exposed to more. And we will modify the materials to her specific abilities."

Mom: "But will the kids accept her?"

Mrs. Sunshine: "We've included kids with Down syndrome and other special educational needs here for many years now. The students with Down syndrome are usually the most popular on campus."

Mom: "What if she won't come in from the playground?"

Mrs. Easton: "We have trained aides in each inclusion class, and the aides deal with the student in those situations so the teacher isn't distracted from the other students."

This was the EXACT conversation I had with Mrs. Sunshine 11 years earlier—only the roles were reversed. She wanted to make sure I knew that Sean had indeed had a profound and lasting impact on her and the school.

Our purpose as we move through life must be to leave the world a better place in our path. *THIS* conversation confirmed that even though we had a few rough patches, we left that school a better place. I've actually met people who have children with special educational needs who have *MOVED* to our neighborhood to send their children to that school.

Intermediate School Saga

Most ignorance is vincible ignorance. We don't know because we don't want to know. — Aldous Huxley

In reality, Sean is not easy. He is stubborn, and he loves to play games, including mind games. The challenge every new teacher faced each year was to simply be smarter than Sean. BUT even with the challenges, behaviorally and academically, Sean left elementary school knowing how to read, write, add, subtract, multiply, how to behave (even if he still didn't choose to be consistent in this area), and he had over 100 friends. Everyone, from the principal down to the janitor (who watched out for Sean), knew him, knew how to talk to him, and knew he wasn't malicious. He received the Presidents Education Award for Overcoming Hardship at the sixth-grade promotion ceremony. The local newspaper covered his promotion from elementary to middle school—the first student with Down syndrome to complete his elementary years fully included at his school. After the promotion ceremony, several parents approached me and told me how glad they were that Sean had been in their children's classes. It was a proud moment for me. This was heaven: Sean had success, and other parents, the educators, school administrators, district administrators—the collaboration worked. Sean's inclusion was a success.

Sean's sixth-grade IEP team was truly dedicated to his successful transition to intermediate school. To prepare the intermediate school principal and teachers, I asked for a meeting to be scheduled, to explain how Sean learned, along with the supports, modifications, and accommodations that had contributed to his success, and to set the stage for his transition.

After school one day at the beginning of February during Sean's sixth-grade year (this was a sacrifice for all of them to go after school hours), they all accompanied us to the intermediate school to meet with the principal. The elementary principal, school psychologist, teacher, classroom aide, the district inclusion specialist, and the inclusion facilitator all attended this meeting. I was offering to send all six of the teachers Sean would have in seventh grade to the Summer Inclusion Institute so they could be prepared in advance, and I wanted them to learn about the supports they would have: a classroom assistant and someone modifying Sean's curriculum for them. I wanted to assure them that along with his classroom assistant, Sean would *NOT* be extra work for them. But the intermediate school principal monopolized the meeting by going on and on about their *special programs* and how I needed to observe so *I could make an informed decision*. Rick and I agreed that I would come to observe the *special class*—to simply placate him. And guess who guided that tour? The same school psychologist, Mr. Patrick, that had assessed Sean to be a 1 year 11 months old when he was in kindergarten—he's baacck.

The Tour

An intensive human rights education for all communities needs to be provided to overcome the old prejudices.—Ruth Manorama

The school psychologist was running a little late, so I was placed in his office to wait. I was sitting right in front of his three-shelf bookcase that had his psychology books and college textbooks on it. I was a little astounded at how yellowed the books were and noticed they were all at least 20 years old! *NOTHING* there had been published in even the past 10 years, so I began to understand why he was not versed in inclusion at all. It is critical that our educators stay current with current evidence-based materials.

In the first part of the tour he explained the Village Concept that the school used. The school is only seventh and eighth grade, but there are around 1,200 students, so they cluster the teachers so the students are in smaller "villages" of 150 students. Their classes are close together, in the same building, and the teachers collaborate so their tests aren't all the same days to make studying easier for their students. I realized I didn't need ONE teacher to volunteer anymore—I needed **six**! *And* the teachers who taught the four core subjects had to all volunteer as a village. They didn't allow for students to hop between villages—this was definitely becoming an exponential problem. They also were on a "tumbling" schedule. So each day began with a different class. Six days into the school year the first class of the day would be period 6, then period 7, then period 1, and so on. He explained how that was confusing to the regular education students, so they sheltered the special education students by just keeping them in the same class with the same teacher all day.

As the school psychologist walked me into the regular education classes, he kept pointing out, "There's 32 students in this class . . ." Sean had been in classes with 32 students for fourth, fifth, and sixth grades. He performed with the after-school choir with around 150 students . . . He loves crowds; the more the merrier! Also, the more students, the more teachers!

Sean had an accommodation throughout elementary school. He is deaf in one ear, and the district provided a FM speaker system that moved with Sean each year from class to class. The teachers would wear a microphone (lapel or headset—it was the teacher's preference which one they would use), and there were speakers on all four walls. So no matter where Sean sat, he could hear the teacher loud and clear out of his good ear. I was concerned that we would be losing this and might have to go to a Personal FM System, where Sean would wear the speaker around his neck, and I was pretty sure he would feel *different* and not want to do this. One village at the intermediate school had all four core classes permanently fitted with FM systems. The science teacher, who was a woman about 6 foot 8, explained to me as we visited her room. "The FM system is great. I know the students can hear me no matter where they are sitting, so they have no excuse to say they didn't hear. It was originally installed because we had a hearing-impaired student. We all liked them, so we kept them after he moved on." I was encouraged that she saw the benefit of the assistive technology for all of her students.

Sean was destined again to be an inclusion pioneer in intermediate school. But this time, we only had 2 years to help them get it right. Two of my friends whose children attended different elementary schools would also be attending this intermediate school the following year with Sean. I was hoping we could band together for our children. Sadly, their elementary school experiences had not been as easy as it had been to include Sean. They had fought all the way through; all 7 years was a struggle, and after one meeting with the intermediate school principal, they caved and allowed their daughters to be enrolled in the special class. I don't blame them and completely understood—especially in hindsight.

The principal really, really wanted to place Sean where *those* kids belong—in the special day class. The school psychologist used the fear-based techniques of persuasion. Only problem, I'm not a fearful person, and being a successful salesperson, I had a positive response to every negative comment. I overcame objections skillfully. But he never acquiesced. He was following the directions he had been tasked to complete. The last stop on our tour was the segregated special day class. Several of my friends' children were in this class, so they all were saying, "Hi," to me and I was a big distraction in the class.

The first thing I noticed is there were no *DESKS* in this class. The seventh- and eighth-grade students were sitting at squatty kindergarten half-circle tables. The students, most of them over 5 feet tall, had to sit sideways in their tiny kindergarten-sized chairs because their legs would not fit underneath the table. And they were *coloring*, with the aide *handing* them colored pencils. They were not even coloring independently. I was appalled. Why weren't they in desks? Why didn't they each have their own package of colored pencils? Why were they still in the same kindergarten station, doing the same things they did in kindergarten, when they were now in *SEVENTH GRADE*?! My heart was racing, I was so angry at the injustice, at the inequity. One girl I knew in that class went to the same tutor as Sean—she could read at sixth-grade level. Thank goodness she had a tutor; that was the only place she was learning!

The teacher, who looked like a high school student, came to talk to me. She was not working with any student; she had her aides working in the stations. She was so excited to tell me how every day they left the campus and that they hardly ever were at the school. Most of their education was community-based, and they were able to walk to many local shopping centers and restaurants. She never mentioned what they learned from walking all over. Perhaps that was their PE class? I could see learning money by buying lunch, but why did they have to be off campus EVERY day? Were they protecting the typical students from being exposed to people who are different? They did have a "special science class" though. I was able to observe that for a few minutes, and that teacher was very nice and as she explained how a rainbow's light reflected the colors we see I couldn't help wondering why the students couldn't be in a regular science class learning the same thing?

We left the special class, and the school psychologist closed the door and said, "Sean would have so much fun in this class."

I was probably a little harsh when I responded, "Yes, he would be a huge behavior problem because he would be bored! And why are they still sitting in kindergarten stations, in little chairs, so little they can't even put their legs under the table?" I was appalled and not holding back. I felt it was my duty to advocate for those children too. And why didn't their parents know what was going on? Did nobody visit or volunteer in their kid's class anymore?

He looked back through the window of the door and said, "Oh, the legs on the tables can be extended. We'll have to do that." It was FEBRUARY! They had been sitting sideways for 6 months! And *nobody* thought that was *wrong?*

I e-mailed the principal and thanked him for the tour and explained that we would be putting "inclusion" as Sean's placement on his IEP.

He probably never responded to an email so quickly in his life. In less than 3 minutes I had a reply. He wanted to meet one more time with just Rick and me. I called Rick, and we compared calendars, but I wanted a district person to attend this meeting with us. I could predict where this was going. Not an "official" meeting. I could see all of the illegal things he would say to us, with no accountability. Since it wasn't an IEP, I couldn't record it. But my husband thought it would be best to honor the principal's wishes to meet without district personnel present. He thought we would be building a relationship with this principal as we had with the elementary school principal if we agreed to his request. For once, I should not have listened to my husband.

At this meeting, the principal began by saying, "I've called my peers at (he named two schools in our district), and I can't find one successful case of inclusion in intermediate school, so this is going to fail. We've never done inclusion here before, so this is going to fail." (*Case?* My son isn't a *case*, He's a STUDENT!)

I used my best poker face. I stayed calm. I detached myself from the emotions I was feeling. The salesperson in me came out to overcome this objection. "Won't it be a feather in your cap when you have the first successful inclusion *student.*"

He responded (and I've never before seen such indignation from a leader), "Feather? I don't need any more feathers! I retire in 2 years. I have all the feathers I need."

And there it was. He just wanted to skate out to retirement without doing one thing different, without upsetting the apple cart—just calmly exit left.

He then went on to explain to us how Sean would need to go to special day class and earn his way out once he had caught up to the regular education students and was able to do the curriculum and work with no modifications or accommodations. (Sean was still reading at a late second-grade to early third-grade level—catching up was never going to happen.) I explained how the district's inclusion facilitator modified his curriculum, and it would be no extra work for the teachers. Completely ignoring my statement, the principal said, "Well, we wouldn't want to overwhelm him by throwing him immediately into a regular class."

(DUH! He's been in a *regular* class for 7 years! What part of this is *throwing*? I think that *I* was throwing the principal into the twenty-first century!)

We left the meeting with the framework set. He was not going to support our choice for Sean's inclusion. He was not going to support or encourage his educators to include Sean. We were on our own. Trying to move the graveyard—getting no help from the inside.

Hiring Help

There are two things a person should never be angry at, what they can help, and what they cannot. — Plato

I decided I didn't have time to do the research on intermediate school inclusion. I didn't have time to dredge up the laws. The elementary school staff didn't feel qualified to write the IEP goals for the intermediate school, and I wasn't getting any help from the intermediate school staff, so I hired an "educational consultant."

A consultant is different than an advocate. While I definitely had a reputation in the school district, and the director of special education knew that I knew the law and Sean's rights, I didn't want to ride into intermediate school on my horse with a perceived adversarial advocate riding shotgun. But I also wanted an iron-clad IEP that I could use to guide them and hold them accountable. I knew the educational consultant from a variety of conferences I had attended. She also taught at the local university's master's level in education program. She had invited me to speak to her class on Sean's successful inclusion experiences in elementary school.

The consultant was the best solution. Not confrontational—well, she didn't have to be. We were working with the school psychologist at the elementary school to prepare Sean's IEP that would be going with him to intermediate school. The school psychologist was grateful for the help and was very positive about the participation of the consultant.

The consultant brought outside eyes. She brought a perspective from someone who had worked with unwilling schools, and she knew how to write the IEP where inclusion was the placement—no questions, no doubts.

She made an amazing observation immediately that I had never considered necessary before. She expressed a concern that Sean did not have a Positive Behavior Management Plan in his current IEP. Well, we had never needed one in elementary school. The support was just *there,* and we were a true team and on the same page. But, she pointed out, it could be a protection for Sean against them trying to punish him unduly in intermediate school and provide them a map to know what to do when Sean exhibited one of his behaviors.

Along with the school psychologist that knew Sean so well, the consultant wrote a Positive Behavior Management Plan (PBMP). The key words are *positive* and *management.* It was not a Negative Behavior Punishment Plan. The PBMP included everything—his triggers, what works to get him back on task, motivators, and incentives that interest him, and the potential staff reactions that may escalate his behavior. It was a solid document.

Behavior Equals Communication

As we accept our children, we free them to be who they are in a world that is trying to tell them every day to be someone else.—Tim Hansel

Sean was far from angelic. He had, and still has, many inappropriate behaviors. Learning that all behavior is a form of communication resulting from an unmet need helped us to not label Sean "bad," but just making "bad choices." Each "bad choice" he made was because he was trying to achieve something. Escape from work or gain attention from the other kids were his most common goals. In order to modify behavior, you have to identify the *need* behind the behavior. Then, give the person an alternate behavior that will fulfill that same need for them more effectively than the inappropriate behavior did. In the autism world, social stories work great to teach what "to" do in those situations that cause a behavior to occur. That method was a little before our time when Sean was in early elementary school, but today it works great with him.

According to David Pitonyak, Ph.D., "Most people just react to behavior itself by punishing for it. A person with a cognitive impairment is not going to figure out a better solution to meet their need on their own just because he got punished. If they knew a more effective way to meet their need, they would have used it in the first place. They were just reacting to an unmet need by impulse. They need help offering a better solution, not punishment without a solution. For a punishment or a consequence or an intervention to actually work, the disabled person would have to be capable of a multistep thought process of way of thinking prior to reacting. They would have to think: If . . . Then . . . Therefore . . . and think of a better solution. NOT happening! You can't take away the things that people use to de-stress and make them earn them back. They should learn to take a break when they feel overworked or stressed, just like the rest of us do.

Pitonyak asks, "What do you people do when you're stressed? How many cigarette smokers or wine drinkers or chocolate eaters are there here? If you are stressed, how would you like it if someone took away all the things that you do to de-stress and made you *earn* them back?" He said people with disabilities should be given a book listing all their favorite things that make them feel good, like listening to music, having a snack, reading, writing a note to someone, jumping rope, whatever. This list should become their break choices so they can learn to monitor their own feelings and take a break when they feel they need one, and regroup.

Positive Behavior Management Plan

After observations and interviews, the Positive Behavior Management Plan was carefully crafted. There is a format that is set, and the answers were filled in:

Behavior(s) of concern (target behavior): Describe the student's behavioral concern(s) in specific, observable, measurable terms.

1. Sean will leave the classroom without permission.
2. He defies adult requests
3. Makes inappropriate comments to adults or peers
4. Becomes combative if cornered or escape blocked

Baseline information: Please describe the frequency, duration, and intensity of the target behavior.

Frequency: One time per week

Duration: Up to 20 minutes

Intensity: Mild to moderate

Events and situations related to the occurrence of the target behavior(s):
Under what conditions does/do the target behavior(s) occur?

Where	**Time**	**Who**
In class groups	Morning	Teachers
Other: Playground	Afternoon	Support Staff
Time	Recess/Break	Peers

Instructional Environment
- Entire group
- Individual
- Transition

Comments: Unstructured time is difficult for Sean. He does better with a routine.

Are there additional conditions that influence the target behaviors(s)?
- Medication
- Cognition

Comments: Sean may make comments to initiate conversation or contact with peers that he perceives as "friendly" but may actually be socially inappropriate. On occasion, his medication (or lack of) has adversely affected his mood/behavior.

Situations that occur before and after the target behavior(s):

What conditions seem to trigger the target behavior(s)?

Low levels of adult attention   Change in staff/routine

Social interaction with peers   Presentation of task or activity

Being physically blocked or not allowed to leave

Comments: Sean has difficulty admitting he has made a mistake, accepting a reprimand, and coping with his feelings. He gets embarrassed by his behavior, and then is embarrassed to join the class so he tends to escape. These situations are difficult for him to work out independently. He may also misinterpret peer and adult behavior/comments.

What is the typical staff response when the student exhibits the target behavior(s)?

Remind of reinforcer   Offer choice   Other: help problem solve

Redirect   Time-out   Office referral

Comments: Sean's teacher will talk to Sean individually away from the group if needed. She will remind him of appropriate behaviors or things to do or say. Offer him choices. Sometimes a time-out in the office is appropriate or the time-out table at recess is used.

Possible function of the target behavior(s):

What function(s) does the target behavior seem to serve for the student?

Escape/Avoid:

Avoid task/activity   Avoid request/demand

Obtain

Obtain item/activity   Gain adult attention   Gain peer attention

Sensory Regulation

None listed.

Comments: Sean reacts to feeling nervous or anxious by leaving the class or group. Recently he walked away from adult reprimand to avoid embarrassment or to get more attention. His inappropriate comments are usually impulsive; he says things that are on his mind without thinking through or not knowing what he should say instead (i.e., immature social skills).

Successful and ongoing interventions:

Describe currently or previously attempted interventions and indicate their level of success.

- Curriculum modification   successful and ongoing
- Pairing of preferred and
  nonpreferred activities   successful and ongoing
- Offering of choices   successful and ongoing
- Part IV Positive Behavior Plan successful and ongoing

Suggest any items, activities, or people that could be used as incentives in his student's behavior plan:

Peer interaction/attention, extra recess time, handball, ball monitor, or other "helpful" jobs

Other comments regarding the current target behavior(s):

Many of Sean's behaviors are due to immature social development and cognitive ability. He craves attention and sometimes may act inappropriately in order to gain peer/adult attention. He also responds well to positive attention and when he is part of the group experience.

Analysis of student behavior:

Under what conditions are the student's behaviors most often appropriate?

Where	Time	Who	Instructional Environment
In class	School arrival	Teachers	Small group
Lunch area	Lunch	Support staff	Individual
Recess break			

Examples of appropriate behaviors: participates in class activities, i.e., science camp; is independent in buying and eating lunch; during playground games, PE; he'll greet staff and peers appropriately, works on simple tasks independently; takes turns at games and class reading, very good gross-motor skills.

Replacement Behaviors:

List the appropriate behaviors that the student will be taught that will replace the target behavior(s) and meet his/her needs.

Appropriate language when greeting or conversing with peers; retreat to appropriate "break" area; seek help from adults

Intervention strategies and techniques:

Teaching strategies, instructional accommodations, and curriculum or materials necessary for teaching the replacement behaviors:

Strategies/Accommodations

Define behaviors with student	Check for understanding
Pair preferred & nonpreferred tasks	Provide choices
Model expected replacement behaviors	Prompt expected behaviors
Other: see notes below	

Curriculum/Materials

Modified texts/materials	Social stories	Break card
Visual schedule	Social skills materials	

Comments: The above teaching strategies, instructional accommodations, and curriculum or materials necessary for teaching replacement behaviors should be utilized, not just in response to an inappropriate behavior, but as an ongoing part of Sean's educational plan.

Teach Sean to identify feelings of anxiety, nervousness, confusion, and embarrassment, and teach coping skills to calm self, i.e., go to an acceptable retreat area, ask for help, or request a break

Environmental structure and supports to be provided to enhance demonstration for replacement behaviors (time, space, materials, interactions):

Time	Space	Interactions
Warn of transitions	"quiet" area	Precorrection
Warn of schedule changes	Preferred seating	Teacher check in
Modeling of behaviors		
		Consistency between settings
		Positive interactions designed to shape student behavior

Comments: Consider providing break card or tokens to exchange for taking a break or going to the "quiet area." Consider providing a peer "tutor" or "guide" to increase success in following the routine or schedule (especially in the fall).

Reinforcement procedures to enhance earning and demonstration of replacement behaviors:

Redirection to reinforcers   Development of reinforcement menu

Reinforcement of approximations of behavior

Based on prior input, anticipated reinforcers the student may earn for appropriate behavior includes:

Peer interaction/attention, extra recess time, handball, ball monitor or other "helper" jobs, earning TV and video game time at home

Strategies for managing recurrence of target behaviors:

Prompt appropriate behavior   Direct to "quiet area"   Provide choices
Remind of reinforce   Remove trigger

Comments: Explore possible current stressors; help Sean verbalize and problem solve.

Communication Provisions:

Between whom	Frequency	Method
School	Daily	Other: Communication among village
Parent(s)	Weekly	teachers and home, method can be agreed upon by teachers and parents.

Plan for monitoring and review of plan:

Data is to be collected on the demonstration of the target and re-placement behaviors.

Frequency of collection:

- Weekly

To continue to monitor the effectiveness of this plan, the plan will be reviewed by:

Date: By first progress report

This plan may be terminated through an IEP meeting when the following criteria have been met:

When replacement behaviors are learned and being applied consistently at school.

Persons responsible for plan implementations:

The following people are responsible for implementation of this plan:

Student   regular education   speech and language
                            teacher   pathologist

| Instructional assistant | parent | special education teacher |
| Site psychologist | support staff | other (i.e., bus driver, campus supervisor) |

This Positive Behavior Management Plan detailed what had worked successfully for Sean in the past, even though it had not been written down before. Having this plan as a part of Sean's IEP would help the intermediate school staff understand what worked and didn't work, and provide a guide and instructions on successfully working with Sean.

Open House

It is imperative that society develop attitudes which enable persons with Down syndrome to participate in community life. They should be offered a status that observes their rights and privileges as citizens, and in a real sense preserves their human dignity. When accorded their rights and treated with dignity, people with Down syndrome will, in turn, provide society with an invaluable humanizing influence. — Dr. Siegfried M. Pueschel

The intermediate school hosted the annual open house about 2 weeks before Sean's transition IEP. Incoming seventh-graders were invited to come and walk the classes and see the electives available, meet the teachers and familiarize themselves with the school. So with Sean in tow, we went to visit.

We took Sean to every elective class to allow him to see the options and to meet the teachers. As we entered the sewing class, the teacher approached me and introduced herself. She explained that her daughter (who was a year older than Sean) had been in the after-school choir with him and how she would come home after choir rehearsals talking about Sean and she had felt that was a positive experience for her daughter. Well . . . with Sean's fine-motor issues I had never considered sewing as a class for him—but hey, they had sewing *MACHINES* in the class, so I stepped out and asked, "Would you be willing to have Sean in your class for a trimester?" Oh my, you would have thought that I had just punched her in the face! She looked horrified and said, "I don't think there is any way he could do what we do here." I explained he would have an aide, and that he worked well with other students. But it was obvious that, according to her, that it was acceptable for her daughter to sing with him, but the fear of him in her class was beyond her.

As I was disappointed that the sewing teacher thought it was OK for other teachers to do inclusion, but not her, we wandered into the video production class. Some student-made films were playing on the screen, and Sean and I became enthralled in the intermediate school minds that must have created these clips; they were funny, stupid, and some were boring. The teacher spied us standing in the back of the room taking it all in. She decided she could save us some time, so she approached, introduced herself, and condescendingly said, "You know we have a class for your son. It's in room number 24, and you don't really have to waste all your time visiting the other classes—it's in the building right across the courtyard outside."

Oh, we were batting 1,000.

I responded, "Thank you, but Sean won't be in that class. He's been in regular education his whole life, and he will be in regular education classes and electives here too." Her expression said it all— she must have misjudged his facial characteristics—maybe he didn't have a disability? He had not spoken, so perhaps he just "looked" disabled? We left her, baffled expression still intact.

Sean was oblivious to all of this and was having fun high fiving his friends in passing that were also checking out the electives. We then visited the computer lab, and that teacher was lovely. She talked about assistive technology to us and that it would be easy to include Sean in her beginning computer class. *Bingo*—an elective!

Next was the theatre where the drama class was housed. That was a done deal—Sean had been performing since he was 3—so drama it would be!

The Transition Meeting

Faith is taking the first step even when you don't see the whole staircase.—Martin Luther King, Jr.

The principal ignored my request to ask teachers to volunteer. Instead, he *assigned* Sean to teachers who were unwilling to include him. Turned out they were in the village that had the FM system installed.

We scheduled the transition meeting. Again, the amazing staff from the elementary school took time out of their lives and came over *AFTER* school hours to attend this meeting. I didn't ask the consultant to come. I was keeping her in stealth mode away from the intermediate school. Sean also was there, and I had one of his friends with us, because I was concerned about him being present the entire time. The plan was for Sean and his friend to go play basketball on campus after Sean met his new teachers and had the opportunity to ask and answer questions.

Present from the intermediate school was ONE teacher who would be his case carrier (resource English—since that was his toughest subject, we opted for resource instead of regular education for that subject—and when school started that fall, this teacher had moved out of state due to a job transfer with her husband's company). The history, math, and science teachers had each come up with a separate excuse of why they could not be bothered to attend the meeting after school hours. Excuses ranged from a child sick at home to becoming suddenly deathly ill themselves during the last class of the day.

Sean didn't have the opportunity to meet one of the educators who would be teaching him the following year. And they didn't get the opportunity to meet him, so I am sure their imaginations of this monster coming to spend 55 minutes a day with them was weighing on their minds all summer. Also present from the intermediate school was the assistant principal of discipline, Mrs. Wright. The school psychologist didn't attend, the principal didn't attend. The message that Sean was not welcome was loud and clear.

To begin the meeting I asked Sean if he had any questions for the resource English teacher, and he asked, "Are the kids mean here?" I quickly explained why he was asking that—that the other students in sixth grade talked about swirlies and being trashed, and she kindly responded, "The kids here are nice, Sean. You will like it." He immediately relaxed.

Then Mrs. Wright asked Sean, "What do you like to do during lunch and recess?"

Sean responded "Play handball."

With a stern, angry voice, she said, "We don't have handball here, Sean. You won't be able to play handball during snack and lunch here." I'm not sure why this was so important to stress to him. I had been on campus during snack and I chimed in, "Yes, but you have basketball, and Sean and his friend brought a basketball so they could practice while we continue the meeting." So I dismissed the boys. Later, Sean's friend asked me why Mrs. Wright was so angry sounding to Sean. I didn't have a G-rated answer for him.

I emailed the teachers to try to meet with them on another occasion, even during their free period. I wanted to prepare them for the reality of having my son in their classes. I wanted them to have the tools to teach my son, and I didn't want them to spend their summer in fear of the unknown. The elementary school invited them to come there and meet Sean and see him in a class. Neither the elementary school nor I received any responses from them, only from the principal that they were too busy to meet with me or drive three blocks during a free period. I e-mailed them with my invitation to send them to the Summer Inclusion Institute. My invitation was met with no response. I sent another invitation—one teacher responded that she couldn't take the day that summer away from her children. Another responded that she had included English-language learners and felt she didn't need additional training. The other two never responded at all.

Sean was set up for failure.

Seventh Grade

Can't is a 4-letter word. Empowered by the brave parents who came before us, we trudge on, Expecting, not Accepting.—Paul Daugherty

Seventh Grade IEP Goals

The consultant also wrote appropriate IEP goals for intermediate school, including language that forced an inclusion placement:

- In collaboration with typically developing peers, Sean will participate and give three facts from the lab.
- In collaboration with typically developing peers, Sean will improve understanding of history concepts and awareness of historical events.

When given an appropriate text, Sean will state the main idea and give five details or facts from the passage.

When given a list of 39 Dolch Basic Sight Words from third grade, Sean will decode the target words.

When provided with teacher-made organizer or assistive technology, Sean will write a four-to-five-sentence paragraph using beginning capitalization and ending punctuation with one visual prompt.

When given a weekly spelling test, Sean will spell the first 100 words from the Fry and Dolch word lists.

When given a set of five coins and three bills (not to exceed $9.99), Sean will calculate the answer.

When given a practical situation, Sean will calculate the appropriate amount of money needed to buy a given item for snack using the dollar-up method.

In a classroom setting, Sean will use a planner with a list of pictures of different feelings to identify emotions.

Sean will be able to produce the target phonemes in complete and grammatically correct sentences and/or questions during structured activities in the therapy setting.

Sean will use selected irregular plural nouns and ask questions using correct syntax during structured activities.

Most important was the notes section of this IEP that included the details of how his education plan was to be implemented.

Utilize a peer buddy to help Sean, especially initially with learning the schedule and routine of the tumbling schedule.

It is not appropriate to push curriculum on Sean if it's too complex cognitively but to modify the curriculum with visuals or prelearning.

Reinforce Sean's prosocial behaviors all the time, and more so initially. Sean does not respond to progressive discipline.

Adults to reinforce peers for ignoring inappropriate behavior.

Team agrees to have teachers give curriculum schedules to inclusion facilitator so she can prepare modifications by fall.

Communication to home/school discussed. E-mail to parents decided as preferred communication.

From Heaven to Hell

The wrong idea has taken root in the world. And the idea is this: there just might be lives out there that matter less than other lives. —Gregory Boyle

The day before intermediate school began, Sean and I met with the inclusion facilitator who modified his materials, and his new independence facilitator at the school who showed Sean where his classes were located and walked the campus. After Sean felt comfortable with where everything was, the inclusion facilitator explained, "Sean has no modified materials for tomorrow. I have e-mailed, called, and stopped in and the teachers are telling me that they do not know what they are doing for lessons this first day or the first week that they decide each day. So he has *NOTHING* modified for him." She was visibly shaken by this lack of cooperation, and I thanked her for letting me know. I was certain this had been done on purpose . . . It was as if somebody told them, "Don't do anything for a week or so, so that his mom will move him to the special day class."

Sean was assigned an "independence facilitator"—fancy name for an aide—and instead of two half-day people, he was going to have one person for the entire day. No more would he have two part-time aides! This was his first time to rotate to every single class.

With the tumbling schedule they also changed the order of the classes every day. Monday began with first period, Tuesday with second period, Wednesday began with third period, Thursday began with fourth period, Friday began with fifth period, and Monday began with sixth period, then it all started over again.

Sean quickly learned *where* his classes were. We did put him in Resource English (RSP) since writing was still a struggle for him. His RSP English class was quite far from the rest of his classes, so he was constantly late to that class, and then he was late for the math class after RSP English, traveling back to the village.

Less than a week into the school year, Mrs. Wright called one day to ask me about Sean's "Positive Behavior Management Plan" and if he should receive lunch detention for being late *all of the time*. My reply, "Is that positive?" The Positive Behavior Plan calls for analyzing *why* the behavior is happening, then come up with a *plan* to change the behavior. My suggestion was that Sean leave the class before RSP English a few minutes early, then leave the RSP English class a few minutes early to be on time to the next class where he was being late. My suggestion was not implemented. And no recommendations were given from the school.

When that phone call was made, they were holding Sean in from his snack time. So he had nothing to eat or drink for snack period.

Later that same day I had another call from Mrs. Wright. The math teacher had decided to keep Sean in at lunch to try to force him to do a worksheet that he had refused to do in class. He told them he would do it at home (an accommodation we still had in place). As the math teacher and Mrs. Wright stood over Sean, trying to *force him* to do the worksheet, he made a bad choice. He wanted to go to lunch, he had not been able to eat his snack earlier, and he was hungry. He had told them "no," using his words, but they didn't listen. He tried to leave, and the independence facilitator blocked the door, not allowing him to leave, so, he kicked her.

When I arrived to pick Sean up, Mrs. Wright explained what happened and that she was suspending him for kicking the independence facilitator. I explained that he forced them to HEAR *"NO."* He had used his words as we worked on for years in elementary school. Now, he had to show them "no," and regress to behavior he had used before he was able to verbalize. The independence facilitator blocking the door is a behavioral trigger for Sean, clearly spelled out on his Positive Behavior Management Plan.

The following week he was suspended for "stealing shoes." He took a boy's shoes in PE while they were changing clothes. Sean would engage in these behaviors when he wanted attention. The boy got his shoes back immediately, but Sean's horseplay was not tolerated, and he was once again suspended from school.

It was less than 2 weeks into the school year. The only recommendation that the elementary school staff made that had actually happened was to include a disproportionate number of Sean's friends from his elementary school in his village. And they selected many who had been good friends to Sean. Two girls called me at home . . . they were not aware that each other was calling me. They were both concerned for the way Sean was being treated. They both independently reported that two of the teachers were being derogatory and condescending to Sean. The teachers were not allowing him to be grouped with anybody other than his independence facilitator—even after they had volunteered to the teachers to have him in their groups. They were particularly concerned about the math and the science teachers.

This is another great benefit of inclusion: while Sean can't always communicate the details of the day, the students there with him certainly can!

I decided to spend a day shadowing Sean and seeing what his day was like. I took a day off of work, and we started in homeroom.

His homeroom teacher was also his history teacher. She was very nice. Sean was sitting in the back of the room—interesting because his IEP specifically states he is to sit in the front as an accommodation because of his hearing impairment and easy distractibility.

Homeroom ended and Sean's independence facilitator was not there yet. He gave me a panicked look and asked, "What class is next?" The teacher had written the day's starting period number on the board but had not said it aloud. I had written it down for me, so I looked at my schedule and told him where to go. He maneuvered perfectly to the next class, resource English. I sat in the back of the room to observe. This was the teacher's first year of teaching, and she seemed overwhelmed, but she was very nice.

Next was history (also Sean's homeroom teacher). During this class, Sean's independence facilitator and I sat outside and talked a bit. I decided to create a daily schedule on my computer, and he could have each teacher initial that he was on time. I would reward him with TV and video game time using that information. His Positive Behavior Management Plan had listed TV and video game time as appropriate and effective reinforcers for him.

Next was PE. Sean is very athletic, and they were learning different sports so he loved that class. Sean didn't want to change clothes after PE. Snack time was next, and he didn't want to miss a moment—and he was a little slow at changing clothes, so he left his PE clothes on. For some reason, this really made the school mad. I personally didn't care either way—after all, he wasn't naked!

After snack, where he flirted with the same girl he had a crush on in sixth grade, he went to math. There was a test being given, Sean's materials were not modified, and he just looked at the 50 problems on one page and simply sat quietly. He didn't even pick up his pencil. The number of problems on the page was overwhelming for him. The teacher scowled at me and said she didn't have time to talk to me, except to say that she couldn't get Sean to do *any* work in her class. I suggested she allow his worksheets to be modified, and then sit down with him and do a few problems "with him" to win him over. She didn't do this.

Sean told me that his math teacher didn't like him and that she was mean. Sean is acutely aware of other's feelings. He has a sixth sense about this and is always aware of who likes him and who doesn't like him.

Next was computer. She was a great teacher, very nice, and the only one who was following Sean's IEP. He was loving learning to type and being on the computer.

The last class that day was science. When I had toured the classes the year before the teacher was the one who had impressed me with her explanation of the FM system. I had thought I would like her as her Web site said she was an air force brat like me. I had such high hopes for her. That day, in addition to her 6 foot 8 inches she was wearing 4-inch platform shoes. I quietly entered the class along with the students and sat at the back of the room. She had each lab table numbered, and she called each student by name and told them what table number to sit at. They were in groups of four.

"Sarah, table 3, Becky, table 6, John, table 3 . . ." At the very end of the roll call, Sean and his independence facilitator were the only ones left standing. She made a huge production using her branchlike arms circling the sky and saying, "And Sean and his aide will sit here," while gesturing at the table in the back of the room . . . far from the other tables . . . not even adjacent to another table. I could see the invisible "R" on the table. I was seething but decided to wait quietly.

She then gave the instructions to the students. The assignment was the same as one Sean had done in FIRST grade, where they had traced and cut out a silhouette of themselves, pasted pictures of things that interested them on one side, then used the letters of their names to create an acronym on the other side. They were to assign a word that described themselves to each letter . . . She had laminated these and now they were grading another class's silhouettes. ONE person was to write, the other three in the group were to just look and see if the instructions were followed: the perfect project to include Sean on.

After she gave the instructions she came over and introduced herself. She stood, looming over me and as calmly as I could speak I asked why Sean was not included with one of the student groups. She used a scolding tone. "Once he has *demonstrated* that he is *capable* of *understanding* the project he will be *allowed* to join one of the groups."

I responded, still trying not to blow up, "So, he has to *EARN* his inclusion in your class?"

She snapped, "I want to make sure he won't grab the project from another student and damage it." I looked at his independence facilitator and asked, "Has he been grabbing things?"

She responded, "I've never seen him grab anything." The teacher, clicking the heels of her platform shoes, stormed away. She was Sue Sylvester on steroids. Mean to the tenth power.

All of the teachers were informed that I would be observing in each class that day. There was no surprise that I was in attendance. Yet the math and science teachers' behavior was abhorrent. All I could think was poor Sean had been so afraid of the students as he was transitioning into intermediate school, but the students were actually nice. It was the *ADULTS* he had to worry about! I thought to myself, *They think Sean is a slow learner? I think THEY are the slow learners.*

ROTATION DAY 1   Date:

Sean McElwee

For Each Check Mark Sean will receive one minute of TV
today, and one minute of gamecube this weekend.

| | | Bucks | Bucks | Bucks |

Homeroom — On Time

Comments:

On Time	Cooperate		
1 Min. Late = 3	1		
2 Min. Late =2	2		
3 Min. Late= 1	3		
4 Min. Late= 0	4		
On Time = 4			
Leave early so you can be on time to English	Bonus Pts.		

1. English — On Time

Comments:

Sean started out strong, but didn't want to finish p "

On Time	Cooperate	Participate	Work
1 Min. Late = 3	1	1	1
2 Min. Late =2	2	2	2
3 Min. Late= 1	3	3	3
4 Min. Late= 0	4	4	4
On Time = 4			
Leave early so you can be on time to Math	Bonus Pts.	Bonus Pts.	Bonus Pts.

2. Theatre — On Time

Comments: *meltdown*

On Time	Cooperate	Participate	Work
1 Min. Late = 3	1	1	1
2 Min. Late =2	2	2	2
3 Min. Late= 1	3	3	3
4 Min. Late= 0	4	4	4
On Time = 4	Bonus Pts.	Bonus Pts.	Bonus Pts.

SNACK

3. Math — On Time

Comments: *Great work with calculator*

On Time	Cooperate	Participate	Work
1 Min. Late = 3	1	1	1
2 Min. Late =2	2	2	2
3 Min. Late= 1	3	3	3
4 Min. Late= 0	4	4	4
On Time = 4	Bonus Pts.	Bonus Pts.	Bonus Pts.

4. P.E. — On Time

Comments: *Very good today*

On Time	Cooperate	Participate	Work
1 Min. Late = 3	1	1	1
2 Min. Late =2	2	2	2
3 Min. Late= 1	3	3	3
4 Min. Late= 0	4	4	4
On Time = 4	Bonus Pts.	Bonus Pts.	Bonus Pts.

Office-get pills (1 Buck)

Lunch-use lunch ticket

5. Computer — On Time

Comments:

On Time	Cooperate	Participate	Work
1 Min. Late = 3	1	1	1
2 Min. Late =2	2	2	2
3 Min. Late= 1	3	3	3
4 Min. Late= 0	4	4	4
On Time = 4	Bonus Pts.	Bonus Pts.	Bonus Pts.

6. History — On Time

Comments:

He is tired and he dosn't want do his homework please

On Time	Cooperate	Participate	Work
1 Min. Late = 3	1	1	1
2 Min. Late =2	2	2	2
3 Min. Late= 1	3	3	3
4 Min. Late= 0	4	4	4
On Time = 4	Bonus Pts.	Bonus Pts.	Bonus Pts.

Meet T.J. & Ayden in front of the office

Complete Lack of Cooperation Earns Compliance Complaint

Light travels faster than sounds. This is why some people appear bright until you hear them speak—Brian Williams

As we attempted to work through the problems of the intermediate school, the staff's absolute unwillingness to work with us and Sean were evident over and over again.

I was invited to speak to a class of college students who were in the special education credential program at California State University, San Marcos. My presentation included the 5-minute video I had created to thank the elementary school staff and to discuss how Sean's inclusion went so well. But I was so heartbroken about how intermediate school was going that I ended up spilling the frustrations and disappointments we were facing to the students. They were becoming amazing advocates as they informed me that if the IEP was not being followed I could file a Compliance Complaint with the California State Department of Education. The teacher even e-mailed me a link to the Web site where the steps on how to file were posted. I reviewed Sean's IEP and, yes, determined that they were not following his IEP or his Positive Behavior Management Plan.

It was only 6 weeks into the school year and I had had enough. I filed an 18-page compliance complaint with the California State Department of Education. Only one teacher was following his IEP, and nobody was following his Positive Behavior Management Plan (thank you, educational consultant, you nailed that one!). They were not providing his modifications and accommodations, and they were simply being mean. I won't bore you with the text of the complaint, but I basically went through every IEP goal and every item on the Positive Behavior Management Plan, listed the goal, then a comment that the goal was not being implemented.

For example: When given an appropriate text Sean will state the main idea and give five details or facts from the passage—to further define "appropriate text" on page 2 of the notes at the top of the page it states: "Team agrees to have teachers give curriculum schedules to inclusion facilitator so she can prepare modifications by fall." The teachers have not cooperated with the inclusion facilitator and have made multiple excuses of why they cannot provide her with lesson plans in advance, including not knowing what they will be teaching until the day of the class.

Copies of the IEP, Positive Behavior Support Plan, and multiple e-mails that had been sent to me from both principals and the school psychologist supporting my claims were attached. It was a very large and heavy envelope when it was ready to be sent the California Department of Education.

Sean continued to avoid changing back into his street clothes after PE. He was now being rewarded with TV and video game time for being on time to class, and he didn't want to risk being late to the next class. So the school decided he needed a *male* independence facilitator. That poor young man was assigned to Sean after he had been rejected and dejected. The daily schedule *I* had created for the tumbling school schedule was working well for him being on time. I had also added a couple of boxes for the teachers to fill in, communicating whether Sean was cooperative and worked in their class. It appeared all his behavior revolved around the placement of the sixth-period science class. Every sixth day his entire day was horrible. But on other days, everything was good until science, then the classes after science were all downhill. Sue Sylvester on Steroids was single-handedly making Sean's whole intermediate school experience a living hell.

So, here came the new male independence facilitator. Mrs. Wright must have told him to "tame that wild child" or something along those lines to set the tone. He was all over Sean. Sean's friends told me the way each class would begin: Independence facilitator commanding Sean, "Get out your book. Sean, get out your book now. Now! Get your book out." Repeating the same command over and over, while Sean was still processing the first request. He does have

about a 7-second mental processing time before he starts moving after a request. This guy gave him no processing time at all.

Sean's friends also told me that Sean would hit this guy—a lot—
but the independence facilitator needed to work all of the hours in
order to collect a full day's pay so he didn't report it—because Sean
would have been suspended, and the independence facilitator would
have been sent home. Until Sean hit him in the nuts.

By the time this happened I had filed the compliance complaint,
the school knew it was filed, and we had a meeting scheduled with
the principal and the district's director of special education for the
upcoming Monday morning. Late Wednesday morning, Mrs. Wright
called me and through clenched teeth said, "Sean has *assaulted his
aide*. He's being suspended for 3 days; come and get him *now*!"

Great. More time from work missed all because these people
would not allow me to work with them in advance. I went to the
school . . . again. Mrs. Wright took me into her office and said to me,
"Sean punched his aide in the face three times."

I asked, "How did he do that? Sean's 4 foot 8, and the IF is way
over 6 feet tall. If he punched him once, why didn't he just stand up?"

"Because he was doubled over after Sean punched him in the
crotch first."

The story continued. "So, what made Sean so angry to hit the guy
in the crotch in the first place?"

"They were in the locker room after PE and Sean was supposed
to be changing clothes. He refused to change, and the aide blocked
the door. Then Sean ran to the other door; the aide beat him there and
blocked it, and that's when Sean hit him in the crotch."

I was so angry now. This guy had violated Sean's Positive Behavior
Management Plan—Sean's trigger for hitting was being blocked in a
room! I said to the Mrs. Wright, "So, you realize that even after I've
filed a complaint detailing where you guys are *not* following Sean's
IEP or Positive Behavior Management Plan that this was a continued
violation of his plan? Sean should not be suspended for 3 days. This
behavior was *caused* by your *untrained* staff member."

She informed me that a meeting had been called for noon the next day with the director of special education and suggested I be there. I told her I had to work and could come for 30 minutes since the meeting time was during lunch, but would have to leave after 30 minutes. Then Mrs. Wright told me the independence facilitator had quit. She then said in the lowest tone, so nobody else could possibly overhear her, "*Really*, I have to know. *WHY* do you want Sean in regular education classes? He's *soooo retarded.*" I saved myself an assault charge and simply walked out of her office. Their behavior toward Sean was retarding him, but I knew she was too slow of a learner to understand that if I had explained it to her.

The next day at the meeting regarding Sean's assaulting the independence facilitator, the principal opened the meeting with this statement: "I don't know what else we can do. Sean's inclusion has failed." I simply sat silent while they talked and continued to demonstrate how they have not supported him.

The school psychologist made the suggestion we change his Positive Behavior Management Plan, since the one he had wasn't *working*. I explained the one he had wasn't being *implemented*. It would work if it was used. He decided to give me a draft of his proposed Positive Behavior Plan to review:

> Sean will face the normal consequences of being tardy, disruptive, or defiant, i.e., discipline referral to office, assigned detentions, opportunity class, and suspensions according to schoolwide discipline policy. Reinforcements included: Offer Sean the opportunity to participate in smaller classes, and/or join the SDC/SH class on community-based instruction trips, e.g., trips to the senior center or grocery store, *AND* raisins or Cheerios for staying on task for 10 minutes.

> Sean was in SEVENTH grade. He could multiply, read, write, and did not need Cheerios and raisins to stay on task! The original Positive Behavior Management plan was successful in elementary school (although it had not even been necessary to put it in

writing before) and addressed the same behaviors Sean was exhibiting in intermediate school. Once again, it was apparent to me that neither the principal nor the school psychologist understood *Positive* Behavior Management as this proposed plan was punitive, not positive. The reinforcements on Sean's existing Positive Behavior Management Plan included earning TV and video game time, which was meaningful to him.

Also proposed was a Hughes Bill. A Hughes Bill is to be used when a Behavior Plan has been ineffective. One of the proposals under the Hughes Bill included twisting Sean's shirt to gain physical control, and a two-person carry, where two people could pick him up and physically remove him from the classroom. Rick explained to them that everything would escalate quickly if they put their hands on Sean, and he would become combative. We once again asked that they implement the current Positive Management Plan and *THEN* if it was ineffective, have someone trained in behavior management observe Sean and assess the situation as to why it wasn't working. And then I asked one question: "Have all of his teachers and his aide been given a copy of his IEP and Positive Behavior Management Plan?" The answer: "No." Well, no wonder they were not following anything in it—they didn't even know *what* was in it!

The school psychologist, Mr. Patrick, then presented me with the results of an assessment he had performed on Sean *WITHOUT MY PERMISSION.* He did this when Sean was in kindergarten too—and all I could think is *who's the slow learner here?* He used the Peabody Picture Vocabulary test and assigned Sean an age equivalent of 4 years 9 months, and Expressive One Word Picture Vocabulary test assigning him an age equivalent of 3 years 9 months. Sean had been assessed by his elementary school 6 months earlier and his receptive language age equivalent was 11 years using the Vineland II. His expressive was 6.4. There was no need for another assessment. He was trying to "prove" Sean couldn't be included. After 30 minutes I left, explaining I would be ready to discuss everything during the meeting scheduled for the following Monday morning regarding the compliance complaint.

The next Monday morning at 8 A.M. Rick and I attended the meeting regarding the compliance complaint. The same cast of characters was in attendance. This time, the principal started the meeting by saying, "We are going to do everything we can to make sure Sean's inclusion is a success." I believe the director of special education did a little *talking* to the principal after I left the meeting on Thursday!

The district had brought in an intermediate school special education teacher from another school who had been successful having her students included in electives and extracurricular activities in her school. She spent 2 days with Sean and *attempted* to work with his teachers peer to peer. I provided multiple examples of Sean's work on modified worksheets to each of the teachers attending the IEP meeting. When they left the meeting, they took the samples with them and never returned them to me.

During the IEP meeting, the science teacher argued about every single suggestion made. We decided she was the main person he was reacting to and decided to drop science and have two PE classes since it was too far into the trimester to start another elective. Another issue that was discussed was Sean was having difficulty following along when there were PowerPoint presentations, looking up and down while trying to take notes. A new accommodation was added—the teachers would print the slides for him to have on his desk to follow along.

Another difference was noted between elementary school and intermediate school: having a classroom assistant versus an independence facilitator. Sean's aggression had been directed at the independence facilitator. The classroom assistants in elementary school were not glued to Sean. They were there to help the entire class. The independence facilitator, instead, was only focused on Sean and had been glued to him. This was making him feel different and smothered, and he was trying to get that person away from him. A third independence facilitator was hired. She was a lovely young woman who was kind and also a graduate student getting her master's in special education.

She brought the balance of assistance without drowning him in attention. And it helped that she was cute too.

We never backed down and required them to adhere to Sean's IEP and PBMP. Sean had been suspended for 8 days total. I brought to one of the meetings excerpts from IDEA that stated: "Schools may remove a student with a disability for up to 10 days for any violation of school rules, as long as there is no pattern of continuing removals . . . Removal for more than 10 consecutive school days, or a pattern of continuing removals that cumulate to more than 10 school days in a school year constitutes a de facto change in placement. Change in placement activates the due process procedures provided in the law, whereby parents may dispute school officials' recommendations." Sean was not suspended again for the remainder of the school year. It was the beginning of the third trimester before things began to seminormalize.

The rest of the year was better supported. But Sean was so emotionally damaged by the hateful math and science teachers and the cling-on male independence facilitator. We decided to move him to resource math class, and take him out of science altogether.

For the second and third trimesters, I tried to have him included in two electives instead of being in two PE classes. Three times he was forced to change elective teachers back to PE after the trimester began because (to quote the school psychologist), "the teacher doesn't want to teach a special education student." I could have filed a civil rights complaint each of these times as they were discriminating against him on the basis of his disability. I thought that I had to have something in writing to file a civil rights complaint to "prove" the discrimination, and I was only getting the information verbally over the phone. Later, I discovered that was not the case. I now regret not knowing that I could have filed anyway. With two PE classes, Sean was in great physical shape! The next trimester he had drama as an elective, performed in a play, and loved that, and the final semester he was in Advanced Drama (because the other drama teacher didn't want him in her class again) and got to perform in several productions. One was a dance number and he was so in sync with everybody else that I couldn't pick him out of the crowd!

IEP Goals added during the additional IEPs during the year

Sean will gain attention of others by calling their names, tapping or using eye contact, persisting and refraining from pushing, shoving or name-calling.

When given adult-led instructions, Sean will follow them within 10 seconds.

Sean will sit quietly and orient himself toward the speaker.

During the greeting with a familiar person Sean will recognize/greet people by stating their name, refraining from hugging or touching that person.

When coming in contact with a person that Sean is not familiar with, Sean will not greet them but instead, walk away quietly.

Sean will accept losing at activities. Sean will accept being called "out" calmly and continue with the game without behavior incident.

When given feedback on attempting an activity, Sean will accept feedback calmly.

When asking a peer (vs. tell them) if they want to play an activity with him, Sean will sustain play with that activity or accept "no" from the peer calmly.

Sean will accept and join into a peer's choice of activity. He will sustain the activity calmly four out of five times.

Sean will answer 20 yes/no questions about factual information at his developmental level.

Sean will answer 10 personal questions accurately (name, age, siblings, etc.).

You Can't Dance

Life isn't about waiting for the storm to pass. It's about learning to dance in the rain.— Vivian Greene

I was in the middle of preparing the compliance complaint when the first school dance was announced. I had accompanied Sean to our community center's dances for a year now teaching him appropriate dance behavior and was confident he was ready for a school dance. I would not have even known the dance was coming up if it had not been for one of Sean's friends who came to our house after school each day (more on this in the Buddy Sitting chapter). He asked me if Sean was going to the dance, and I dug through Sean's backpack looking for a permission slip matching the one Sean's friend showed me. I couldn't find one, so I photocopied his friend's permission slip. I went onto the school's Web site looking for information on the dance and saw the link to the school newspaper—and landed on the page that listed the staff. The editor had titled herself, "The Retarded Editor." Nice. I sent the principal an e-mail about that and checked the next day—her title had been changed back to just say "Editor." The principal never addressed that with me.

I sent Sean to school the next day with the $3 fee and the photocopied permission slip. When Rick got home that day he immediately asked Sean if he had gotten his dance ticket. We wanted to put it somewhere safe so it wouldn't be lost. Sean said, "No, I'm bad, so I can't go to the dance." Sean said, Mrs. A. told him he was bad. Rick e-mailed the principal because we didn't know who Mrs. A was, and he responded, "Mrs. A. is the school secretary. Students who have 'been bad' (i.e., getting suspended) also automatically lose the privilege of going to the next dance as well. This was explained to students in the discipline assembly at the beginning of school, but I'm sure it had little or no significance to Sean at the time." One more thing to add to the compliance complaint.

Recovering Behaviorally

Every obnoxious act is a cry for help. — Zig Ziglar

In seventh grade Sean learned how to hit people. This was the only way he had been successful in getting the people at the intermediate school to *listen* to him; it worked for him, and he was using it. And being sent home was not a motivator to be "good" anymore. He didn't *WANT* to be there with the hostile educators, so being home was now a good option to him. Even if it meant sitting on the stairs for the entire day.

I sought out and found a private social skills class to enroll Sean into. Most of the students in the class were on the autistic spectrum, but Sean needed to relearn how to accept criticism, enter a room full of people without being embarrassed, and learn some replacement behaviors for hitting. He stayed in this class for a year, 1 hour a week at $89 an hour.

The behavior analyst would ask the parents to fill out a card before each session with anything their child had done inappropriately that week. Then she would trigger the problem behavior—in Sean's case demanding angrily for him to quickly do something that was hard for him like write a sentence—and then show him a better reaction than hitting or yelling. It worked, and Sean successfully stopped hitting people. His replacement behavior when he was angry and wanted to hit someone was to "walk away."

We were experiencing the results of Sean's aggression at home too. He was reacting to the rejection and nasty behavior of the intermediate school staff, and was being noncompliant, aggressive, and having horrible tantrums. We requested behavior support at home and the Department of Developmental Disabilities (regional center in California) provided a behavior consultant who performed an assessment and provided us with some intervention strategies. We were using negative reinforcement and trying to reason with Sean when he was refusing to do his chores or homework or anything else. I'm not sure why we thought they should be providing positive behavior supports at school and it was all right for us to be punitive by removing TV and video game time or limiting his outside activities, etc. Isn't that the way we were all raised? When I was in high school I'm pretty sure I was grounded more often than not. But punitive techniques only made Sean more noncompliant, and once we started using positive reinforcement, everything changed! We still have to remember to keep it positive many years later, but it's really a better reaction in every situation.

The Down Syndrome Association began karate classes this year too. The karate sensei was an occupational therapist, and he instilled a sense of responsibility in his students and constantly drilled when it was appropriate to use karate. When Sean hit someone or did something inappropriate at school, Sensei had him do sit-ups, or push-ups and in a very kind tone of voice reminded Sean what was expected of a karate student.

Ditching Eighth Grade

No trumpets sound when the important decisions of our life are made. Destiny is made known silently. —Agnes de Mille

Around March in Sean's seventh-grade year, I e-mailed the principal and asked if we could ask the eighth-grade teachers to volunteer to have Sean in their classes, and I offered to send them to the Inclusion Institute the upcoming summer to provide them with the base of information they would need to successfully include Sean. I was hoping for Sean to have one successful year there. He did not reply to my e-mail. I had a friend who was a substitute teacher, and she confided in me that Sean was the talk of the teacher's lounge. His teachers would "out" his every mistake to each other and bash him mercilessly. Because of this, all of the eighth-grade teachers were forewarned, and they were steeling themselves—not preparing themselves—for the arrival of this little monster in their classes.

The hostility from the administration and staff was so incredibly bad that we made the decision to go ahead and send Sean to high school. I was certain that all of the eighth-grade teachers would display the same amount of hostility as the seventh-grade teachers had.

This decision was tough to make. Sean had around 150 friends that watched out for him in his grade. He would be thrust ahead and while many of the students would *know of* Sean, they would not have had him in any of their classes and wouldn't have his back. But I also knew that if he had 1 more year of hostility, he might never recover emotionally.

You're probably wondering *how* I made this happen. Remember, Sean did kindergarten twice? Well, our district has a transition program that happens from age 18 till the students turn 22. If Sean continued going through the grades, he was destined to miss one year of that program. That was my justification . . . and ironically, nobody at the intermediate school tried to stop me.

Buddy Sitters

Meeting the world with a loving heart will determine what we find there. — Gregory Boyle

The school district provided no after-school daycare after sixth grade. I still worked full-time, but needed some sort of supervision for Sean after school each day. I wanted him to have as *normal* of an after-school life as possible. I was lucky he had three good friends who agreed to be his buddy sitters.

One of the boys' mothers committed to picking up Sean each day along with his designated buddy sitter and bringing them to our house. They would arrive at our house around 3:30, and we were always home by 5:00. They were to get a snack (we left several choices each day to choose from), and then just play—basketball on the driveway, video games, whatever—but fun was the point.

The schedule was set, and the boys made $5 an hour. We paid them when we got home. If there was a minimum day they were paid for the additional hours too.

These three boys were extremely responsible. One time one of them was sick and he called the other two boys and arranged for one of them to fill in the next day—then he called me and explained who would be with Sean and why. This was a great responsibility for the boys, an opportunity to make money, and they all had fun with Sean.

The other benefit was having the mom who drove observe the after-school walk to the car. About 3 months into school she called me to let me know that Sean was being bothered by a student. As he was walking to her car, a boy that none of the buddy sitters knew would taunt Sean and say mean things. One of Sean's friends warned the boy, "You don't want to mess with Sean; he's really strong."

Then the mom called me one day. She told me that she witnessed Sean and the bully walking away from the school—she was too far away to hear what the boy said to Sean, but he was mouthing off to him. The bully walked ahead of Sean, and she saw Sean take a melted Otter Pop out of his backpack, rip the end off with his teeth, and pour it over the boy's head! She ran over quickly and told Sean to get in the car before the boy could beat him to a pulp. We decided to change the place she picked Sean up—to right in front of the principal's office. I never heard of any other encounters with this boy again.

This is the ONLY time in Sean's entire life that anybody ever messed with him.

Freshman Year

Consider how hard it is to change yourself and you'll understand what little chance you have in trying to change others. —Jacob M. Braude

Freshman IEP Goals

Sean will have class material at the ready by the "tardy bell" and persevere at lessons for at least 30 minutes with aide prompting.

Sean will follow adult-led directions within 5 minutes.

Sean will accept feedback calmly 75 percent of the time.

Sean will produce his target sounds ("sh," "ch," and "r") in structured sentences.

When given a set of eight coins and five bills (not to exceed $9.99) with the aid of a calculator Sean will calculate the answer.

When provided with a teacher-made organizer or assistive technology, Sean will write a four-to-five-word sentence using beginning capitalization and ending punctuation with one visual prompt.

In a science lab setting, Sean will participate and give five facts.

Sean will answer questions using possessives and comparatives.

Given stories/readings at his instructional reading level, Sean will read and write or have the aide transcribe answers to *who/what/where/how* questions.

Sean shall produce his behavior sheet for each period with teacher prompting.

While Sean was still in seventh grade, I asked to visit the high school to observe Sean's "options," and I was hoping and praying we would never encounter such hostility again.

The educational consultant came with me and the high school's psychologist took us to observe the "Severely Handicapped Special Day Class." The class was divided into two groups while we were observing. One group was working on counting money. There was a worksheet that listed prices of grocery items. They had to add up the items they "chose" to purchase from the list, then they had to count out the money (play money) they needed to purchase the items. It was a good hands-on math lesson, very concrete, very practical.

The other group was cooking in their kitchen. They were making cinnamon toast. There was a list on the wall of the items they had cooked all year. And nothing on the list was healthy. They had made toaster waffles, smoothies, lemonade, pizza, cookies, etc. Not one salad, and other than the smoothies, nothing on the list included fruits or vegetables.

Also part of their curriculum was to do laundry. And every day after lunch they would gather recyclable cans and bottles out of the campus trash cans. YUCK! On Tuesdays, they would take a week of recycling across the street to the recycling center and redeem it for money. With that money, they purchased the supplies for their cooking projects. The class included freshman through seniors. The seniors were able to have an unpaid "work experience" working in businesses in the shopping center across the street from the school. This was the second year this class had been housed on this campus. Previously, all of the students in special day classes had been located at either the segregated school site or another high school that was about 5 miles away. I asked about going out into regular education electives, and the teacher mumbled something about the students were with her class all day.

The school had resource classes, and they also had "modified" classes (MOD). This was a level of special education I had never heard of before. These classes used the same textbooks that the regular education students did. Their materials were modified, the class size was smaller, and every class had an aide assigned to give more personal attention to the students. The educational learning pace was slower. For Sean, additional modifying would be handled by the same inclusion facilitator from the district who had been providing his modifications since third grade. There were still four core subjects—math, science, English, and geography (later, history and government), and Sean would change classes every period. Electives would be general education electives, the same as the regular education students would take. The day we observed there were cheerleaders and athletes in uniform that were students in these classes, I felt it was a semi-inclusive setting.

I saw no choice. I couldn't risk the hostility of the regular education teachers for Sean's sake again, so for the first time in 8 years of public education, I selected a special education placement in the MOD classes.

We didn't tell Sean he was going to high school until the day of registration 2 weeks before school started that summer. He was very apprehensive. The anxiety of another new school was making him very nervous as we waited in the registration line. As he looked around he didn't recognize *any* of the other students waiting in line either, but as we entered the registration area, Sean saw something that changed his attitude. He looked at me and whispered, "Cheerleaders!" And these adorable girls were very sweet to him! He was being welcomed!

Sean had the four MOD core curriculum classes with modifications. He also had PE the first semester and keyboarding. Drama was on his IEP, but for some reason, he didn't have drama on his schedule when school began. The district allowed him to keep his own aide who was with him throughout the day in all classes.

I selected the special education program because *I* didn't want to experience the prejudice and hostility that we encountered in seventh grade, but especially I didn't want Sean to be treated as *less than human* as he had been. Somehow, I thought that *special educators* would be more accepting of Sean in their classes and have more training on positive behavior management and be able to deal with Sean's avoidance behaviors. Amazingly, there was one teacher—who was Sean's math AND science teacher—and he also ended up being Sean's case carrier, and he was as bad as the *REGULAR* education teachers had been in intermediate school! Mr. Spicoli. He first refused to work with the Inclusion Facilitator who modified the curriculum—and instead, would give Sean five-page tests with all but five problems crossed out in pen—and call that a modification. It took until the end of November to get this teacher to work with us.

The director of education had requested that the next time I felt like I needed a compliance complaint to remedy any IEP goals that were not being followed to let her know first. The compliance complaint had generated a lot of extra work for her and her staff, and she wanted to avoid that in the future. I made a call to her and after she met with this teacher, he began to cooperate a little more. After Sean received appropriately modified materials, then he began to experience success in both math and science.

The Basketball, the Bagel, and the Bus Driver
Best way to stand out in a crowd? Be yourself.—Byrd Baggert

I had always driven Sean to school, but for the first time we decided to put him on the Little Yellow Bus to go to high school. One day, the second week of school, Sean picked up a basketball off our lawn as he walked to the bus from our front door. This was completely premeditated as he had tried to put another basketball in his backpack earlier that morning (and I discovered him trying to make it fit along with his notebooks).

Later, I was told the story: Sean arrived at school, his aide met his bus, and he got off the bus with a backpack, a basketball, and a bagel. The other student on the bus had a donut.

When Sean got to math class (his first class), his teacher, Mr. Spicoli, took the basketball away from him, then told Sean to throw away or put away the bagel. And the fight began. Sean refused to throw away the bagel. The teacher told him to put it into his backpack and Sean got angry and threw it down on the carpeted floor. Then he refused to take his book out, and that's when the teacher called me and told me Sean was being suspended. It took me 20 minutes to get to the school.

When I arrived, the teacher had called the school safety officer (who is an actual sheriff), and he had physically removed Sean from the class and taken him to the office. As I entered the office, Sean and five adults were in the assistant principal of discipline's office. Before Sean saw me he was laughing hysterically—if you think about it, it was pretty funny—he had successfully gotten FIVE adults to drop everything they were doing and pay full attention to him. Because he wouldn't stop laughing they suspended him. (I was thrilled that he had not hit anyone.) Present was the assistant principal of discipline, Mr. Jonas, the math teacher, Mr. Spicoli, the school psychologist, Mr. Calkins the school safety officer, and his aide. I was trying to figure out where Sean got the bagel. We didn't have any bagels at home, so I had no idea where that had come from.

I started to walk to the car with Sean, and he didn't want to leave. The safety officer took ahold of Sean's arm, as if he was strong-arming a criminal, and was going to walk Sean to my car. Sean agreed to walk with me unassisted, but the way the sheriff physically handled Sean concerned me.

I later called Mr. Jonas and told him if there was a "next time" that Sean was in his office, I would like to have Sean sit outside so I could hear what happened and discuss possible consequences without Sean present. I was always careful to not undermine any authority figure in front of Sean. I never wanted him to think he could get away with his behavior. I told Mr. Jonas that I wanted him and the safety officer at Sean's IEP meeting that we had scheduled for the following week.

Sean had a glorious day of time-out on the stairs, at home, writing his spelling words 10 times each, doing 10 math worksheets, no TV, and no video games.

Later, I found out how Sean had acquired a bagel. There was another special education student on the bus with Sean. I met her father for the first time at the school's football game that Friday night. I asked him if perhaps his daughter had given it to Sean on the bus, and he said, "No, the bus driver took them to the donut shop and bought them for the kids." *WHAT?* The bus driver, who had Sean on his bus for only 4 days, took him off the bus, walked into a donut shop, and bought him a bagel? Thank God he didn't get a donut. He has a huge digestive issue with sugar! (It causes almost immediate diarrhea.) This dad told me the bus driver had asked *him* if he could do that, but I didn't walk Sean out to the bus, so he couldn't ask me—well, he could have called me. He had my house and cell phone numbers. Sean suffered the consequences of the bus driver's bad decision and was suspended, and the bus driver suffered no consequences—except I decided I would drive Sean to school from then on. So, 4 days on the small bus was enough for me! Sean got the Mom Taxi Service the rest of high school.

The bagel incident was on Tuesday; he was suspended for Wednesday, and that Friday I came to observe him, a whole 7 days into the school year. Since I was going to be there observing the classes all day, I also volunteered to help ASB (associated student body) prepare for the first dance of the school year by putting wristbands on the students before school, during snack, and at lunch. I arrived at 7:15 A.M. for my first shift of mayhem.

The students stood in their alphabetical line while one mom verified their names off their ASB card and checked their names off a list while I struggled to put the paper adhesive wristbands on as tight as possible. I was instructed to do this so they couldn't take them off and give them to their friends—friends who didn't have an ASB card (which allowed them to get in free) or friends who didn't attend our school and weren't allowed to go to the dance—the Disco Dance— the first dance of the school year, which was being held that night— after the first football game.

And because it was a disco dance, they were dressed in disco clothing for the day on Friday! We were instructed to tell the kids they were not allowed to "Freak" dance while we put the wristbands on. Well, since *I* attended high school during the Disco era, I felt it important to provide them with some guidance, along with the dance rules. "In the '70s we did the Hustle—so tonight you can do the Hustle, but you can't Freaky dance!" It was fun. Most of the students laughed, then you saw the ones who were determined to Freak dance roll their eyes.—I should have tattooed them with a Sharpie!

Those polyester shirts, leisure suits, platform shoes, and Afros. Wow, did we really look *that* ridiculous back in the '70s? AND HOW did that girl find my favorite dress almost 30 years later?

OK, so being there all day I got a great flavor of the school and students. During lunch, I saw that the severely handicapped special day class arrived to the lunch area a full 20 minutes before the rest of the student body's lunch period began. They went back to their classroom after only 10 minutes of overlapping with the regular education students, who didn't hang out with them. A mom volunteering next to me (who didn't know me from Adam) said, "I love seeing those Down's kids here with all the other kids. That's really neat."

I said, "Yes, people with Down syndrome should be included in all aspects of school and community life."

She said, "I just haven't *seen* it before. I'm glad our school does that."

NICE! I liked it, even though she had no clue about people first language, her heart was in the right place!

Trailing Sean through His Day

I've failed over and over again in my life. And that is why I succeed.
—Michael Jordan

Communication with Sean's teachers is crucial. When Sean was younger he could try to tell me about his day, but his articulation was so bad I didn't understand most of what he said. Now, his articulation is much better, but he *would not* tell me about his day anymore.

"What did you do today?" "Nothing." Pretty typical of a high school student.

When I wasn't putting on wristbands for the dance, I shadowed him from class to class. I observed how his modifications and accommodations were being applied. I had short discussions with the teachers, and some long ones with his aide.

This was the first time Sean was not fully included in all regular education classes. Yes, it felt like a huge failure to me. Sadly, the reality had hit; it was easy in elementary school to work with and teach ONE teacher how to include Sean and deal with his quirks. And in 7 years, they also had the benefit of collaborating with his teachers from previous years as well. But I learned in seventh grade to work with six different teachers, with six different personalities, six different attitudes, and six different prejudices. Add a principal and school psychologist who didn't support his placement, I simply was not up for the job.

Thankfully, the high school had layers of special education classes. Resource classes were for the students who simply struggled. MOD (modified) classes were for students with true learning disabilities. Perhaps they had autism, Asperger's syndrome, and dyslexia. They may only struggle in one subject, or in all core subjects. There were cheerleaders and students who were football players and on other sports teams in his classes—Sean was the only one with a *visible* disability. They still studied the same curriculum that the regular education students did, but it was modified, and they took each section a little slower. Sean's materials were modified still more. But he was learning English, pre-algebra, geography, and science.

The severe handicapped special day class was where most of the students who have Down syndrome were placed.

I had the opportunity to talk to Sean's aide quite a bit. She reported that Sean had been testing his teachers as he usually did at the beginning of the year. I had opportunities to talk to all of them during the day, and we instituted his daily checklist to earn TV and video game time. Turned out that TWO of his teachers had siblings in their

40s that have Down syndrome! But they also seemed to have low expectations—and I felt that was an obstacle to overcome. Sean rises to other's expectations, and if they're low, well, that's where he rises to. When the expectations are high, he manages to surprise everyone!

His MOD English teacher had a sister with Down syndrome who was in her 40s. In her class we discovered he was very good at doing Word Search exercises, and she allowed the other students to look at Sean's worksheets see where on the page he was finding the words. For Sean to be helping the other students with their class work was a huge esteem builder for him.

The parents of the geography teacher, Mr. Ainsworth, were some kind of amazing people and had adopted boys with disabilities—before special education laws were enacted. He had an adopted brother with Down syndrome in his 40s and another brother (his words) with retardation and autism, and is an independent living aide for another brother with cerebral palsy and legal blindness. Mr. Ainsworth was the only teacher who recognized what I was going through and truly comprehended why Sean was in his class.

I also discovered that Sean was having a real problem with his locker. Our school had over 3,000 students, so they had very tiny lockers which were stacked three tall. Sean's locker was on the bottom, and he had to squat to unlock it. I had an accommodation of a key lock instituted because I was certain the combination lock would be frustrating for him. In intermediate school they didn't have lockers. The school provided two sets of books, one set for home and one set to stay in the classes. That had been great so he didn't have to lug books back and forth. With the other frustrations occurring I asked each teacher if Sean's book could just stay in the class, and any time he had homework that he needed the book for if they could send it home that day. That arrangement ended up working for the rest of his high school years.

Sean's aide had a daughter with Down syndrome who was around 12 years old. Her daughter was in a wheelchair. I don't know what other medical issues she might have had to end up in a wheelchair, but she is the only person I have ever heard of with Down syndrome who was in a wheelchair. She had been his aide the first 2 weeks of intermediate school before she was replaced with the *male* aide.

Sean's aide discussed *placement* during one of our conversations. During PE class as Sean ran the mile, his aide told me that she wished Sean was in the severely handicapped special day class (SH-SDC), "because they go somewhere off campus every day." It would be more fun for her. Then she began to list the benefits for Sean if he were in *that* class—she told me how they were learning to order off a menu and pay for their food. How they were learning to cross the street. Learning to cook, do laundry, and learning money. I told her that we do all of that at home. Sean started doing his laundry when he was 11 (took me months to get him independent with that!), he vacuums, he changes the sheets on his bed, he cooks in the microwave. And he's had an allowance since he was 5, and in seventh grade, he saved for 6 months to buy himself an X-Box 360! (And he's been able to cross the street safely for years)—Not that learning these skills in school are not necessary, and I'm glad it's available for those who need it, but we were able to teach Sean those skills at home, and I know others need more practice, or their parents might have several other children to deal with—but that's not our situation.

Then she said how she wished her daughter was *high function-ing enough* to be in the severe SDC class at the high school. I tried to encourage her that it didn't matter what level of functioning her daughter is, that she could still could be in that class (my goodness, what's the definition of *severe* if a person with Down syndrome is in a wheelchair—isn't that severe?). Her response told me everything about her attitude toward Down syndrome, "Oh no, she's a baby, she's our princess. She's at a 2-year-old level. All I want them to do with her is color. There's no reason to teach her ABCs and numbers. She doesn't need to know that stuff."

I found that attitude so foreign to me! So repulsive and all I could think is how she was subjecting her other children to the care of their sister for the rest of their life. Her daughter's independence was never a dream, never a possibility.

I simply said to her, "Well, you have a big extended family and you know she will always be taken care of. Rick and I are *it* for Sean, and when we go, he's on his own. So, I have to make sure he is as independent as possible."

Special Ed—Not So Special

People don't want tolerance, they want dignity. — *Rick Warren*

Sean's case carrier was also his MOD math and MOD science teacher. He was a total surfer dude, in his late 40s, tall with long blond, crazy, unruly hair. This was the guy who "referred" Sean for suspension for bringing a bagel into his class. His students liked him, including Sean. He was very nice to Sean in class. But then he asked me if Sean would be better served in the "severe class" because he would learn more life skills there. I explained that it was my job to teach him life skills, and I didn't dwell on his suggestion.

The PE teacher seemed to be fine. He treated Sean like the other students, and Sean was getting a great workout each day. Sean's last class of the day was Computer Keyboarding class. That teacher was completely frustrated with Sean's behavior and lack of participation. He explained that Sean was not cooperating and was disrupting the other students. I discovered that his aide went home before 7th period and he had no support during the keyboarding class. I sat down next to Sean, which I had not done in the other classes, and discovered that nobody had shown him that he needed to push the "control-alt-delete" keys to access the keyboarding program! I observed the teacher sitting in his desk the entire class, never getting up one time to talk to or help any student. It was a self-learning module. I wasn't worried about it after Sean got into the program—he had computer keyboarding for two trimesters the year before—but he was so bored to have the same thing again. I asked the student sitting next to Sean if he would help Sean get logged on each day if he needed help, and he agreed to do so. After that, Sean wasn't a disruption. He was able to actually do his work—but he mostly didn't choose to do his work. He figured out how to access the Internet and would search High School Musical web sites most of the time. But he was no longer a disruption. At the end of the semester, Sean's grade was a D. The only D he got in high school. Oh, yes, he was supposed to have modified grading too.

It is critical to build relationships with the teachers and try to not be adversarial. I wanted to educate them, not reprimand them. My reasoning for choosing the MOD classes was because the teachers were special educators and *should* be trained in educating special education students, behaviors and all. I mistakenly thought they would not be as challenging as the intermediate schoolteachers—but I was wrong about one—the case carrier/math/science teacher, Mr. Spicoli.

I also discovered on this day of observation that none of the teachers had read his IEP or his Positive Behavior Support Plan. I talked to the school psychologist, Mr. Calkins, who said that each teacher had been given a "folder," but they acted like they didn't know what he was talking about. I later discovered they had not received copies of either document. They were working blind—well, not really; they thought they should teach Sean just like the other students, and that their work was already modified enough so he should be able to do it.

Every time I talked to Mr. Calkins, he was extremely busy with other students who were having meltdowns and always made excuses of why he has not done what was being asked of him. Later that year I discovered the other parents of special education students had given him a nickname: "Side Step." Boy, was that accurate!

Snack and Lunch Entertainment
You've only got three choices in life: Give up, give in, or give it all you've got! — Unknown

Sean's aide shared with me that he had been behaving inappropriately at snack and lunch. Since we skipped him past eighth grade he didn't have a lot of friends, so he was doing some inappropriate attention-seeking behaviors. The behaviors she observed:

- He was punching students—well, I guess if nobody is talking to you, that's one way to get attention!
- Hugging students (who don't want to be hugged). He was trying out that stereotype that all people with Down syndrome love to hug—and he was hugging the hot girls in high school!
- Throwing student's backpacks and books, taking students' hats, throwing their hats in the trash, wearing their hats, or playing "keep away" with the hats.
- Throwing water bottles at students or throwing water bottles on the grounds.
- AND with his camera phone he was taking pictures of the girls! I didn't know he even knew HOW to use the camera phone! I had that phone for a year and didn't know how to take pictures with it! So, for me, a proud and embarrassing moment all at the same time!

She said the students were looking to her and asking her to take him away from them. Sadly, this was all because I had jumped him ahead 1 year. The students were not his friends or peers who knew him or that he had known since kindergarten. These were all strangers, and he had no friends. He did know some of the students that were in the severely handicapped special day class from Challenger Sports over the years. But they went to lunch early and left early and were off campus much of the time. I had set my son up for social failure. I had to find a group for him to belong to. The entire reason he was behaving so heinously was because he had no *sense of belonging*. I also had a lot of *awareness* to build at the school, but I had 4 years to do it in and that was the bright side.

Every summer at the Inclusion Institute Richard Villa stressed the crucial importance of *belonging*. Using Maslow's Hierarchy of Needs he demonstrated how students must first feel *safe*, and then that they *belong* in order to be able to learn successfully. Having a *sense of belonging* is a critical part of accepting oneself, and a critical component of being able to function in any situation. Feel outcast—you can't even begin to succeed.

I was hoping Sean's sense of belonging was close to being realized. The first football game and dance were that night.

The First Football Game

If you want something in your life you've never had, you'll have to do something you've never done. — *J. D. Houston*

Before the football game our church youth group had a tailgate party in the parking lot. I dropped Sean off with them and went to my volunteer duty of putting on more disco dance wristbands. After wristband duty, I found Sean in the stands watching the game and really getting into it. I went to sit with my friends in another section and periodically checked on him. He moved up and down the stands and was getting to know a lot of kids who were being very friendly with him.

I had to leave the game before it was over to take my place at the entrance of the disco dance to check wristbands as the students entered the dance. I touched base with Sean to explain that after the game was over he had to go to the gym for the dance, and he confirmed he knew where the gym was.

The Disco Dance

Here's to the kids who memorize the lyrics faster than the vocabulary words. — *Unknown*

1,600 kids went into the gym for the disco dance—it was a frenzy, and the game wasn't even over yet! AFTER the game ended (we lost), Sean came to the gym—he's a huge sports fan and I knew he wouldn't leave till the game ended—even if he was the last person left in the stands!

I saw him enter through another door (he didn't see me), then I took my place to observe him in the gym. With all those gyrating teen bodies it quickly heated up to over 85 degrees in there (and began smelling really bad, really quick!).

I wanted to keep my eye on him. To prepare for the high school dances I had been taking him for 2 years to our community center's monthly dances. He learned how to dance there and knew that it was appropriate to dance in a group. There was no asking girls to dance in this setting, it was just a dance-with-everybody scene.

The gym was set up for the dance with tarps protecting the wood floors from damage. The DJ had two huge video screens set up projecting videos of motocross, break-dancing, and other random stuff. They had brought a few raised square platforms that were about 6′ x 6′ and lit up, reminiscent of the disco dance floors that I had danced on many a night in my late teens and early twenties.

Sean entered the gym and stood next to one of the lit dance platforms and was mesmerized staring at the screen. He put both hands in his mouth and began to chew his fingers!!! Not just a fingernail chew—he had both hands *crammed* all the way into his mouth! He stood, stared, and chewed for at least 5 minutes. I was thinking how I should have put his cell phone on vibrate so I could zap him into getting his fingers out of his mouth! He was tired. It was around 9:30 and he was used to going to bed around 8!

FINALLY some kids came over and motioned to him to dance with them! And the fun began! They all claimed one of the raised lit platforms and began to dance. Different groups of kids danced with him, all girls at one point, girls and boys, then the football players all were up there, and one was picking Sean up onto his shoulders—he loved that! Occasionally, Sean had the platform by himself—and was break dancing with a crowd around him clapping! (OK, his break dancing was not so hot, but a great attempt.) He stayed on that platform till the dance ended. I was able to see everything he did, and I was so relieved that he had many people dancing with him all night.

Then around 11, he was pooped. He was sitting on the platform, and a girl came over, sat by him, and they somehow were having a conversation over the loud music!

It was fun to watch, and the sense of belonging was felt by both

Sean and me. I had hope that the next week there would be more kids who would *know* Sean and would *hang out* with him at lunch and the breaks.

He did begin to be more accepted. To stop the photography of girls with his camera phone I filled it up with pictures of our household, lamps, the dogs, anything so the memory card would be full and there wouldn't be room for any more pictures. His aide wrote me a note in his communication notebook a week later that some students Sean was hanging out with were going to take a picture of him with their group. One student held the camera and said, "Oh, the camera is full. Let's delete some pictures so we can take more." The camera phone was no longer a problem—he was making more friends.

First High School IEP Meeting

Treat everyone with politeness, even those who are rude to you—not because they are nice, but because you are.—Unknown

Since Sean's high school teachers had no input into his IEP, I wanted to meet and have them write more appropriate goals for this year. It took a few weeks into the school year to get it scheduled. I brought freshly baked cookies as I had in elementary school. Mr. Spicoli began the meeting with a scolding tone and said, "The ASB director, Mrs. Dreier, reported that Sean was totally inappropriate at the disco dance." I was shocked! I told him that I was there and saw everything he did all evening and that was completely inaccurate. I didn't want to waste time in the meeting exploring that false accusation further and we moved on.

Mr. Spicoli then listed everything Sean had done wrong in the past few weeks: the bagel, bringing the basketball to class, on and on. And then he punctuated his diatribe with, "And his placement is inappropriate. He should be in the severely handicapped class." I wanted to cry. I thought I put Sean in *special* education so *I* didn't have to deal with this prejudice again. I should have just put him in regular education classes. It would have been the same outcome—then the other teachers spoke. The computer keyboarding teacher chimed in with how Sean was not cooperating and was not staying on task. Then he left before I could say a word. He had to go back to his class. The PE teacher was not present. The English teacher quickly stated that Sean was fine in her class, and she was getting to know what his levels were and she understood his difficulty with writing. She was obviously uncomfortable with the opening statements. Then the geography teacher, Mr. Ainsworth, spoke, "Sean is an absolute delight to teach. I thoroughly enjoy having him in my class." WOW! We've got ONE teacher on board! This guy made my day, and truly gave me the only glimmer of hope—the hope I needed. Sadly, no new goals were written in this meeting and the inappropriate ones that were written at the intermediate school were still in place for the remainder of the year.

More Issues

Think not of yourself as the architect but as the sculptor. Expect to have to do a lot of hard hammering and chiseling and scraping and polishing.—B. C. Forbes

Because he had an aide during snack and lunch, I was privy to *everything* Sean did. I soon realized that he wasn't doing anything any different than the other students were, but because he always had eyes on him, he was busted and couldn't get away with anything. While I still wanted to know about any behaviors so we could nip them in the bud, I certainly didn't need to know every stupid teenage thing that he did.

During lunch one day he was sitting with one of his friends he had known for a long time, a girl who has Down syndrome. All around them on the campus boys and girls were making out, hugging and kissing each other. As they sat on the bench eating their lunch, his aide observed from a short distance. She saw Sean lean over and give his friend a quick peck on the lips! The aide came unglued, ran quickly over, and told him he couldn't do that! Why not? Everybody else is doing it? The sad thing is Sean couldn't get away with anything. He knew he wasn't behaving any differently than other students and it was pretty confusing to him why he should not be allowed to do what everybody else is allowed to do! (On a side note, I called the girl's mom and told her what happened—she was on the same line of thinking as me—everybody else is doing it, why not our kids?—and she decided to ask her daughter, "So, I heard you kissed Sean McElwee."

Her daughter replied, "Yep!"

She asked, "Was it good?"

"Yep!" Whew, that was my biggest concern—that it was a consensual kiss. (And a good one at that!)

I came back to observe once again a week after the first observation day. Sean had banner behavior, cooperation, participation, and they believed it was because I was there. I explained to them it wasn't because I was there, it was because I threatened him, and told him that he couldn't go to the football game that night unless he was perfect that day. He needed positive motivation to make good choices, and earning access to the football game was very motivating to him.

During snack that day they had a pep rally. Sean was selected to go up on stage during the pep rally and participate in an arm wrestling contest. He arm wrestled a football player. He won (it was fixed) and won a really cool shirt that I didn't think he would ever take off! The other students cheered for him. He bowed and took his cheers with grace and pride. He felt like he belonged. He was becoming known and accepted.

Mr. Spicoli continued to be contrary and took every opportunity to tell me he believed Sean BELONGED in the severely handicapped class. This man did not have to modify Sean's materials. Sean had a one-on-one aide, so he took no additional time away from the other students. Sean was successfully doing PRE-ALGEBRA problems in his class. The teacher simply didn't *want* Sean in his classes. The only accolade I can give him is that he did not show his prejudice to Sean and was professional with Sean, but he was not professional with *ME*. I frequently asked Sean about him, and Sean said he liked him! At least he wasn't *mean* like the intermediate schoolteachers had been.

A Case of Mistaken Identity

Truth is truth, even if no one believes it. A lie is a lie even if everyone believes it. —Thomas Jefferson

Before the next school dance in March the case carrier/math/science teacher e-mailed me and told me that I had to chaperone Sean at the upcoming dance because of his *inappropriate behavior* at the disco dance. I e-mailed back and said that I wanted to talk to the ASB director, Mrs. Dreier, who had reported Sean as "inappropriate" because Sean was *NOT* inappropriate at the first dance at all.

Mrs. Dreier called me. I explained to her how I was standing on the landing in the gym and kept Sean in my sight the entire dance. The only inappropriate thing Sean did was to chew his fingers the first 5 minutes that he was in the dance. She told me that she observed a student running into the middle of the dancers, and then running out of the dancers! She said he was running into people, and that it was dangerous behavior. She asked another student, "Do you know who that is?" The student said, "His name is Sean McElwee." She said that "Sean" was completely nonresponsive when she talked to him—duh, she was calling him the *wrong* name! And this student would just run back into the crowd after she told him not to. I asked her where in the proximity of the entrance this student was and she answered, "The far side of the gym." I told her that she had the wrong student—there were around five or six other boys with Down syndrome at the school and it was probably one of them. I explained to her that I didn't know all of the students with Down syndrome since Sean had not been in classes with them, but either way, it was a case of mistaken identity.

I also explained to her that while Sean was in sixth and seventh grade our community center had dances every Friday night. I had volunteered at those dances, took Sean, and worked with him to teach him how to dance and how to behave appropriately. I would be chaperoning every other dance from then on so I could defend Sean if he was inappropriately accused of bad behavior again.

Due to Mr. Spicoli's prejudice, and gossiping about Sean in the teacher's lounge he kept Sean from being accepted by the regular educators who taught the elective classes. (My friend who was a substitute teacher also worked at the high school occasionally and had witnessed him in the teachers lounge.) I did not know how he presented Sean to other teachers, coaches, etc., but his general tone was negative.

The Disability Discount

Our prime purpose in this life is to help others. And if you can't help them, at least don't hurt them. — Dalai Lama

Sean was a master manipulator from the beginning of his life. He has an uncanny sense of people's feelings and can read people and play them. In school, he would act like he couldn't do something in order to get somebody else to do it for him. I had to watch carefully each year at school for the girls with the maternal instincts and make sure they didn't baby Sean into being a baby. But when he was around sixth grade, I realized he also had a way of manipulating strangers.

One day after school, Sean accompanied me to a store where I needed to get my cell phone replaced. He was thirsty, and there was a fast-food restaurant next door. I gave him two dollars and told him to get a medium soda, then come back. A few minutes later he returned with a *giant* soda that would have cost over three dollars. After I was done at the cell phone store, I took Sean to the fast-food restaurant and apologized to the man behind the counter and offered to pay the rest of the amount for the soda—and discovered he had *given* Sean the soda *free*. My big concern was that Sean would think this was normal and expect free drinks everywhere, and the man refused to take my money. And Sean did learn that lesson well.

A few years later, he would take the public bus home from school, and the bus stop was right by his favorite fast-food restaurant, Taco Bell. So, to enhance his four-block walk to our house, he would stop by for a burrito and a soda. I finally started limiting the amount of money he was allowed to carry with him so he wouldn't be able to stop there, ruin his dinner, and end up getting fat on beans and cheese. But he still showed up with a soda cup and burrito wrapper anyway! He told me, "They give it to me."

I left work early one day and stopped into the Taco Bell just after Sean arrived off the bus, and there he was, eating a bean and cheese burrito and drinking a huge diet soda. I asked him if he paid for it, he said, "Nope!" So I went to the sweet little Hispanic lady behind the counter and asked, "Did he pay for that burrito and soda?"

She responded, shaking her head no, and waving her arms, "No, no, it's OK, it's OK."

I explained, "No, it's not OK. He will think he can get free food everywhere, and plus, he'll get El Gordo (fat) if he keeps eating burritos every day." But alas, they still gave that "poor disabled boy" free food. And Sean took advantage of it every time he could.

We experienced this when we took Sean and his friends with disabilities bowling. The lane would be $15 an hour for anybody else, and they paid $6. He would get entrance to events free. It was embarrassing how often he would receive free items, like the people giving him free things were granting themselves some sort of sainthood. So we began calling it the *disability discount* whenever Sean got a break.

A Huge Shock

It is grief that develops the powers of the mind.—Marcel Proust

Sean's aide passed away in January of his freshman year. As I was dropping Sean off to school, Mr. Spicoli was standing outside and asked me if I could come in for a minute—he sent his class to join another teacher's class and told me that Sean's aide had a massive heart attack during a baby shower the day before and did not make it. She left seven children, including her daughter with Down syndrome who was in a wheelchair. We sat there together in shock, trying to make sense of it—she was only 48 years old.

We all attended her funeral. There were around 600 people there. Sean sat next to Mr. Spicoli. Sean handled it well. We explained that she was living with Jesus and since he had been going to church his whole life he accepted that answer.

The school did not replace his aide until close to the end of April. I didn't want to make a big deal out of it—it wasn't their fault that she passed away. The new aide, Mrs. Spencer, was a very sweet grandmother who had been an aide in the SH class. She volunteered to replace Sean's aide when nobody else was selected, and she saw the substitute aides were creating an inconsistent experience for him. When she started, she didn't receive any direction from Mr. Spicoli or Mr. Calkins on what Sean's IEP or Positive Behavior Support Plan said, and even that she was to supervise him from a distance during lunch and snack. NO DIRECTION until 3 weeks after she began.

While he wasn't being supervised during breaks, Sean got into some trouble during snack and lunch. I never did get the whole story, but students told Mr. Spicoli a few different stories. Sean was blamed, and he got suspended from school—again. IF he had had the supervision he needed by his new aide she could have intervened and stopped him before it went too far. I asked Mrs. Spencer what happened, and I discovered she had been on her own break. I needed those adult eyes to discern and step in to stop situations from escalating to the point of Sean being suspended. I made a written request that she be provided with Sean's IEP, Positive Behavior Support Plan, and that she take her break at a different time so she could observe him during lunch and snack.

As I looked back on that school year, every one of Sean's suspensions revolved around Mr. Spicoli's recommendations. I knew we needed to remove him from Sean's team.

Golf Team
There's never a loser until you quit trying.—Mike Ditka

Parents and students were informed of what was happening at school by a daily email newsletter. It was nice to know what was going on. The golf team's tryout location, date, and time was only published one time in the daily newsletter. Sean had been playing Special Olympics Golf for the past 6 years, and in Special Olympics, he was pretty good. Rick planned to take Sean to the after-school tryouts and e-mailed the golf coach to let him know Sean would be there. The day of the tryouts Sean was suspended, once again. He had yelled at students in Mr. Spicoli's math class, and walked out of class. The suspension letter that he came home with stated, "Due to suspension from school, other extracurricular activities may not be participated in."

Later after this suspension his aide told me that Sean was having a hard time that day because there were substitutes in three of his six classes. "Change in staff" was listed in his Positive Behavior Management Plan as a "situation" related to the occurrence of a "target behavior." ALSO, in both math and science classes, he was given nonmodified work to do, which is another "situation" related to the occurrence of a "target behavior."

ALSO, there was a game as a reward in Mr. Spicoli's math class, which constitutes a "change in routine," which is another "situation" related to the occurrence of a "target behavior." The Friday before this suspension there was a note in Sean's communication notebook from Mr. Spicoli. "Last 10 minutes of class Sean wanted to play a game with students who had already started playing. They said, 'No,' and he then told one of them, 'I will kick your butt.' He then played by himself."

On Tuesday, the day of the golf tryouts, he didn't want to be left out the game *AGAIN*, and he had to finish his work to be able to play. Having nonmodified work created stress that he would not be able to finish.

This incident could have been predicted if his Positive Behavior Management Plan was being implemented; i.e., if the worksheet he was given would have been modified. If he was provided with an "escape pass or token to be exchanged as an option" as listed on his Positive Behavior Management Plan, Sean would not have gotten angry, yelled at the students, and left class. Walking away was one of the replacement behaviors to hitting that he had learned—and learned well. I had requested that an "escape pass" be developed and provided, with rehearsals, to set the expectation of what Sean is to do when presented with the escape pass so he can leave the room without being disruptive and given a chance to calm down so he does not escalate. Mr. Spicoli didn't have to suspend Sean for yelling and walking out of class. As I look back on this, I wonder if he purposely presented him with non-modified materials to provoke Sean's outburst so he could suspend him; thus disallowing him the opportunity to participate in the golf tryouts. (The lesson had been modified and provided to Mr. Spicoli, he just didn't' give Sean the modified worksheets.) Yes, I was becoming paranoid.

Rick e-mailed the coach, who scheduled a private tryout for Sean to attend. Rick was very impressed with the coach, but Sean did not perform well that day. The coach was very gracious. It turned he out had a son with autism who was around 5 years old. Sean didn't make the team, but even though Mr. Spicoli had attempted to stop the tryout, the golf coach had allowed him to try anyway.

Electives

Success is the ability to go from one failure to another without losing enthusiasm. —Winston Churchill

I explained to Mr. Calkins that Sean needed to belong to a group in order to begin to be successful in school again, both behaviorally and academically. His freshman IEP had stated he would be in drama, but the first day of school when he wasn't in Drama I Mr. Calkins convinced me to wait till the second semester and we would investigate drama at that time. In January, we had an IEP to plan his second-semester schedule.

In advance of the IEP, I had multiple conversations with Mr. Calkins asking about Sean becoming a team assistant for one of the teams. He suggested Sean *join* the track team. That was funny to me since Sean can't run fast, he can't jump far, and he can't jump high—he could probably do the shot put, but that's about it. He assured me that Sean wouldn't "compete" but could work out with the team, and that would give him the sense of belonging that I was seeking and that Sean needed.

The IEP meeting included the drama teacher and one of the track coaches. The drama teacher explained to us that Drama I was a year-long class, and Sean had already missed half of the year. He convinced us to wait till fall, and then Sean could be in his class. I was so disappointed, and I knew Sean would be too. He loved performing. The mistake I had made on his IEP was not including any goals that had to be achieved in the drama class. That mistake would not be made again when we wrote the IEP for his sophomore year.

The track coach tried to discourage us from putting Sean in track. He explained there are 300 students on the track team (wow!) and that they couldn't *watch* Sean after school. He said that if Sean wandered off, they didn't want to be liable for him. It was confusing to me that Mr. Calkins would have suggested the track team, and then bring in the coach to discourage us. It always made me laugh that people thought that it would be harder for Sean if there were more students involved—he loved crowds from an early age and large numbers of people never was an issue for him.

I explained to the coach that Sean didn't wander, and as long as he was being *included,* he would never leave the arena. Plus he had a cell phone, and we could find him if they couldn't. He left telling me that he would talk to the head coach.

A week went by and we had no answers. I e-mailed the track coach and received the following response:

I apparently sent my answer back to Mr. Spicoli about the size situation and track in general. I told him that I have observed Sean in physical education classes, and that he would need an adult to supervise him if he would *make* the track team. We have approximately 300 athletes in track and field, and I could not offer the same type of supervision that Sean gets in physical education, in track. Sean would require a person to supervise him for the time he would be in track as there are 16 different events going on at the same time. Sean has a very short attention span, as I have witnessed in physical education, and I do not have the manpower to do the proper supervision. I do not want to create an anxiety situation where Sean would wander off and I would have to be calling you to tell you I do not know where your son is. Sean is welcome to try out.

Sean is welcome to try out? Of course, he wouldn't *make the team.*

Mr. Spicoli was perturbed that I had e-mailed the coach and forwarded me the e-mail thread between him and the track coach, proving that he had done his due diligence. The track coaches e-mail to the Mr. Spicoli:

We will be having tryouts the first week of the new semester. Sean is welcome to try out, but he must remember this is a varsity sport and there are standards that he must meet like anyone who tries out for track and field.

Response from Mr. Spicoli:

As you know Sean is a Down syndrome boy. Thanks for your input, parents have been informed of this. I was wondering if there was a way he could be a part of the team for seventh period only if he doesn't meet the standards (water boy, sand raker, helper . . . etc., and perhaps work out with the team when possible. It would be a good inclusive thing to do for him.

I was astounded. My thoughts are that the case carrier should be an advocate for their students. Introducing him as a "Down syndrome boy" made my skin crawl. I already didn't like his punitive nature. Because of his reactions to Sean's poor choices, Sean had already been suspended for 8 days this school year.

The bad thing about jumping Sean ahead 1 year was not only

were his friends a year behind us, but so were their parents! Their parents were *my* support and also there to fill me in on what the *real rules* were. One year later, when my friends' teens were in high school, I found out from them that the track team was a *no-cut sport*. That means anybody can join the team, but only the best compete with other schools. The ones who *join the team* would simply compete with each other. That's why there were 300 students on the track team! When I found this out, it was past the time limit for a civil rights complaint to be filed. Too bad, because this was clear-cut discrimination on the basis of Sean's disability, and I had the e-mails to prove it.

The Dream Team

Integrity is a choice. It is consistently choosing the purity of truth over popularity. — Byrd Baggert

From out of nowhere I get a call from the varsity baseball coach, Coach Watkins. He told me that Sean could be the assistant for his team! And this was the turning point for Sean.

For seventh period, he would report to the baseball field, put out the bases, and be on the field with the team till the end of seventh period. They were adamant that he had to leave once seventh period ended and could not stay through the entire practice.

Rick went to observe one day after Sean had the position for a couple of weeks. He was trying to be stealth and was looking through the outfield fence. He was there a little early and Sean wasn't on the field yet. He started looking around to see where Sean was when all of a sudden, Sean jumped out of the Port-A-John placed near where he stood and yelled, "Boo!" at the players standing there. All roared with laughter. Rick observed Sean not doing much on the field, but he loved the camaraderie of being with the team.

I went to watch the games and the first two home games Sean was in the dugout with the team and the coaches. The first game he sat on the bench next to a coach, but the second game he was on the fence in the dugout side by side with the players watching the game and cheering the players on. I was thrilled to see Sean accepted and becoming a true member of a group—developing a sense of belonging.

The day before the third game, Coach Watkins e-mailed me that Sean was too much of a distraction in the dugout, and he was concerned for his safety with the foul balls going into the dugout that he preferred Sean to sit in the stands during the games, and because he had no aide after seventh period, Rick or I needed to be there to *watch out* for him in the stands. Sean ate lunch with the baseball team. He had his group. And I was no longer receiving reports of his bad behavior during snack and lunch. Finally, the high school experience was coming together!

We *thought* Sean had successfully assisted with the baseball team that spring. He was accepted by the ballplayers and included in their pep rallies. One rally was a dance competition between all of the spring sports teams. According to the players, Sean was the reason they won this competition. Wish I had been there!

The baseball players would all say, "Hi." They would high five and knuckle punch Sean between classes and during lunch—he was extremely happy for the first time in 2 years and finally had a true sense of belonging. They honored Sean at the baseball banquet with a baseball signed by the varsity team and the coach.

It's important to praise those who stand out and do the right thing, so I wrote the following letter to two of the boys' parents who sat next to Sean during the baseball banquet:

> I just wanted to tell you all what amazing young men you have raised. Last night at the baseball banquet, Sean was originally seated at a different table, and I'm not sure how, but he ended up between your two sons at the senior's table!
>
> I went to see if Sean had wormed his way into that seat, and both of your sons assured me that was where Sean was welcomed and belonged right where he was.
>
> After the buffet line was visited, I went to see if Sean had gotten any meat—and there was J. cutting Sean's meat for him like it

was no big deal—not many young men would be so accommodating in our age of image.

As the night went on, I was relaxed that both of them, and the
other young men at their table, were so comfortable with Sean,
accepting of his joking nature and truly paying attention to him,
knuckle knocks and high fives all around.

It's been a couple of years since I have seen Sean so accepted
and so included, and I wanted to tell you both that you should
be proud of your sons. They exemplify the true depth of character
that will take them far in their lives.

Photography

Follow the trail to your dreams, not the path of others' expectations.
—Byrd Baggert

The second semester Sean's elective was Photography I. The
teacher did an awesome job of including Sean and accommodating
him. The class was learning to use 35 mm cameras and developing
black-and-white film. As an accommodation, Sean was allowed to
use the digital camera that we had bought for him earlier that year.
The teacher gave him great assignments and had him photographing
teachers for the yearbook and other assignments. He was embraced
and included in this class. We thought we were on the right track to
success.

Football Assistant

*We must scrupulously guard the civil rights and civil liberties of all
citizens, whatever their background. We must remember that any op-
pression, any injustice, any hatred, is a wedge designed to attack our
civilization.—Theodore Roosevelt*

Each day the daily announcements were e-mailed home so students could review them, and so parents would know what was going
on at school. During the spring of Sean's freshman year, there was an

advertisement from the football coach on several different days that was asking for football team assistants. It also stated that as an assistant, you could earn a letter in football as a team assistant.

So I inquired about this assistant position on behalf of Sean. I cannot begin to count how many newspaper articles I have seen over the years covering the football team assistants who have Down syndrome. I thought this was a position reserved specifically for Sean!

After getting no response from anybody that I contacted I decided to call Mr. Calkins. He said he would look into the football assistant position for me, and then a couple of weeks went by with no word. Then one day when I returned home from work the following message was on our answering machine:

Hi, Mrs. McElwee, I am one of the assistant principals at the high school. I oversee all athletics, facilities, and business, and I've had an opportunity to speak with the school psychologist this morning and the head football coach regarding Sean's participation in seventh-period football.

At this time, the coach is declining that opportunity for a number of reasons:

We're very concerned with the numbers of that class, supervision, safety, him getting injured. We've also had concerns with Sean this year in baseball with some of the behaviors and distractions it has caused the coaches and the players for those teams. So at this time, we're going to decline that opportunity to Sean. We do have numerous other opportunities for him during seventh period that we can put him in that's more conducive to him that will make him feel comfortable and excited about coming to school at the same time, and, at the same time, provide our other students with the same type of opportunities. Feel free to give me a call back or you can e-mail myself or the school psychologist and we'd be happy to do it that way as well.

I know that Mr. Calkins has talked with you and e-mailed you regarding this and I wanted to confirm from an administrative standpoint that we're going to stand by that decision. Thanks so much. Bye-bye.

I had *not* heard from Mr. Calkins, so this was the first I knew that he was being denied this opportunity. I believe they spent more time trying to figure out what to say so they wouldn't be violating the law than they did to try to find a way to make it work for everybody. One of their excuses was "not enough supervision." Sean had a one-on-one aide, and she would be there during seventh period. How much more supervision could a person need?

In the daily e-mail announcements there was always a "Word of the Month" as part of a Character Counts program. The word this month happened to be "Moral Courage." There was no courage and no morals being used to make the decision to exclude a student on the basis of his disability.

Once again, I should have filed a civil rights complaint—but I didn't.

On Safety

The world is a dangerous place, not because of those who do evil, but because of those who look on and do nothing.—Albert Einstein

Safety became the mantra for denying Sean access to assisting for sports, both for football and for being on the field or in the dugout during baseball games.

They also named *supervision* as an issue. I did not know until his sophomore year that his aide was sitting in the bleachers and not accompanying him onto the baseball field. (She was afraid of getting hit in the head with a baseball.) I jumped onto my e-mail list of parents of people with Down syndrome and asked them what supports they had when their sons had been team assistants. They had a variety of examples: other students, an aide, and even in a few situations, a job coach. We inquired with our WorkAbility program, and they insisted their job coaches all stopped working at 3 P.M. and were not available after-school hours. I then made the suggestion that they find a student who could be Sean's aide and help keep him on task. I envisioned it being an injured player who wasn't able to practice but was able to attend the practices. After we determined there was no support after-school hours, we kept our requests to just assist during seventh period. We didn't want to lose the team spirit as it was.

Coach Watkins later explained that Sean was trying to get the attention of the players while he was assisting because he had a lot of time after he put the bases in place until the seventh period let out. I suggested that they give him more to do and talk to the boys and let them know that if they allowed Sean to be a distraction (by talking and messing around with him, instead of concentrating on practice), then Sean would be fired. That worked. The players understood that Sean's continued success relied on them helping him to stay on track.

I offered, time and time again, to sign a liability release. I was not afraid of Sean being hurt. If you live with the fear of being hurt, then how can you ever grow and expand your horizons? I felt like he had a better chance of being hurt in the school parking lot walking to the car than during a sports practice. I explained my reasoning for not being afraid, "Sean has played Challenger Little League Baseball since he was 5 years old—for 10 years now. In this league, the players throw the ball; but it hardly ever hits its mark. They bat; and hardly anybody ever catches the batted ball—they THROW their bats! Nobody, in the 10 years Sean has been playing on *ANY* of the eight teams in his league has ever been hurt. I certainly am not worried about him being hurt on a high school field, where they know how to throw to another player, they know how to catch, and they know not to toss their bats." I've seen the angels our kids have protecting them. There was one Challenger Baseball game when they were still young enough to have buddies. A player hit a line drive, and it was heading for one girl's face—her buddy put his glove out and caught the ball right in front of her nose. Her mother ran onto the field and hugged that buddy. The parents in the stands cheered. I just couldn't tell them that there are angels protecting Sean. They would have thought that I had lost it—well, I guess they probably thought that already!

What the Law Says

(Code of Federal Regulations, Title 34, Volume 2, revised as of July 1, 2007, from the U.S. Government Printing Office via GPO Access, CITE: 34CFR300.107, page 25)

TITLE 34—EDUCATION

CHAPTER III—OFFICE OF SPECIAL EDUCATION AND REHABILITATIVE SERVICES, DEPARTMENT OF EDUCATION

PART 300, ASSISTANCE TO STATES FOR THE EDUCATION OF CHILDREN WITH DISABILITIES—

Table of Contents

Subpart B, State Eligibility

Sec. 300.107 Nonacademic services.

The State must ensure the following:

(a) Each public agency must take steps, including the provision of supplementary aids and services determined appropriate and necessary by the child's IEP team, to **provide nonacademic and extracurricular services** and activities in the manner necessary to afford children with disabilities an **equal opportunity for participation in those services and activities.**

(b) Nonacademic and extracurricular services and activities may include counseling services, **athletics,** transportation, health services, recreational activities, special interest groups or clubs sponsored by the public agency, referrals to agencies that provide assistance to individuals with disabilities, and employment of students, including both employment by the public agency and assistance in making outside employment available.

(Approved by the Office of Management and Budget under control number 1820-0030) (Authority: 20 U.S.C. 1412(a)(1))
Available for confirmation at http://edocket.access.gpo.gov/cfr_2008/julqtr/34cfr300.107.htm

After reciting the above statute during one IEP meeting, I explained that if not having an aide in the after-school extracurricular activities was the objection being used so Sean could not participate, then according to the statute, they needed to provide him an after-school aide.

The district representative (not the inclusion specialist; she was unable to attend that day) said that our district did not interpret the law in a way that they were required to provide an after-school aide for Sean to participate. Well, the law explicitly stated it, so how do you respond to that statement? I didn't know how to respond so I stopped asking for after-school support.

As I am finishing this chapter (2 years after Sean's graduation), there are articles all over the place about the U.S. Department of Education's clarification of schools' obligations to provide equal opportunities to students with disabilities to participate in extracurricular activities and athletics.

A couple of quotes from one article: "Sports can provide invaluable lessons in discipline, selflessness, passion and courage, and this guidance will help schools ensure that students with disabilities have an equal opportunity to benefit from the life lessons they can learn on the playing field or on the court," said Education Secretary Arne Duncan. And, "Participation in extracurricular athletics can be a critical part of a student's overall educational experience," said Seth Galanter, acting assistant secretary for the Office for Civil Rights (OCR). "Schools must ensure equal access to that rewarding experience for students with disabilities."

A little too late for Sean but at least this was clarified for other students in the future to never be told that their school district had the right to their own interpretation of the law. I truly believe the statements that Arne Duncan made—that sports provides invaluable lessons in discipline, selflessness, passion and courage—and think that Sean's behavior would have been different in every area of school had he been allowed to participate with additional teams every semester. His behavior the final semester during baseball was always better than the first semester of the year—he had that seventh period to look forward to all daylong. You may find the full text of the clarification here: http://www2.ed.gov/about/offices/list/ocr/letters/colleague-201301-504.html.

Preparing for Sophomore Year IEP

Don't let negative and toxic people rent space in your head. Raise the rent and kick them out! — Robert Tew

The intermediate school psychologist had written Sean's IEP at the intermediate school, assuming Sean would be there for eighth grade. It was weak, not truly measurable, and I had hoped that the teachers would have rewritten the goals and objectives earlier in the year, but they did not. For the sophomore year IEP, Mr. Spicoli had taken the existing goals and simply copied them to continue into his sophomore year. Sean had achieved all of the goals AND that was even marked on the document that he had *MET* the goals, including the dates they were met!

My consultant was back on the scene, and she wrote some appropriate goals for Sean's sophomore year *INCLUDING* two drama goals.

To begin this meeting, Mr. Spicoli began by listing—once again— *EVERY SINGLE* thing that Sean had done wrong the entire school year and punctuated it with an emphatic, "He is in the wrong placement! He belongs in the severely handicapped class." He claimed that Sean would never have any success in the MOD classes. I asked him what his definition of success was and his response, "Mastery." I explained that Sean wasn't required to "master" any subject, and any progress, no matter how small, was still progress. Sean had built a staircase out of Popsicle sticks in the math class, using measurements for the rise of the staircase. It wasn't pretty, but I had been impressed that Sean learned that at all. If that was the only thing he learned, it was more than he would have had the opportunity to learn in the severely handicapped class.

As the meeting went on, the other teachers came in, reviewed Sean's accomplishments in their classes, then left. They didn't get to hear what each other had to say, but the tone was considerably more positive from the English teacher and the elective teachers than the meeting in September had been.

The high school speech therapist was new to our district. Over the next few years, she would come to every IEP meeting, no matter the reason for the meeting. Many times as Sean was denied services, she would sit quietly with tears streaming down her face. Silently she supported us, and I understand that she couldn't speak up since she had no tenure yet. She added a very encouraging note to Sean's progress report and read it to the team during this meeting:

Sean is wonderfully polite with beautiful manners. He opens the door for me and always lets me enter first. Such a gentleman! Sean made my day last week when, at the end of our session, he said, "Thank you for helping me." I don't hear that often, and I so appreciated him saying that to me. Sean may struggle academically, but socially, he certainly possesses better manners than the majority of the "typical kids" on this campus. I applaud your efforts as parents in raising such a nice young man.

Angels flock to Sean and by osmosis, we are blessed.

As we were wrapping up the meeting, I said to Mr. Spicoli, "I would like to ask one favor of you . . . could you please stop listing everything Sean has done wrong all year? I am acutely aware of every transgression and don't need to be reminded." Then I joked, "I'd hate to be married to you; you remember everything and use it as weapon!"

He laughed and said, "Many people don't want to be married to me!"

I continued, "And please stop telling me you believe his placement is wrong. His placement is not going to change based on *your opinion.*" He pushed his chair back and stood up, aggressively towering over me in my chair. He was aggravated. "I cannot be censored! I cannot be told what *to* and *not to* say! Sean's placement *is* wrong. Maybe I should step down from being his case carrier." (YES! That was my goal!)

I responded, "Maybe you should, because the least Sean deserves is a case carrier who believes his placement is correct."

Whew! We were done with him! Well, not quite. We decided that Sean did not need science any longer. (We had made the decision for Sean to earn a certificate of completion instead of a diploma—more on this later.) So Sean would only have this man for math the next year. Mr. Ainsworth took the role of Sean's case carrier—the man who said, "Sean is a delight," in the first meeting of the year. That's who Sean deserved as a case carrier, someone who thought he was a delight, not a delinquent.

You know, the more I think about it, the more I wonder why our kids have to be so "perfect" when we live in a world that has to include warnings on electric hair dryers, "Do not use while in a bathtub full of water." Sean had kissed a girl on campus after watching the other kids kissing. But it wasn't OK for *him* to do it. He had emotional meltdowns and other teens did too, but it wasn't OK for *him* to do it. And, Sean was always caught. Because he was under a microscope he didn't get away with anything. I could go on and on, but the point is, society puts much higher demands on our *special* children to be perfect and yet makes concessions to those who *should* know better! Sean had to behave *better* than the typical students, and even equal to their behavior was not good enough. What is wrong with this picture?

I was determined that this battle was not about winning or losing—it was about what was best for Sean—and to achieve what was best for him to help him achieve his goals was the new definition of winning. *His* happiness, and not being exposed and forced to interact with nasty mean people was critical. And I didn't need to be interacting with them either.

Summer

Leaders bring out the best in others. — Byrd Baggert

I was still determined that Sean should have a fun summer and not attend summer school. He had aged out of his previous summer camp program, and I learned from another parent of a teen with a disability about another camp where 15-year-olds could be in a Camper in Leadership Training (CILT) Program. Sean applied and was accepted into this volunteer position! I wanted to be sure of success and asked the WorkAbility Program at our school to provide a job coach for Sean. I was told they don't do that. Another local program funded through our regional center (Department of Developmental Disabilities) provides for aides in after-school programs. We requested this service, and Sean was granted an aide, which we then renamed "job coach." Sometimes you have to get creative! The agency hired a young man who, coincidentally, had worked at this camp the summer before as a paid camp counselor. So Sean had the perfect person to teach him his job.

This camp was extremely inclusive, and Sean enjoyed working with the kids and had a great summer. Each counselor uses a pseudonym. Sean selected "Panda" as his name. Sean was also an inspiration to parents who sent their children with Down syndrome to the camp. They were able to see the possibility that their children would be able to contribute in the future too, and not just be receivers of services. This summer Sean matured significantly being put into a position of responsibility.

Sophomore Year

You can get someone to remove his coat more surely with a warm, gentle sun, than with a cold blistering wind.—John Ruskin

Sophomore IEP Goals

When verbally and visually prompted, Sean will use an appropriate rate of speech.

When presented with daily living situations common to Sean's environment of home, school, and community, Sean will predict the outcome of actions and their consequences.

When visually and verbally prompted, Sean will answer six out of 10 orally presented questions, each containing one of the following concepts: before, after, yesterday, tomorrow, on the weekend, next week, some, none, equal, around, through, beside, between, first, next, last.

When visually and verbally prompted, Sean will answer orally presented *WH* questions.

Given two cues from his instructional aide, Sean will replace chewing on his fingers with an alternative form of oral stimulation, such as chewing on a chewable pencil topper.

Sean shall write his name in cursive.

With the aid of a tracking device such as a "book mark," or "line tracker," Sean shall, with shadow aide assistance, copy or highlight notes for later retrieval.

When given a prompt by the teacher, Sean shall write at least a three-sentence paragraph.

Sean shall seek assistance from an adult to resolve conflict with peers.

Given adult assistance, Sean will demonstrate self-controlled behaviors in real or simulated situations with no more than one verbal prompt.

Sean shall arrive at class on time with all required materials.

Given modified materials and/or peer assistance, Sean shall provide five health facts per chapter.

Sean shall have class materials at the ready by the tardy bell and persevere at lessons for at least 30 minutes with the aide prompting.

Sean shall read a one-paragraph monologue and follow a two-step direction during skits as instructed in drama class.

Given modified materials, Sean shall use and select units and tools of measurement.

Given modified materials, Sean, with aide assistance, shall solve addition/subtraction problems.

Given modified materials, Sean will select and apply directional concepts in a variety of contexts.

Sean shall, with the assistance of a shadow aide and a calculator, grasp the concept of simple interest/percentage and taxation using the four basic operations at a modified level.

In word problems and real-life situations, Sean shall be able to find coordinates on quadrant graphs with aide assistance.

What a difference a new case carrier made! Sean made it through his entire sophomore year without being suspended even one time. THIS was the first time in his entire school career he made it through an entire year and was not sent home even one time—either officially or unofficially!

His elementary school friends were now a part of the freshman class, and Sean was quickly becoming quite The Big Man on Campus.

I was involved with the Parent-Teacher Student Association (PTSA) in two positions this year as the special education chairperson AND as the volunteer coordinator. The volunteer coordinator was a very visible position. I knew every school activity before anybody else did, and I worked closely with the ASB director, requesting and coordinating the parent volunteers for dance chaperones, school events, grad night, and more. Because I was coordinating the volunteers, I was on campus often and was able to observe Sean walking through the campus and see that he was greeted by just about everybody—and embraced by the baseball players.

I thought the year was all set—he had a regular education health class, regular PE first semester, the 1-yearlong Drama 1 class, and second semester he would be the assistant to the baseball team again. He was in regular education 50 percent of the time. The English, math, and history classes were in the Mod program and were the same teachers he had freshman year so they were familiar with Sean, and he with them. The aide that took over the prior year was back, and she had a great feel for how to work with Sean. And he really liked her, and that made a big difference.

We needed one more communication tool. Sean was getting homework from four classes each day, and I was spending a lot of time digging through his backpack trying to figure out what he needed to do. Other times, he would do the homework and forget to turn it in. So they created an assignment checklist. Each day, his aide wrote in the homework assignments along with when they were due. I checked that they were completed at home, and when Sean turned them in, the aide checked that off too. If she saw it was completed and he was forgetting to turn it in, she would prompt him. He also had a separate folder with homework to be turned in so he wasn't searching high and low for the work in his backpack.

His aide also wrote very detailed notes in his communication notebook. So detailed that Sean was frequently surprised when I asked him about things that happened during the day. He was sure I was a mind reader. Then he figured out it was all in that little spiral notebook in his backpack. He tried a few tricks to foil us—once he ripped the cover off the notebook. I just sent a new one in his backpack. Another time when he had made a bad choice he decided he would throw the notebook in the trash so I wouldn't see the note! But his aide was watching, and she fished it out. She was stealthy at putting it back in his backpack when he wasn't looking! She learned quickly that she had to be smarter than Sean.

Sean's new case carrier, Mr. Ainsworth, was amazing, and became Sean's favorite teacher—and mine too. He even came to our house for Sean's fifteenth birthday party!

But in December, Mr. Ainsworth dropped a bomb on what I thought was finally a perfect year. He was not in agreement, but had to communicate with me that the drama teacher, Mr. Rains, did not want Sean to continue for the second semester in the yearlong drama class. AND the baseball coach was reconsidering Sean being an assistant for his team! So, we called an IEP meeting. I needed more information in order to prepare for this meeting. I knew that Sean had had a couple of small issues in drama, but hardly anything compared to the previous 2 years. Between the communication notebook and his daily checklist, I felt like I was in the loop, so I went through every daily checklist from the beginning of school and only 6 days had less-than-perfect marks from the drama teacher—and I had notes in the communication notebook that correlated to those dates.

I thought maybe he was worse in drama than was being communicated . . . so I went to observe.

Drama about Drama

That is still the case in this country for too many students, the soft bigotry of low expectations. If you don't expect them to learn, if you don't expect them to succeed—then it becomes a self-fulfilling prophecy.—Tavis Smiley

I went to observe drama class immediately after the Christmas break in January. When I arrived, Sean's aide helped me find a place to observe where Sean would not see me. The students were reciting the monologues they had been assigned. One girl's monologue was the fear of being raped. During her emotion-packed performance, one boy laughed and heckled her. Sean had the best behavior of all 40+ students. He listened raptly to each student's monologue while other students had side conversations and didn't pay attention to the performances. When she finished her monologue, Mr. Rains called the boy out.

"Do you think rape is funny? It's not funny."

The class ended, and the drama teacher asked me to stay and talk to him. I didn't know the next period was his free period. He spent the entire hour talking *at* me. I had already started this book, so when the extremely frustrating conversation concluded, I transcribed the conversation. It was over nine pages long, and I will only include some of the most incredulous comments here.

Being a salesperson, my entire career is based on overcoming objections. All the drama teacher did for 1 hour was hurl objections at me. As I responded with reasons why his objections were unfounded or offering solutions to potential problems, he not only ignored me, he didn't even respond and was not open to one suggestion. I have never had a conversation like this before or since. I utilized my professional skills to detach myself and respond as unemotionally as possible. When I left his office, I was boiling but did my best to not show it or react like it. The tone of the conversation was almost deadpan as we held our emotions in check.

I began, "Since school started, Sean has only received less-than-exemplary scores six times on his daily checklist in your class. Six times—on predictable days—his birthday, the day after his birthday, the day before Thanksgiving break . . . etc., from your class."

The drama teacher said, "I was being *kind*. There was one time that Sean rolled himself in the stage curtains, and then he refused to leave the stage. And one night he came to a performance and during the intermission got on stage and danced—one of my senior students had to get him off the stage." *(I had dropped him off and left him like any other sophomore's mother would have left her kid to attend a drama performance! After talking with some of his friends later, it turns out the senior who got him off the stage was the one who TOLD him TO GET ON the stage in the first place!)*

I expressed my disappointment that he had not told me about Sean's inappropriate behaviors before and he explained, "I don't have time. I have 40 students in each class, and I should have less than 30. You know that boy who was laughing about the rape monologue? *EVERY* day I have to get after him. He's a real problem. I have students who do drugs and have all kinds of issues; I don't have time to spend with Sean."

I asked, "Is that disruptive student being removed from your class too?"

He didn't respond.

He began to tell me a story of an issue that occurred in October (3 months earlier) that I was aware of because Sean's aide had written it in his communication notebook. Mr. Rains has a policy that when a group is performing a scene or a skit that they must all be present or they will have to postpone the performance in class. Sean had participated in writing a scene where he was playing Zac Efron and was being taken on a date by Vanessa Hudgens, and the scene included a fight with his parents. He had quite a few lines he had learned, and when the day of the performance came, one of the students was not there—I had been under the impression that student was ill—so he was disappointed that he wasn't able to perform as he was expecting—and like many actors, threw a bit of a tantrum. This is what I knew had happened, then the drama teacher filled me in on *why* the other student wasn't present to perform.

"One of the students from Sean's performance group is a senior. She's an aide in my class. She realized that day that she had to get signatures from various teachers and staff in order to submit her application to college and that was the last day she was able to get the signatures or she would miss her deadline. She was upset and crying and asked if she could do it during my class, so I let her."

A senior student's irresponsibility trumped my son's scene that would have only taken 5 minutes for them to perform—THEN she could have gotten her signatures. But no, instead, *her tantrum* gained her a pass, which disappointed Sean, and, in turn, *he threw a tantrum*. Hmmm . . . I see that both Sean and this young lady had the same behavior that day. So, I said, "So, her lack of planning was rewarded, and Sean, who was ready to perform his scene, was the one who was punished."

He didn't respond to that and started in, "And NOW that I was so nice to *let* Sean into my class, there's four more kids from the severely handicapped class who want to be in drama! I have to put my foot down; I don't have time for those kids to be in my class. Not all kids with Down syndrome are the same. I should have never set the precedent, but that's who I am. I'm a nice guy."

(*In whose book are you a nice guy to prejudge students with disabilities and keep them from participating in your class?*) I responded, "You are right, not every person with Down syndrome is the same, but they *ALL DESERVE the SAME opportunity.*"

Ignoring my response he continued explaining how during the second semester the students tried out for, rehearsed, and performed a play. "I purchase copy written scripts so I can't change anything about them. I can't create parts. And I don't want anybody picking my scripts for me. Sean can't memorize five lines; he can't be in the play."

I responded, "Sean *can* memorize five lines, and he has memorized *MORE* in the past! I'm not asking to pick your scripts, I'm not even asking for a speaking part for Sean! *EVERY* play has background people; he would be thrilled with being cast as a background character. He would be thrilled to play a rock."

"It would be better for Sean to be in another class. If he's only got a background part, then he's going to just sit here for a week or two till we get to rehearse his scene. He would be bored, and there's nobody to watch him. I'm afraid he's going to get into trouble. We've got curricular saws, real swords, and all kinds of props on stage that he could get hurt with. He could get a lot more out of being in another class. What about choir or dance class?"

I was staying calm and keeping my voice steady. "You completely underestimate the benefits to Sean of being in your class. Even sitting and watching you direct other scenes, telling the students to 'stand this way, say it like this,' and giving them direction, he will learn from that! He also will benefit from hanging out with the other students and mirroring appropriate teenage behavior."

"So what good is it going to do for him to learn how to act? He's NOT going on to Drama II! I won't allow it."

I ignored that and addressed the lame supervision excuse. "As for supervision, what's his aide doing? I'll sign a liability release. Has Sean touched the circular saws yet this year?"

"I heard you would sign a liability release, but what good does that do if he breaks an expensive piece of equipment or part of a set?"

"I will pay for anything he breaks."

"What about rehearsals after school? Who is going to supervise him then? I just don't have the time to work one-on-one with any student! AND the kids do rehearsals at their homes; I can't send Sean to somebody's house unsupervised."

"I will come to every rehearsal and sit in the back of the theatre. I can sit in another room at the students' houses if they need me."

"No. No, the kids don't like adults hanging around. That wouldn't be right. And don't you have a job?"

"Yes, I have a job, but I am willing to take off of work early and do whatever it takes for Sean to be successful. If being in the house doesn't work, then I'll sit in my car in front of the house, and they can come get me if they need me."

"No, that wouldn't be right. He needs somebody to be right there all the time."

"Then I can pay a 19-year-old boy I know to supervise in the teens' houses." (*Is nothing I offer enough for you?*)

"Well, that wouldn't be right that you would have to pay somebody!"

My patience was wearing. "I'm trying to make suggestions on how to make this work, and nothing seems to be OK with you."

He kept going with his deadpan voice, "Doesn't Sean have a lot of after-school activities?"

"Yes, he has many activities, but when the play is being rehearsed, we can just put the other activities on hold."

"I don't have to do a play for Drama I. I could cancel it and not even have one."

Trying to be helpful I said, "I have a network of about 500 families of kids with Down syndrome. There's also a group in L.A. called the Born to Act Players that is an acting troupe of adults with disabilities. I could contact the drama coach there too—If you would like, I can send an e-mail and find out what other drama teachers have done in their schools. Would you like me to help you?"

"Why don't you take Sean to L.A. for that group? He could do drama there instead of here."

"Seriously? You want me to drive to L.A. every Saturday when this is available here at school? Sean plays sports on Saturdays. I can do the research for you on what other drama teachers have done in their classes to successfully include students with disabilities, and then give it to you typed out or in an e-mail, or whatever form works best for you."

"No, I don't have time. I have to work nights. My wife wants me home. She's always mad at me. This job is sometimes 18 hours a day when we have plays. I have too many students, and everything takes so much time. Maybe I won't even do a play for Drama I this year. There are no scripts that have 40 characters, except musicals, and they can't do that in Drama I. There aren't that many afternoon rehearsals anyway."

"Wow, sounds like you're at a crossroad."

He continued, "No, I love my job. I just don't have time for special-needs kids. I have my four teacher's assistants who are seniors, and I assigned them to Sean, and he takes all their time. They haven't been able to work with the other students at all. I've had them do the skits with Sean because the way I grade it wouldn't be fair to the other students for Sean to be in their groups."

This was the first time I had heard that he had segregated Sean with his teaching assistants. "That's why he has an aide. Why aren't you utilizing her? He should have been performing with the other students from the class, not the class aides."

"She's not a trained drama coach."

"So, you are saying that for Sean to be successfully included in your class, he needs an aide that is a trained drama coach. You realize that the school district has to provide the accommodations for him to participate. When we have Sean's IEP next week, you need to tell them that so they can provide a trained drama coach for one period per day."

He continued complaining. "And of the four seniors who are aides, Sean has really taken to one boy, and he's told me he's tired. Sean is wearing him out."

Making another suggestion I said, "So change which Drama I class Sean is in next semester, put him in period 2 instead of 3."

Then he got punitive. "I thought about that. Period 2 is pretty mellow compared to period 3. They're my worst class. I've done a lot of special grading and made a lot of accommodations for Sean. I guess I'll have to start marking him down on his daily behavior sheet to get him out of here."

In a warning I responded, "Well, now then, that would be retaliation."

"It would not, but would be the fair thing to do. I shouldn't have been so nice. I should have said no. I didn't mean for him to be in class all year. I meant for him to just be in first semester. I thought I had made that clear when we met last year. I could tell you are good parents, and I thought I would let Sean in because you are good parents. And now it's biting me in the butt. I just know that Sean can't stay in my class for next semester."

Trying my best to not come unglued at his irrational behavior, I said, "Well, he can, and he will still be, in your class. Drama is on his

IEP, and we won't remove it as his elective. When he was in elementary school, he was fully included in regular education classes. He was accepted, embraced, and included by everybody in that school. He participated in every after-school activity. When Sean got to intermediate school, the teachers didn't want to include him. The principal was about to retire and told me they had never done inclusion before, and it was going to fail. The teachers were out and out mean to Sean."

He said, "Oh, that's not right!" (*But you kicking him out of your class is right?*)

"No, it's not, and you would think that when I went to observe that they would have been nice to him when I was there, and they were still awful to him, even with me in the class! They created all kinds of behaviors, and it's taken him 2 years to recover from that year of rejection and hostility."

He finally found one positive to share. "You know the kids are great with Sean. I never have a problem with them being anything but nice to him. Thespians are the most accepting of people's differences." (*What's your excuse as a Thespian since you are not accepting at all?*)

"I know that, which is why your rejection is so shocking to me. Next year, we have to do Sean's transition plan. And as a part of that plan, he says what he wants to do for a living. I can see Sean being a motivational speaker. He needs to be able to stand up in front of people and not be afraid. He needs to have drama in order to reach that goal. So, he will continue in drama in order to reach that goal."

He found one more positive. "If there's one thing about Sean that he isn't—that's afraid. I really like Sean, he's so real. He comes up and says, 'Dude, you're funny,' or 'I love you.' Most of the other kids are too cool for that.

"What about a speech class? There has to be a speech class here on campus. He's *NOT* going on to Drama II. That's my class, and you have to audition for it. What about dance class?"

"We're asking for dance as his PE class, and that would be 'in addition to' your class, not 'instead of.' I've heard that three other kids with intellectual disabilities haven't been allowed into the dance class, so we'll see if that even happens."

Finally the bell rang, I thanked him for his time, and left—even though he never said Sean could continue in his class. I was utterly exhausted after an hour of back-and-forth.

This was so unbelievable to me, the drama teacher, who, in one breath, said, "Thespians are the most accepting of people's differences," and in the next, "but Sean can't be in the play." I was so discouraged. Sean loved to be on stage and had been ever since he was 3-years-old. I had been in drama in high school, and it was one of my biggest social experiences in school. Sean's opportunity to belong to another group was being taken away from him. Once more prejudice was limiting his opportunities.

I called the school district office and spoke to the inclusion specialist who had been supporting Sean's inclusion over the years and explained that somebody at the school's administration needed to explain special education law, ADA, and civil rights to the teachers at Sean's high school. That the denial of electives to students with intellectual disabilities stops with Sean, and that I was ready to take this further. She said she was going to be out of town and unable to attend this meeting, but she would make sure an assistant principal would attend Sean's IEP (two attended), along with another representative from the school district so we could solve this problem once and for all at the high school.

As we entered the IEP meeting, it was obvious there had been a meeting before the meeting. I am sure the drama teacher had been *talked to* before we arrived. I had brought an entourage of support, including the drama coach who had taught Sean in a private Improv class he had taken outside of school and a mother whose son with special educational needs was also not allowed to continue in drama at the school. I invited my mentor, whose daughter had been the first fully included student in the district (and had graduated a few years earlier), my educational consultant, and Rick. This was the first time I had more people attending an IEP meeting than the school.

Mr. Rains seemed to have changed his tune. He complained he had too many students but agreed that Sean could be in his class the rest of the year. We talked about the play, and he said that he wouldn't be responsible for Sean during after-school rehearsals. Our educational consultant asked him, "Are you responsible for the other students when they are here rehearsing after school?"

He said, "Yes."

She said, "Then you have to be responsible for Sean too."

We discussed an aide for after school. I had a copy of the Title 34 federal regulations from Section 504. These regulations provide for supplementary aides and services for nonacademic and extracurricular activities. I said, "If you believe Sean needs an aide for rehearsals after school, then the district has to provide one."

The district representative said, "That's not the way we interpret those regulations here."

When I was reviewing the IEP notes, I found a discrepancy from what she said and what was written in the notes. It says, "District administrator explained that if an extracurricular activity is required, an aide would be provided, the drama teacher states that after-school practices are voluntary, not required." That was not said at the IEP meeting. I even reviewed the tape. There were other notes in this IEP document that were untrue, and I should have taken it home and reviewed it before signing it. Lesson learned. Mr. Rains said, "I can get one of my student aides to supervise Sean." And the objection of supervision went away.

There was some discussion between Sean's independent drama coach and Mr. Rains about techniques that work with Sean, and he showed a little trepidation regarding Sean's stubbornness. I took the opportunity then to address the administrators.

I said, "It has only been 3 years since this school has had severely handicapped students on campus. How much in-servicing of the regular education staff has occurred since the SH-SDC class was established here 3 years ago?"

Blank stares, then the district administrator said, "Well, the first year there was a 1-hour in-service during a teacher in-service day."

My response, "And no more?" I looked at Mr. Rains and Mr. Ainsworth and they both shook their heads "No." I looked at the assistant principals and said, "The administration at this school has got to provide basic in-service training for your regular educators on including students with special needs in their classes. A 4-hour course on behavior and interpreting behavior would be beneficial too—when a kid runs away is he being bad? Or is he communicating something? Behavior equals communication. Most likely, he's trying to communicate that he doesn't understand what he's been asked to do—or it is too hard—or whatever. Knowing that behavior equals communication and having some basic tools to address that would go a long way in empowering them so they aren't afraid of having our kids in their classes. Right now, what's happening is the school psychologist comes to an IEP, a parent asks for an elective for their student, then he goes and talks to the teacher who is immediately scared because they don't know anything about people with disabilities, and they say, 'No' out of fear. *THEN* the school psychologist has to come back to the parents and make stuff up about why the kid can't be in that class. The regular educators have to also know that the IEP drives the placement, and they can't say 'No' because they are afraid. Please, when a student with special educational needs is going into a regular ed class, please spend some time educating the teacher about the students' needs—don't just give them an IEP and be done with it."

Mr. Ainsworth was nodding in agreement with me through my whole diatribe.

Mr. Rains was not happy about keeping Sean in his class and was not about to make this easy for Sean or Rick or me.

A couple of weeks later, Sean's aide wrote a note in his communication notebook that said, "Sean needs to memorize a monologue as his audition for the play. I took him to the library, and he picked a book of monologues to choose from."

I looked through the book of 1-minute monologues—all excerpts from plays from the '30s and '40s, many F-bombs, and other unsavory language, so I sent it back with a note. "I feel fortunate that Sean doesn't use the F-word now with it thrown around as much as it is at school. I don't want him to memorize a monologue with the F-word in it." The requirement was the monologue had to be from a theatrical production.

So, Sean chose a monologue from *High School Musical*. While it's a movie, it has also been created into a theatrical production. He memorized it over the weekend. When he went to school on Monday, Mr. Rains had a fit and declared that *High School Musical* was not a theatrical production and was unacceptable as a monologue choice. After a lot of back-and-forth, he chose a monologue for Sean.

I typed the monologue in a larger font for Sean and sent it to class with a note asking what play it was from in case it had been made into a movie so Sean could see how it was performed. He never responded. And the monologue he had selected was not from a theatrical production. He assigned it, even though it did not match his requirements—the requirements he was so staunchly defending. He took something that could have been so easy and made it huge deal. All because he wanted to be *right,* and he wanted to prove over and over again that Sean did not belong in his class.

Sean performed his monologue audition, his aide wrote me a note that he did well, forgot one line, but recovered and remembered it . . . The monologue he memorized was 12 sentences long! This proved that he could memorize more than five lines.

A couple of weeks later the daily checklist began coming home with blanks for drama class. I asked Sean what he was doing in drama and he said, "Making posters." I asked him if he was in the play, and he said, "No." I assumed that there would be a certain number of students who would not have a part in the play, so I accepted that, knowing the guy didn't want Sean in his class, much less in his play.

Then his aide wrote this note in his communication notebook, "Sean and I are enjoying WATCHING ALL the OTHER students rehearse."

I e-mailed the inclusion specialist:

"It never fails to amaze me how blatantly people's character is revealed where Sean is concerned—he certainly divides the angels from the avoiders." I filled her in on the note from his aide, then asked, "I was wondering if in all of your free time <ha-ha> you could pop over during 3rd period (9–10 A.M.) and see what's truly going on." I continued filling her in on another opportunity for Sean to participate in the student body. "Also, Sean came home with the forms to run for ASB commissioner of Boys and Girls Athletics! He has a campaign manager, and they will be attending the mandatory information meeting next Monday during snack—I fully expect some backlash about this from the staff—hope I'm wrong, but wanted to give you a heads-up in case it does happen. He's capable of performing all of the duties of the job . . . if he even gets elected in the first place."

The inclusion specialist had traditionally been great about responding to my e-mails, but 4 days later, there was still no response. I wrote a note to Sean's aide asking her to call me.

Sean's aide called me during lunch on a Friday. She said the inclusion specialist had been out to see the Mr. Rains on Wednesday but missed seeing him. The inclusion specialist had told her to stay out of the drama drama and not talk to the drama teacher about the problems, and I said, "She's right, you are Switzerland. We'll take care of this, but I have to know one thing—Is Sean the *ONLY* Drama I student who doesn't have a part in either of the two plays?"

She replied, "Yes."

Friday afternoon at 5:30 the inclusion specialist called me obviously upset, but, of course, she couldn't admit that Sean was being discriminated against. She said when she went out to the school she saw *some* of the kids rehearsing, but not all of them—eluding that Sean *might* have a part but wasn't rehearsing at that moment. She said she had e-mailed the teacher after she visited on Wednesday, but he had not replied to her yet (this is Friday around 5:30). I asked her what her next steps were, and she said she would be speaking to the principal on Monday.

Drama Continues

Behind every resentment, grievance, and projection of anger lies a miracle if I will open my heart. — Marianne Williamson

Dress rehearsal was scheduled for a Saturday. Sean and I ran into a fellow drama student at the store, and she greeted Sean and said, "See you at rehearsal." I told her Sean wasn't in the play and he wouldn't be there. She was shocked. She told me that she didn't see him rehearse, but thought that he was in another performing group and that was why.

We had been notified by Sean's aide that Sean would be passing out the programs during the play on Tuesday night. We cancelled his karate class for him to fulfill that obligation. Then on Monday, we were told Sean was to come on Thursday night to pass out programs instead.

Thursday was a stressful day for me. I had a conference that morning for my job and had to get up at 4 A.M. I rushed from the conference to pick Sean up at school at 3 P.M. and rushed him to an interview at 4 P.M. The interview was for the state Youth Leadership Forum. (He was not selected to represent our area.) The note from his aide said to have Sean at the theatre at school at 6:30. Sean had to eat in the car after his interview. I went home to change clothes quickly, and my car was out of gas so I took Rick's car and drove Sean to the school. It was simply a long, stress-filled, nonstop, exhausting day for me.

We arrived at the school on time, and Sean went into the theatre while I waited in the line outside with other parents and the students in drizzling rain—I was about the eighth person in line. I was soaked by the time I finally entered the auditorium. Rick had decided not to come; he didn't want to see Sean pass out programs.

When I first entered the theatre, after being pushed aside by incredibly rude students (about 30 students rudely pushed ahead of the parents waiting in line), I walked through the door and a female student handed me a program! Sean was not handing out programs. My first thought was he was doing something inappropriate (and proving the drama teacher right). I couldn't see him, and I thought perhaps he had pushed his way backstage, was not listening, and was getting into trouble. I was exhausted and stressed out so my mind was racing and thinking of the worst-case scenarios!

I asked the girl who handed me a program, "Isn't Sean supposed to be doing this?"

She said, "No, he's in the play now."

I said, "What? He hasn't rehearsed. When did this happen?"

She said, "Oh, he just rehearsed three times now. He did great."

I asked where Mr. Rains was, and she said to check the sound booth. As I headed up there I realized I'd better get a seat—the place was filling up fast. I was quickly texting Rick to get there ASAP since Sean was now in the play. The student must have told Mr. Rains that I was looking for him because all of a sudden he appeared and had some other guy with him (a witness perhaps?). I lost it and said, "When the #%&* did you decide to put Sean in the play?"

He said, "Today, during class, his aide and I decided he should be in it."

I said, "*WHY* didn't she write me a note, or you call me, or e-mail and tell me? Rick is at home. I don't have my camera, and Sean didn't get to rehearse!"

"I've got over 120 kids. I can't call every parent—I don't have the time! He just rehearsed now; he did great. You're bumming me out. I can't do anything to please you. I can go tell him that he can't be in the play now if you want me to."

I was losing it. "NO! You would devastate him! Which play is he in? (There were three plays listed in the program.) When is it? Does Rick have enough time to even get here? I see his name in the program. When did you print the programs?"

He said, "We printed them this afternoon. He's at the end of the second play. I'll stall so Rick can get here."

Rick was on his way but the camera wasn't charged, and I had left him with my car that was out of gas so he still had to stop at the gas station.

I said, "Don't stall. These people don't want to sit here and wait—go and start the show. Hopefully Rick will get here in time."

The drama teacher said, "Now you're bumming me out."

He had more to say, but I jumped in. "I'm bumming *you* out? Sean's friends wanted to come, and I told them he wasn't in the play. His grandmother isn't even here."

He butted in, "You have to understand where I'm coming from."

I said, "You have to understand where *I'm* coming from—every time I turn around at this school, someone is trying to keep Sean from participating."

He cut me off again. "I know. And it's wrong."

I was astounded. He had tried his hardest to remove Sean from his class. He had not cast Sean in the play till the last minute to keep him from being at rehearsals, and now he's acting like everyone else was the bad guy? I asked him to *please* go and start the play. But he didn't walk away. He kept complaining on and on about how he had worked last Saturday for 10 hours rehearsing these plays, and how he didn't get paid for his overtime. He'd been at the school every night till after 10 P.M. after working a whole day . . . How he didn't have to do a play for Drama I, and next year he's not going to do one; it's just not worth it…blah, blah, blah.

I said, "I've been upset for the past 2 weeks since I found out that Sean was the *ONLY* Drama I student not cast in any of the three plays!"

He said, "Who told you that? He's not the only one not in the plays. I kicked six or seven students out of the plays."

I said, "*THEY WERE IN* at the beginning at least! Sean was *NEVER* cast till this minute. You only did this so I couldn't file a civil rights complaint."

He said, "No, I did it because the other students found out he wasn't in the play and they were all over me."

God bless those kids again!

I don't even remember what he said next, but he was not leaving. I asked him three different times to *please go and start the show.*

I even said, "I am about to start crying. Please, go start the show." And he would *NOT* walk away! I had to stay with the two seats I was defending from the crowds so I could even see Sean's performance. I finally sat down and turned away from him, and then he left. I wonder today if he was trying to get me to be physical with him. He was truly baiting me.

AFTER the play ended he came over and apologized to Rick (not me) and said, "Sorry, man, I like to see my kid's plays too." Then he said something about how good Sean did with his part.

I said, "Well, now will you allow the four students from the SDC class to be in your class next year?"

He said, "What four kids? What are you talking about? Where did you come up with that number?"

I replied, "When I came in, in January, you said that there were four kids from the severely handicapped class that wanted drama, and you didn't have time for them."

He said, "I never said that! Where did you get that?"

I stated, "You certainly did say that—it's been burning in my ears ever since."

Rick just looked at him. He's good at giving the silent treatment. I had nothing else to say, and he kept standing there. I finally said, "I don't have anything else to say to you."

Then he walked away and joined the kids backstage celebrating the end of their show.

I wish I had thought fast enough when he told me he had 120 students and didn't have time to call all the parents. I should have said, "There was only ONE student who was cast at the last minute, so only *ONE* phone call was needed." But I didn't think of that until the next day. I was so angry. I was angry Sean didn't have the opportunity to rehearse. I was angry because I had planned to file a civil rights complaint—Sean being the ONLY student excluded from the play was pretty blatant, and a cut-and-dried win. I thought the drama teacher had taken that opportunity away from me—what I didn't know is I could have filed the civil rights complaint anyway because he did not allow Sean to rehearse during school or allow him to attend the rehearsals after school hours. Once again, I found this out past the 180-day time limit to file.

Sean's Part in the Play

Success is determined not by whether or not you face obstacles, but by your reaction to them . . . And if you look at these obstacles as a containing fence, they become your excuse for failure . . . If you look at them as a hurdle, each one strengthens you for the next.—Dr. Benjamin Carson

At the end of the play titled, *Fifteen Minute Hamlet* (which would have been funny if I had not been so angry), a female student escorted Sean to center stage (the stage was dark, but he could have done this without an escort). The spotlight came up, and he was holding a sign that read, "Encore!'" And he enthusiastically said, "Encore!" The spotlight went off, and the girl escorted him offstage—he didn't need a guide, and if the teacher had allowed him to attend the rehearsals, then he would not have had one. Since the drama teacher had the girl leading Sean on- and offstage, it made Sean appear to be more disabled than he was in front of everybody in the audience.

Prima Drama's Revenge

In the end, dear friend, it is always between us and God, not between us and them.—Mother Teresa

During the next PTSA meeting, the principal asked to see me privately and he informed me, "I will be sending you a letter regarding your profanity." Mr. Rains had filed a complaint that I had used profanity with him. I should have framed the letter. The teacher never appreciated Sean's talent, drive, and desire—he was definitely the slow learner in this chapter.

Baseball Assistant

Integrity is the glue that holds our way of life together. We must constantly strive to keep our integrity intact. When wealth is lost, nothing is lost. When health is lost, something is lost. When character is lost, all is lost. — Billy Graham

The night before the IEP meeting—the same meeting where the drama teacher was protesting Sean's continuation in his class—I received an e-mail from a friend of mine to come by her house in the morning before the meeting and pick up a letter that some of the baseball players were writing on Sean's behalf.

Here's what the letter said:

TO Whom It May Concern:

Although we could not retrieve all members of the 07–08 varsity baseball team on such late notice, we believe they would agree and feel the same way about this situation. We are writing on behalf of Sean McElwee. Sean was a blessing for the Varsity 07–08 baseball team. He was always there for a friendly smile, hilarious joke, or an inspiring pat on the back. Sean showed us that sports isn't all about winning or losing; it's about loving the game and coming together as a team. Sean truly brought last year's varsity baseball team together. Whether it was the juniors or seniors, or starters and subs, we all had something in common: Sean. Sean was in no way a distraction for our baseball team whatsoever. If anything, he loosened our team up. After 6 months of being out of high school, we look back and realize Sean brought out the best in us. Not only did the game become more fun, but daily life as well. Sean would brighten up our day. Just to see him and know how happy he was to be there made us feel so lucky to be able to compete and be able to enjoy the game of baseball. He inspired us to try our best, not only in baseball and school, but life in general.

To take away Sean McElwee's joy of being with the varsity

baseball team not only will take away his happiness, but take away the inspiration to the players, the people in the stands, and even the opposing team. You really have to think and realize how much this means to Sean. We understand that there are positives and negatives; however, it seems crucial to allow Sean to be a part of this baseball program. He was the happiest kid in the world, with a smile always on his face whenever he stepped onto the ball field. We strongly believe that the benefit of allowing Sean to be a part of the baseball program far outweigh the reasons for not having him there.

If the main reason for not allowing Sean to take part in the baseball program this year is because he may be a distraction, this statement obviously is not true. Last year, the baseball program had one of its most successful years in the last decade as we went to the second round of CIF playoffs. To Sean, baseball is not just a game, it's his happiness, his joy, and his getaway to his tough everyday life. Why would you want to take that away from him? Sincerely,

The 2007–2008 Varsity Baseball Team Members:

(eight boys signed it)

We were surprised that the baseball coach, Coach Watkins, was at the IEP meeting. We thought the decision that Sean would not help was made, and we were ready to ask about other sports for Sean to be involved with.

Coach Watkins explained that Sean could assist with the team after all. I made the suggestion that another student be Sean's aide on the field since his aide was afraid of going out onto the field. This student aide would be able to keep him on task. We discussed giving Sean a list of duties to perform, and I suggested a motivator that he tell Sean if he does his duties right for a month, without arguing, then he could ride with the team on the bus to an away game. I would meet the bus there and sit with Sean in the stands.

I also was able to make sure that "Assistant-Baseball" was added to his transcript. (The year before it was not listed, and we needed it for a possible future program at UCLA Sean wanted to apply to after high school.)

Coach Watkins finished up and I said, "Thank you so much. We really appreciate this opportunity for Sean to have a second chance. Here's a letter that some of the guys wrote on Sean's behalf."

He said, "Oh, I know about that. The team has been really after me." And he made the hand gesture with one hand open and the other one punching it as though he was being *beat up* by *the team.*

The boys really *went to bat* for Sean, and in our eyes, that's the part that makes the most difference! The adults didn't get it, but the teens—they *totally got it*!

School Site Council—Insider Information
Goals are like the stars—they are always there. Adversity is like the clouds; it is temporary and will move on. Keep your eyes on the stars.—Theodore Roosevelt

The election for the parents to serve on the School Site Council was held at a PTSA meeting, and I was elected to serve. This year serving on the council was particularly important as they were preparing the school for reaccreditation through the Western Association of Schools and Colleges (WASC). I was given a report on the school's programs, class descriptions, and demographics to review. On that list I discovered a class that I had not been made aware of during IEPs or on any elective or general education list of classes. Read 180 was the name of the class, and the description intrigued me. "Read 180, a reading intervention program that is a comprehensive system of curriculum, instruction, and assessment for struggling readers. Read 180 utilizes adaptive technology to individualize instruction for students." Other than writing, Sean's greatest weakness was reading. I thought this class would be perfect for him.

We asked for this class during this same IEP meeting. This was a *SPECIAL EDUCATION CLASS*. First, Mr. Calkins told me that the students had to be reading at a sixth-grade level in order to be in this class. Sean was reading at a low third-grade level. But that didn't sit right with me, so I did a little research. I was certain this wasn't a program the school had created, but one they had purchased. So I searched the Internet for Read 180, and found that Scholastic was the creator of this program—and they had a hotline for teachers to call and ask questions. I called and asked the person on the phone about the program. She explained that the program utilized the computer and made reading "a game," and Sean loved games. I asked what level a reader had to be at in order to benefit and she said, "First grade." I explained that I was told my son would have to be reading at a sixth-grade level in order to participate, and that he has Down syndrome. Also, I speculated that the program came in different packages, and perhaps the school had purchased the program starting at the sixth-grade level.

She was appalled. She explained to me that program comes in one package, with the same levels, and that there isn't any packaging for different grade levels AND the program was devised for students with intellectual disabilities like Sean. Only after it had been in used in schools did they find it beneficial for other students who were having difficulty reading. She e-mailed me the Web sites with the descriptions and the evidence of all learners, and I forwarded it to the school psychologist.

Sean was denied entry to enrollment into this *special education class* for the next 2 years. First, they told me they were considering cancelling the class and going with another program. Each IEP I asked about it they told me they didn't offer the class anymore. I never believed them, but had no way to prove they were not telling the truth. After Sean's graduation I found out that they only allowed this program for English Language Learners. It could have helped so many more students.

Being denied this program caused me to talk about it with other parents during a Challenger Baseball game. A couple of parents told me about a tutor who had been successful in teaching phonetic reading to teens with disabilities, and we hired her. Sean attended her program for a year. Unfortunately with Sean's phonological processing disorder and hearing loss, sight reading was all he was able to accomplish. It was the effort that counted, I truly believe you have to try everything to know whether it will work for your child or not.

Social Skills Class
God sometimes removes people from your life to protect you. Don't run after them! — Unknown

Another class I saw on the WASC Report was Social Skills. We had discontinued Sean's private Social Skills class by now since he had not hit anyone for quite a while. But I thought that it might be a good choice of an elective. Social Skills was listed as a special education elective, so during the same IEP meeting, I inquired about it. Mr. Calkins explained that it was for students with high functioning autism and Sean's social skills exceeded theirs. Not deterred by that, I explained that he had been in a private social skills class with peers who also had high functioning autism and the education came from the teacher, not the peers. And then I asked, "Who is the teacher?" Oh no! It was Mr. Spicoli! I almost fell off my chair. I believed that *HE* needed social skills training, so how could he be *teaching it?* We decided that Sean didn't need that man for one more class and never asked about it again. But several of my friends did inquire about it for their teens that were in the SH-SDC class, and they were denied the class. A special education elective, denied to special education students. *Unbelievable.*

The R-Word
To argue with a person who has renounced the use of reason is like administering medicine to the dead. —Thomas Paine

Sean knew he had Down syndrome, but he didn't know that people also used the word *retarded* to describe his intellectual disability.

He never heard the word used at our house, but when he arrived at high school, the regular education students used it quite frequently. They used it inappropriately to describe stupid situations, and they would call their friends that when they did something inappropriate or silly.

Sean only knew this word in the context that his high school classmates used it. So when he used it with a friend, I wasn't surprised that he used it inappropriately. Sean frequently copied behaviors and phrases his typical peers modeled. But I was shocked at the proposed consequences.

Sean was hanging out at lunch with one of his friends from the SH-SDC, and they were goofing off. His friend did know that the R-word was used to describe her intellectual disability. She did something silly, and Sean said, "That was retarded." She burst into tears, and Sean had no idea what he had said or done wrong. The aides for the SDC-SH class came running, and she told them Sean said she was retarded. I received a phone call telling me what Sean had done and suggesting he have consequences for this incident. I was boiling. I said, "Sure, you can give Sean consequences for joking with his friend and using the R-word inappropriately. But you must give every other student on that campus the same consequences when they use the R-word inappropriately." I never heard one more word about the incident, but once again, Sean's behavior was expected to be better than the typical student's behavior.

Winter Formal

Each friend represents a world in us, a world possibly not born until they arrive, and it is only by this meeting that a new world is born.
—Anais Nin

During Sean's sophomore year two girls knocked on our door with balloons and a big poster that said, "Will You Go to Winter Formal with Us?" One of our neighbors, Ashley, and her friend, invited Sean to go with their group of friends—14 teens—in a Hummer

Limousine to Winter Formal! Of course, Sean said, "YES!" He jumped up and down, then he hugged the two girls individually, then both at the same time.

WELL, Ashley found out the *NEXT* day that her GPA for first semester was only 1.83—she was usually a B student, but blew it the first semester that year. The school's policy is you can't go to the dances if your GPA is below 2.0!

I found out after the fact that she went into the assistant principal's office, crying—not upset that *SHE* couldn't go, but upset about how this would affect Sean since she's the one in the group that he knew the best. She explained to the assistant principal (while crying), "I don't care that I can't go to Winter Formal, but I invited Sean McElwee, and he's going to be so disappointed!"

I'm not sure which assistant principal it was, but he replied, "Sean's my buddy. You guys are going to have a blast." Then he waved his magic wand and removed the restriction so she could buy the dance ticket. Her mother was blown away and told her daughter, "It's just because of Sean that you are getting to go to Winter Formal." Mom AND the school wouldn't have let her go because of those grades. I think you could say that Sean was a "Friend with Benefits," and the girl benefited from the "Disability Discount."

The Winter Formal was a lot of fun, Sean went to dinner with them all beforehand, and then rode in the Hummer limo to the dance, then had dessert at an after party with the group. I didn't chaperone and had no reports of mistaken identity from anybody that night! Then his junior year he went to Winter Formal with this same group of kids in a limo—again. As a mom, I felt so *normal* not knowing what happened that night—other than the report that Sean danced the entire way in the limo and back! While Sean wasn't fully included in all academics, the social inclusion was coming together nicely. He was happy; he was accepted. He belonged. He was having a blast.

ASB Commissioner of Athletics Election

Life is like a roller coaster. It has its ups and downs. But it's your choice to scream or enjoy the ride. — *Unknown*

While the drama drama was occurring, Sean had come home with the election packet for our school's upcoming ASB (student council) election. He wanted to run for president. While that was very ambitious, and I was proud of his desire to lead, I also saw the extremely long list of event planning that I knew would be an onerous job for any student. So I carefully read each of the other elected position's job descriptions and came to one that was a perfect fit for Sean. The job description included:

- Teach positive cheers on the announcements.
- Distribute skinny balloons for all home football games.
- Responsible for recruiting two mascots or assigning ASB students to designated football games.
- Act as one of the official representatives of the high school (attend a variety of school activities).
- Create a sports rotation schedule every Friday for ASB members.
- Be in charge of solicitation from coaches an athlete of each varsity sport and recognize these students (i.e., breakfast-rally-assembly-announcements).

I asked Sean what he thought about the Commissioner of Athletics position and told him he would *have* to attend every home game for every sport, and he was thrilled. THAT was his favorite activity—sports!

I asked Ashley and another girl, Megan, in our neighborhood if they could be co-campaign managers for Sean and help him with the election. They were all over it. Megan designed a great T-shirt for the campaign team, and Ashley created campaign posters and flyers to hand out. While Sean was a sophomore, they were both juniors and were allowed to leave campus for lunch each day—but they were going to sacrifice off-campus lunches and stay on campus for an entire week helping Sean campaign!

I didn't want anybody to know that Sean was going to run until the day of the information meeting. That way, there would be no preplanning by the school staff on how to disqualify him. Call me paranoid, but by now, I was pretty suspicious of the intentions to limit Sean in any way possible.

The information meeting that was posted on the application forms said the date was March 16, but then an e-mail daily announcement came out saying the meeting was changed to March 9. So, Sean and his cocampaign managers went to the meeting—and discovered the daily announcement was incorrect. The meeting was to be on the 16th—and Sean was discovered! NOW, the ASB director knew his intentions of running. And here came the disqualification tactics!

I truly believe that the ASB director, Mrs. Drier, and Mr. Spicoli were colluding with each other. Sean still had him for math.

I had been aware that Sean had frequently been late to math class, which was the fourth period and after snack. The school had a policy that the first 20 minutes of fourth period would be "Super Silent Reading" and students had to read a book or something for those 20 minutes. Sean, not being the best reader, didn't feel like he was missing much by being late, but he always made it in time for the math portion of the class. And this had been going on all year with no consequences—until now.

On March 9th, the same day that Sean and his co-chairpersons went to the ASB room for the mistaken meeting, Mr. Spicoli decided to assign Sean a detention for being late. Sean had been late all year—and NOW Mr. Spicoli decides to punish him?

I didn't receive the detention letter in the mail until Thursday, March 12th. "Parent Notification of Student's 3rd Tardy. Teacher assigns the student to detention."

COINCIDENCE? I think not! He had actually had three tardies months ago, so why was he being punished now? Detention was on Saturdays. The students would have to sit quietly, doing homework for 4 hours. Sean couldn't sit quietly for 4 hours. And he never had

4 hours of homework. If he didn't serve the detention or if he misbe-haved during the detention he would be suspended. I believe the goal was to suspend Sean.

One of the qualifications for running for ASB was "no suspen-sions" and this was the FIRST year since fifth grade that Sean had not been suspended! His self-confidence had been restored through inclusion as the assistant on the baseball team and the presence of his friends who were now a year behind him in grade level. He was actually becoming a popular guy in his own right!

I sent an e-mail to the inclusion specialist to try to fend off any additional discrimination before it was too late. She decided to come and attend the information meeting with Sean, and she stayed after to talk to the ASB director. I have no idea what was said. She also took care of the detention and arranged for Sean to have an in-school off-the-record consequence for his continuous tardies.

Giving Back

Volunteering is the ultimate exercise in democracy. You vote in elec-tions once a year, but when you volunteer, you vote every day about the kind of community you want to live in. — Unknown

I had been busy Sean's sophomore year as the ASB Director, Mrs. Dreier's, volunteer coordinator. Every event that needed parent vol-unteers I solicited volunteers via the school e-mail list and scheduled the volunteers, even accounting for extra people for the inevitable last-minute dropouts. The ASB director had to have confidence that I was reliable by March. After she found out Sean was planning to run for commissioner of athletics, she called me on the phone.

"I haven't been able to sleep ever since I found out that Sean was running. Do you think he can do the job?"

I began to read the listed duties. "Yes, he can pass out balloons, and he can attend all the sports events at the school. I do have a question for you, however. On the weekly sports rotation calendar, can I create an Excel spreadsheet with the home games for him on

Thursday nights? Then he can bring it to school on Friday, and the ASB students can fill in their names on the games they can attend."

"Yes, that's OK."

"And the solicitation from coaches for their star players, can he do that via e-mail?"

"Yes, that's all right too."

"OK, since I can help him with those two things, he is capable of everything else with no help. You don't have to worry, I won't let him drop the ball on anything, and I've already talked to Mrs. Spencer. She also won't let him drop the ball at school." She was still not satisfied, but didn't say anything else.

Newsworthy!

History has demonstrated that the most notable winners usually encountered heartbreaking obstacles before they triumphed. They won because they refused to become discouraged by their defeats—B. C. Forbes

The local Down Syndrome Association was excited about Sean's election bid and contacted the newspaper. The reporter assigned to cover Sean's election was a really nice guy and determined to be objective. Sean worked his magic with him. This man came to Sean's Challenger Baseball games, came to our house, and played video games with Sean. He went to the high school varsity baseball practice and interviewed the players and by his determination, he concluded that Sean was able to perform the duties of the ASB commissioner of athletics.

The reporter attempted to contact Mrs. Dreier and wanted to interview all of the students running for all of the various elected positions. Mrs. Dreier never called him back. He contacted the interim principal who became very angry. The interim principal told me that no student candidate should get additional publicity, and it was unfair that Sean was being covered by the newspaper—I was worried they would disqualify him on the basis of this newspaper story—and that would have made a great follow-up story if they had.

The campaigning began. Ashley and Megan created flyers and re-cruited 10 more students to pass them out the week of campaigning. They all wore the cool shirts Megan designed for the campaign team that said "Vote for Me Sean McElwee."

Sean was getting a ton of attention, and he loved it. Then the girls came over to our house to talk to me—upset and shocked. Random students were coming up to them and saying to them, "Can he do the job? I don't think he can do the job." They explained over and over again that Sean could do the job requirements, but the doubters kept coming—and it seemed to the cocampaign managers that it was an idea planted by a teacher—they were sure the students had not thought of that by themselves.

Election Day arrived. It was the day after the play (when Sean was added at the last minute). I was so worried that he would win. I was worried he wouldn't win. The results were to be posted after school. I couldn't look. So I let Ashley and Megan call me at the end of the day when the winners were posted.

Sean lost. They were so disappointed. He lost to a very popular junior girl who was a volleyball star. She was a worthy competitor.

The newspaper reporter smelled a rat. He suspected that the elec-tion was fixed! Both of Sean's campaign managers were shocked—they said so many students said they would vote for him. The reporter tried to get the results and wanted to know by how much of a margin Sean had lost by. The school refused to tell him but assured him ev-erything was counted by Scantron, and there was no way to cheat the system. The reporter wrote a great follow-up article and called our house to interview Sean again. He asked Sean, "What are you going to do now?" Sean's response, and the last sentence of the article: "Run again next year—for president!" That's my boy! He never gives up.

That night we took the co-campaign managers out to dinner and milk shakes. They had worked hard on the campaign, and we appre-ciated them so much.

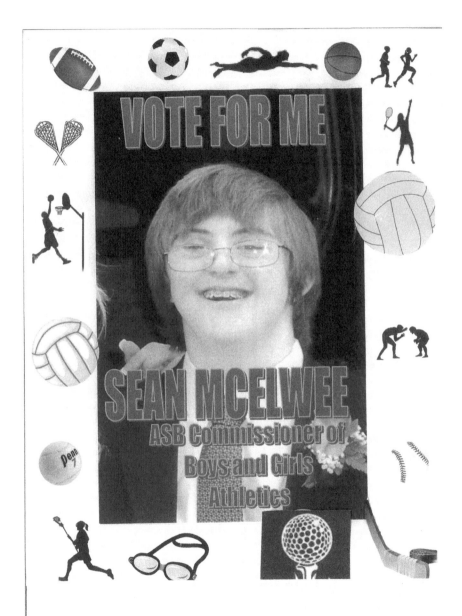

Shirt Designed by Megan Schley

That Poor Disabled Boy

Heroes build up. Cowards beat up. — *Byrd Baggert*

Before the election the reporter had wanted to take photos of Sean campaigning, but the school would not allow the photographer on campus. Instead the reporter sent a photographer to our house to take photos for the article covering Sean's election. Since the position was "Commissioner of Athletics," they thought a picture with one of his four basketballs would be good—unfortunately, the photographer picked the ratty old basketball that was peeling like a bad sunburn. If I had been home that would not have happened. Of course, the main photo for the article was Sean holding that nasty peeling ball—I was mortified.

The week after the election was spring break, and I was able to relax. Sean recovered beautifully from the disappointment. He was learning how to accept that the experience is the victory. The first day back to school after spring break was a PTSA meeting held at noon. The interim principal was angry at me over Sean's newspaper coverage AND the profanity I had used on the drama teacher, and was not hiding it. He was outright hostile to me during the meeting. About halfway through the meeting, one of the secretaries came in and said something to him. He walked out of the room, then returned to the door and gestured for me. I had no idea what he wanted, but I was sure it was not good. (He had already informed me I was getting a letter about the profanity earlier in the meeting.) We left the room, and he said in a very stern voice, "There's a presentation, but we can't call students out of their classes."

I was completely confused, "Presentation?"

"Yes, there's a man that has brought something for Sean. He's in the office and wants to present it to Sean. But he can't be taken out of class for this presentation."

Like I knew this guy was coming? Thinking fast, I said, "Lunch is in 10 minutes. Can we get a message to Sean to come to the office at the beginning of lunch?" He agreed that would work, and I went into the office to see who was there.

There in the office stood this handsome African American man who was way over 6 feet tall wearing an expensive suit, and he was holding a basketball and a gift bag with a huge grin on his face. He was the regional sales manager for Mercedes Benz. He had obviously been a college basketball player, and he was in the office with a brand-new basketball for Sean. He had read the first article about Sean's bid for election but had not seen the follow-up article and wanted to know the outcome of the election. I told him that he had lost but was planning on running again next year. He was so disappointed for Sean but loved his determination to try again. This man had come to the school the previous Monday but found the school was on spring break and actually took the time out of his busy schedule to come *again* so he could present Sean with a new basketball.

A few minutes after the lunch bell sounded, Sean arrived in the office. Seeing me, he thought he had done something wrong, but I quickly told him everything was all right. I introduced him to the Mercedes Benz Regional Manager. The manager talked to Sean, told him that he had seen his article in the newspaper, and was impressed with Sean—and he thought he needed a new basketball (*how embarrassing!*). Sean was very gracious. He also had a gift bag full of Mercedes Benz promotional items including logoed golf balls, a belt, golf tees, and more. Then he asked me to take a picture of him with Sean. What a nice man to come out of his way to go to the school and recognize Sean! Sean was thrilled to add the basketball to the four he already had! I wanted to avoid any issues with Sean having the goodies and basketball at school, so I told Sean I would take them home for him.

Funny how a complete stranger could be so touched by Sean's story and understand the importance of Sean's election. The Mercedes Benz regional manager assumed that it reflected the acceptance of differences at the school when, in reality, the school personnel could not grasp the revolution Sean was forcing them to accept.

Principal Selection Committee

The difficulties you face in life do not come to destroy you, but to show you what you're made of and just how strong you are! — Unknown

The week before the play and the ASB election the monthly school site council meeting was held. The interim principal gave us an update on the Western Association of Schools Accreditation (WASC) process. The paperwork had been submitted, and the WASC committee would he holding parent interviews as part of the accreditation process. I asked whether parents whose children have IEPs would be included in the interviews. He had not considered that and made a note to do that.

Next on his agenda was the principal selection committee. We needed a new principal due to a scandal that had occurred toward the end of Sean's freshman year. And no, it didn't involve Sean or any special education students. The interim principal explained that a committee had been formed consisting of teachers and parents to conduct an interview with each of the principal candidates. I asked how the parents were selected, and he said it was through the PTSA. I had not missed one PTSA meeting, so I asked when that was voted on. He curtly responded, "The PTSA selected the parent members of the committee." When I left the meeting I e-mailed the PTSA president, and she said the request had come in between meetings, so she and another parent volunteered.

I requested the criteria for the selection process from the interim principal and received the following via e-mail:

The assistant superintendent of personnel services has established the selection process for the committee. The committee is as follows: Three teachers selected by the teachers at the school, two parents selected by the PTSA. One student selected by the principal and the school office manager. Our teachers are in the process of making their selection. The office manager will represent the classified staff.

I was certain from my past experience that the new principal would be the key factor in instituting inclusion change at the school. I was adamant that a parent who had a student with an IEP be included on the team. I thought the parent should have at least one regular education and one special education student, since only two parents were being included on the committee in the first place. I did not want to be that parent, but felt as the special education chairperson that it was my duty to ensure that my son and his special education peers be represented. I moved this up the ladder and e-mailed the assistant superintendent of personnel services:

> Dear Assistant Superintendent of Personnel Services,
>
> As a member of the school site council and the PTSA special education chairperson, I was made aware that there would be a selection committee for the new principal of the school.
>
> Friday, I was told that the committee had been formed, and that no parent of a student with an IEP was included on this committee.
>
> Approximately 10 percent of the students at this high school have IEPs. The students who are considered to have "significant" disabilities have only been educated at this school for the past 3 years.
>
> Myself and other parents of students with IEPs believe it is critical that a parent of a special education student be included on this committee. It is important that the principal hired possess the skills and belief system to unite the regular education and special education teachers to become a team and empower the regular educators (especially the elective teachers) to feel confident and prepared to include students with disabilities in their classes.
>
> I appreciate your consideration of adding one more parent who has a student with special educational needs (IEP) to the committee. It is inherent in public schools that a culture of inclusiveness be maintained. To that end, it is very important that a

parent of a student with disabilities be represented on this selection committee.

Sincerely,

Sandra McElwee

High School PTSA Special Education Chairperson

She responded:

Thank you for taking the time to express your interest in the selection process for the new principal of your high school. The parent/teacher committee is one part of the process. As I believe you are aware, parent representatives on the committee are selected by their PTSA. Those representatives have now been determined. Parent representatives serve on behalf of all the parents of the school, not just one particular group. I am sure that the representatives selected will represent your school well.

Thank you again for your interest. I am confident that the selection process will identify an outstanding candidate for principal.

The panel members will be asked for input on questions to be asked. I suggest that if you have a question to suggest, please communicate that to the interim principal. I am confident that the array of questions to be asked of the candidates will be comprehensive. Thank you again for your interest in this important selection.

I submitted the following question to the interim principal and the PTSA president, hoping one of them would ask it during the interviews with the principal candidates:

How would you lead an educational staff in a paradigm shift from segregation of students with intellectual disabilities to inclusion in all of the electives, campus life, and sports as assistants or participation where appropriate?

I was later assured by both the PTSA president and the interim principal that the question was asked of the candidates. The announcement was made that the principal had been selected. He was being promoted from an assistant principal position at another high school—the school that had housed the severely handicapped classes in the past. The school that was known for including students with disabilities in electives. I had high hopes.

Junior Year

*If you have to judge people, judge them on what they can do not
what they cannot.*
*Judge them based on who they are, not who they aren't. Otherwise
you are judging based on your own shortcomings.—Aanonymous*

Junior Year IEP Goals

While participating in class discussion or instruction Sean will make
appropriate remarks and ask questions that are relevant to the topic
at hand.

Sean will produce the following phonemes at the sentence level
while in the speech room "sh", initial "r," voiced, and "th."

Sean shall produce his behavior sheet for each period with teacher
prompting as documented by the teachers initialing the sheet. Sean
will show the sheet to his parents every evening to earn video game
and TV time as determined by his parents.

Sean will demonstrate an understanding of the following concepts by
pointing to the appropriate picture while in the speech room before,
after, whole, half, medium-sized, right, left, in order, most/least.

When given a dotted-lined paper, Sean will copy his full name cur-
sively, forming each letter and connection correctly.

When given a simple application, Sean will independently print his
name, address, and phone number legibly.

When given a simple journal question (what is your favorite holiday? Or, my favorite holiday is Thanksgiving), Sean will answer the question in a complete sentence with correct punctuation and spelling independently.

When given the class vocabulary list, Sean will verbalize the definition of a majority of the words from the list.

Given modified materials and/or peer assistance, Sean shall provide five health facts per chapter.

When given a request, Sean will comply with the adult's request.

Sean will have class materials at the ready by the tardy bell and persevere at lessons with aide prompting for at least 30 minutes.

When presented with situations common to Sean's environment of home, school, and community, Sean will answer "*How*" and "*Why*" questions.

With the aid of a tracking device, such as a book mark or line tracker, Sean shall, with shadow aide assistance, copy or highlight notes for later retrieval.

Given aide assistance, Sean will demonstrate self-controlled behaviors in real or simulated situations with no more than one verbal prompt.

Sean shall arrive at class on time with all required materials.

When presented with picture cards requiring the use of irregular plurals and is+ verbs, Sean will produce grammatically correct utterances.

When given a prompt by the teacher, Sean shall write at least a three-sentence paragraph with at least 70 percent accuracy in English writing conventions.

Given daily homework assignments, Sean will complete and turn in 85 percent of all assignments in a timely manner

Classroom and/or Curricular Accommodations/Modifications

The student will be exposed to the general education curriculum in order to develop positive social skills, and/or gain academic competence in the curriculum. The student will require accommodation and will receive MODIFIED curriculum for the following classes: English, U.S. history, math, dance, health.

Sean will be provided with a shadow aide throughout the day, preferential seating, and positive behavior plan, modified grading, modified curriculum, extended time on tests, and other accommodations as identified by consensus of the IEP team. His grades will reflect his modified work as indicated on his report cards.

The day before school, Sean looked at me and just said, "Off campus." I had no idea what he was talking about, so I asked him what he meant by "off campus." He responded, "For lunch." Oh boy, juniors get to leave the school for lunch. I started to bargain with him, "If you can be on time to class after snack and lunch for the next week, then next Friday you can go off campus." He agreed, but he didn't mean it. The next day he called me before the lunch bell rang. "Mom, can I go off campus?"

"No, remember, if you are on time every day for lunch and snack, then *next Friday* you can go off campus."

"I'm going anyway!" The bell was ringing as he shouted that into the phone, and then he hung up on me. His aide called next. "He's leaving the campus! He's leaving the campus!" I told her to just let him go.

"I'll fix him tomorrow, and I'll send him with a lunch and no money. Let me know via the communication notebook if he makes it back on time." He did. But he had been late to the class after snack already that day, so he knew he wouldn't be getting off campus for a long time with the "earning" rule. He still hated that Super Silent Reading time. I sent his lunch the next day—and the stinker took it over to McDonald's and ate it there!

We had a new principal, Mr. Witherspoon. And I was filled with hope that everything would change for our students with special educational needs. Sean was not the only student who was not allowed in electives. Many of my friends' teens were limited by the elective teachers' fears of including their kids in electives. I had been so hopeful that Sean could be included in electives, even if the core academic classes were too much of a battle to gain access to.

Before the end of Sean's sophomore year I had done a presentation to our PTSA about the Spread the Word Campaign—eliminating the derogatory use of the "R" word. (retard, retarded, 'tard, etc.). Mr. Witherspoon had come to that meeting to introduce himself so I was privileged to have been able to meet him.

I had tried to get a Best Buddies Program going for 2 years—but the first principal had been reassigned because of a scandal, and the interim principal didn't institute anything new. He was maintaining the status quo while holding down the fort for the previous year. Mr. Witherspoon had previously been an assistant principal at another high school in the district that had a Best Buddies Program, and he was on board to get one started at our school.

I talked to him regarding the students being disallowed to take electives, and he was working on the inside to turn the ship around.

We had had enough of Mr. Spicoli and had requested another math teacher during the IEP planning for his junior year. Turned out there were two MOD math teachers, and the other one was a woman. She had come to Sean's IEP and sat down and started off by saying, "I don't think I can teach Sean. He is a disruption in class and can't complete the work at this level." I was astounded. I knew that Mr. Spicoli was poison and had tainted Sean's image at the school. Even though he had been professional and nice to Sean's face, he was sabotaging him behind his back and his opportunities to broaden his horizons.

I addressed her concerns. "His current math teacher isn't allowing the inclusion facilitator to modify materials for Sean, and he expects Sean to do the same level work as the other students." I then introduced her to the inclusion facilitator who explained how she could modify Sean's materials if the teacher would provide her with the lessons and worksheets in advance. This teacher was great, and once she experienced Sean for herself, she changed her mind.

Sean's electives included video production and dance, and he loved both classes. He still wanted to be in drama, but I never brought it up again. The drama teacher became so nasty to Sean during the second semester the prior year that he was creating behaviors that we did not want to dredge up again.

Since we had skipped eighth grade, Sean missed the health class that was part of the eighth-grade curriculum. The high school health teacher was one of the assistant baseball coaches and was also married to Sean's English teacher. Since we were skipping science Sean was able to take the health class his junior year. He learned a lot about why to not do drugs, and about sexually transmitted diseases, although I'm pretty sure that went right over his head.

Sean didn't get suspended once his entire junior year! And the same girl that took him to Winter Formal the year before took him again this year. Limo and all.

Baseball had been uneventful during his sophomore year since he had a student aide on the field with him and she kept him on task—and Coach Watkins had created a list of duties for Sean to complete and instructed the team that if they let Sean distract them, then Sean would be fired.

Baseball season was beginning to ramp up when the coach sent an e-mail to all the players and parents that his wife had a baby . . . a baby boy with Down syndrome. His bond with Sean was strengthened. For the first time, Sean was invited to the team dinners that were held the day before each game. We even hosted a team dinner at our house—and those boys ate a lot! We set up two 6 foot long tables in our garage so everybody could sit down and eat together. When they had all gone through the buffet line and sat down I heard Sean yelling. I went into the garage to see what he was yelling about as they all bowed their heads and Sean led them in a prayer—and he made them all hold hands too!

Sean loved having them all at our house (even if our next-door neighbor sat on his driveway glaring at everybody playing basketball on our driveway the entire time!).

In the fall of Sean's junior year, my good friend called me and told me her son had been invited to participate in a WET Workshop (Workforce Exposure & Training) by his school's school psychologist. I contacted our WorkAbility representative, and she sent the information home with Sean. The flyer said, "This workshop will simulate conditions and situations in a working office to help students to prepare for future employment." More information on what to wear, including golf shirts and nice pants for men, then the attendance policy. "Only one absence will be allowed during this short 3-week training or the students will be terminated from the program. In addition, if a student is late for the WET Training Program, they will be terminated . . . Upon successful completion of class, each student will have a personal PowerPoint of their skills, career goals, and accommodations and will receive a certificate of completion." I was very excited about this part since it fulfilled requirements for the UCLA Pathways program that Sean was aspiring to attend after high school.

The WET Workshop was a paid work experience that essentially trained the students in the program after school, on their home campus, for 3 hours a day for 4 weeks in the month of February. They would learn the proper way to answer a phone, take a message, shred paper, file, and other skills related to working in an office. This program was being funded by a federal grant and was facilitated by the Department of Rehabilitation. Sean was excited to have the opportunity for a real paying job. I e-mailed that he was interested, and then received the following letter:

> Your child's special education teacher has referred your son/daughter to the district's Cooperative Program with the state Department of Rehabilitation. This program is for students with a learning disability or other disabilities (medical or emotional) that could benefit from assistance during their junior and/or senior year of high school and beyond in figuring out what they want to do when they get out of the public school system . . . This year, the school district is allowed to refer 40 of our juniors and seniors to this program. Your child has

been lucky enough to be referred by their teacher . . . Tax dollars fund this program. The goal of the cooperative program and the state is to help your child get the training he/she will need to get and hold competitive employment . . . The State of California is experiencing a financial crisis at the current time. All types of state-funded programs may be cut back, including this program. That is why it is incumbent upon you to take this opportunity to help your child connect to the services the Department of Rehabilitation can provide by completing the attached application and returning it to me as soon as possible . . .

The letter was signed by the woman who was also over the district's transition program and the Work Ethics Career and Real-Life Experience (WE CARE) Program, Ms. Roberts. I filled out the application immediately and turned it in for approval. The acceptance letter came along with instructions to attend a mandatory information session.

We went to the information session at one high school's auditorium, and my friend and I realized our sons were the only ones there with Down syndrome. Most of the other students were also in the MOD classes and had invisible diagnoses, such as autism and learning disabilities. But we also knew that our sons were the only ones with Down syndrome in the MOD classes. Every other student with Down syndrome in our school district attended either the segregated school site or the severely handicapped classes. Ms. Roberts addressed the parents and students at this meeting in a very condescending tone. She didn't use People First language. And she was scolding the students in advance about being late, not dressing properly, etc. I will never forget one part of her presentation: "If you have not explained to your student that he/she has a disability, then you'd better do this so they can develop self-determination." This was so disturbing to me. Sean and his friend both knew they had Down syndrome, but many of the students in that meeting most likely did not know they had any sort of disability for the sake of their self-esteem.

For this woman to assume the job of informing them in such a public forum was unforgivable.

My friend and I didn't think much more about our sons being the only two students with Down syndrome at this meeting until my friend received an IEP request for this program. During the IEP meeting, Ms. Roberts explained to the school psychologist, "This program does not provide aides. This student has an aide, so he is not an acceptable candidate for this program." His aide was only present during snack and lunch and Sean was the one who had one all daylong. My friend decided that this woman was prejudiced against students with Down syndrome. She told me that Ms. Roberts spoke in a degrading manner using nonperson-first language in the meeting and talking to the school psychologist as though my friend wasn't even in the room. My friend didn't fight the decision because she didn't want her son exposed to someone like this woman.

I decided to wait and see before I made any decision. I reasoned Ms. Roberts was not present during the day-to-day workshops. She just oversaw the program, and Sean wouldn't be exposed to her directly. A couple of weeks went by and I didn't get a call for an IEP, so I thought everything was moving forward for Sean to participate at our school.

Sean continued to go off-campus after lunch. And he was late going back to class because of it. He also still hated the Super Silent Reading period and was late every day after snack to that class. That had become a real problem since he had more friends on campus and was being a social butterfly instead of taking his schoolwork serious.

Just before Christmas break we had an IEP meeting to discuss strategies to motivate Sean to be on time to class after snack and lunch. We had just begun the meeting, and Ms. Roberts entered our meeting. I was appalled and stopped her dead in her tracks. "I'm sorry, I wasn't informed that you would be attending this meeting." I did not want her to hear about Sean's being late since that was grounds for being terminated from the WET Workshop. I was certain she would use that information as an excuse to disqualify him. The new school psychologist, Mrs. Nolan, told me that she had been called by Ms. Roberts and asked for an IEP and she had simply invited her to this one. I told Ms. Roberts if she wanted to wait outside that we could meet about the WET Workshop after we were done with the meeting we were having. She didn't wait, and she left. I thought I would get a call to reschedule a meeting with her, but the call never came.

It was a week before Sean was to start the WET Workshop. We had put his karate class on hold for the month of February. We had purchased nice slacks and golf shirts as stated in the requirements. Sean was excited and ready to start. I just needed to find out *where* on campus the class was to be held since I had not received any notification yet. I e-mailed the school's WorkAbility representative and she responded the next day:

> Dear Mrs. McElwee,
>   I am sorry to notify you that Sean does not qualify for the Department of Rehabilitation. Therefore, he is not eligible to attend the WET Workshop. If you have any questions, please feel free to contact WE CARE at (phone number).
> WorkAbility Case Manager
> WE CARE

I was livid. Nobody had notified us that he didn't *qualify*. Not qualifying meant that he wasn't *disabled enough*. I saw the other students who *did* qualify, and they had significantly fewer disabilities than Sean. I went up the ladder to the principal in charge of the WorkAbility program who said she would look into it for me. A few hours later she called me back. I could not believe what I was hearing. She said to me, "Sean wouldn't want to work in an office anyway. From what I'm hearing about him, he would prefer a more physical job. Why don't we do some assessments to determine his interest levels and find him an appropriate work experience?"

I was so disappointed and discouraged. Sean was being discriminated against *within a special education program!* It was bad enough to experience discrimination within regular education programs, but *special education* too?

The school's WorkAbility case manager performed some assessments and sent home the results. The report said that Sean would make a great plumber. We tried to remember that when our toilets were overflowing. There was no follow-up to find him the perfect work experience to train him to become a plumber. I didn't let the subject drop. I scheduled an appointment with the principal in charge of the WorkAbility Program and the school's case manager to see about Sean working at the Taco Bell across the street from the school, or another site. As I waited for the meeting to begin, I asked the case manager if she supported any other students at the school, and she responded, "By the time I am done with reports and filing each day, I just don't know where the time has gone. I don't have time to talk to local businesses about setting up jobs." I realized I was wasting my time.

Ms. Roberts wasn't just the program manager of the WET Workshops, but she was also the director of the district's Transition Program. My friend and I both felt she had discriminated against our sons on the basis of their disabilities, and at the time, we were worried about what would happen when they got to the transition program. We lucked out; she retired before we got there.

You Aren't Smart Enough to Be Elected

Getting knocked down doesn't make you a failure—staying down does.—Unknown

Sean's final comment after losing his bid for ASB commissioner of athletics was, "I'm going to try again next year."

Sean picked up the election packet immediately after the announcement was made and brought it home. He tried to convince me once again that he should run for president. *Riiiggghhhttt.* I was successful in convincing him again that the ASB commissioner of athletics was a more appropriate position for him to run for.

Although Sean didn't win his attempt the year before, he must have come close to winning because the director of ASB was pulling out all the stops to eliminate him as a potential candidate his junior year.

As I reviewed the packet, I noticed a few *new* eligibility requirements for running:

- Must have an A or B in English based on previous semester grade (*overall GPA required for any extracurricular activity in our school district is 2.5.*)
- Students must pass a writing sample (graded on a rubric standard)
- Students must be able to read fluently from an excerpt that ASB provides (grade 10 literature text)

I immediately e-mailed the special education inclusion specialist asking her, "How do *you* spell D-I-S-C-R-I-M-I-N-A-T-I-O-N? READ FLUENTLY??"

I scheduled a meeting with the Mr. Witherspoon and brought a copy of the prior year's application requirements and the new application requirements and had highlighted the *new* qualifications and explained to him that I felt like these new qualifications were added specifically to eliminate Sean from running.

He told me he would talk to Mrs. Dreier, and later e-mailed me that Sean did not have to complete those requirements. I didn't feel it was fair that Sean didn't have to do it but other students would have to, so I asked via e-mail that they remove those requirements from the packet altogether, but received no response.

Spread the Word

Men often hate each other because they fear each other; they fear each other because they don't know each other; they don't know each other because they cannot communicate; they cannot communicate because they are separated. — Martin Luther King Jr.

Coincidentally, I had a collaborative campaign starting at the school with the PTSA and the Best Buddies Club, "Spread the Word to End the Word." Also known as the "R-Word Campaign." The purpose of the campaign was to educate students and staff of the inappropriateness of using any derogatory form of the word *retarded*. I had been on the campus a lot the previous 2½ years and heard that word almost every time I was there coming out of students' mouths. Usually it was preceded by the "F" word. Students had even used the word while sitting next to me in the stands at baseball games—and they knew I was Sean's mother. It was obvious they had no idea that what they were saying was hurtful, and this campaign would educate them otherwise.

I knew that we needed to have the teachers and staff to be supportive in order for the campaign to be effective. One of Sean's friends told me her volleyball coach during a practice told the girls they were "acting retarded." Another one of Sean's friends told me their teacher asked if they had come to school on the "short bus." So the teachers needed to support the campaign too by not using the R-word themselves in order to model appropriate behavior for the students.

Special Olympics supplied me with a presenter to present and explain the campaign to the teaching staff, a beautiful young woman who was hearing impaired, and who had a younger brother with Down syndrome. She also was a filmmaker and had just produced an award-winning documentary.

As I waited with her outside the staff meeting, she began to get very nervous. She could see through a window that the room was full and asked me how many educators there were—130. She had only expected there to be 30, and she was pretty stressed out about there being that many people to present to. The principal came out to get us when it was time for her presentation. As we entered the room I saw Mrs. Dreier sitting right by the door we were entering. She also saw me and out loud said, "Oh gawd." I heard it. Mr. Witherspoon heard it. Thank goodness my presenter was hearing impaired! Had she heard Mrs. Dreier's comment, she would have been mortified, and with her nerves so bad, she might not have been able to present the campaign.

After the presentation, Mr. Witherspoon e-mailed me that he had great feedback from the staff, and he thought it went well. I replied that I thought it went well too, and that I appreciated the opportunity. Then I asked his advice. "I am still disturbed by Mrs. Dreier's comment when we entered the room. It's apparent there is some animosity there. Should I talk to her or let it go?"

He responded, "I'll talk to her."

Two weeks later we began the R-Word Campaign. I arrived with the supplies and to help the best buddies get set up. The students had an opportunity to sign the R-Word Pledge Posters. The posters would later be laminated after all of the signatures were on them, and then would be hung in the gym as a reminder of the pledge.

The campaign was extremely successful. Over half of the students signed the poster pledging to stop using the word. One young man said, "I use this word all the time. I didn't ever think it would hurt someone's feelings till today. It's going to be a hard habit to break, but I'm going to do it." Another student said, "Thank you for doing this. My little brother has autism, and I'm sick of hearing the word all the time here at school." Mr. Witherspoon's son, who went to another high school, told his dad that at his Club Rugby practice, a student from our school corrected another rugby player when he used the R-word and said, "That word is banned at our school now." After Sean graduated, I was told that there was a zero tolerance policy instituted in regards to the R-word. Making a difference can be so easy sometimes.

We were setting up the table with the pledge posters and getting the campaign started for snack the first day. I had acquired a CD of video Public Service Announcements, and there was going to be one per day playing on the morning video announcements.

Mrs. Dreier walked past the table as we were preparing and was loudly huffing in my general direction and obviously agitated. She walked past again a few minutes later and huffed again. So I asked her if we could talk. She invited me into her office, but did not sit down. Instead, she stood, feet firmly planted, arms crossed—all body language said she was *ANGRY*. I asked her, "Are we were OK? Have I done something to offend you? If so, I would like to apologize—"

Cutting me off in midsentence she dove right in. "Yes, you have offended me! *You* told Mr. Witherspoon that I made a comment when you entered the staff meeting, and I did *no such thing*."

I said, "I didn't have to tell him. He *heard* you." Then I quickly decided that this was not an argument I needed to have so I added, "But I'm sorry if I did anything to make it hard on you."

She continued, "Well, I went into that meeting and told myself I was going to say nothing. I didn't make a comment. I know I didn't."

I acquiesced and said, "Well, I'm sorry, there must have been a misunderstanding." And I brought up the one thing I really *did* want to talk to her about—the application packet. I began, "The new requirements to run for ASB are pretty discriminating, not just for Sean, but for all of the students in the special ed programs, RSP, and MOD classes."

She got very defensive and said, "*My* students created the new requirements, not *me*." I was gasping as I said, "You missed a great opportunity to teach them about discrimination—and that those rules are discriminatory." (*Seriously? These kids had been with Sean since kindergarten; they didn't create those requirements without direction from her.*)

She emphatically said, "This class is like an AP class—it's a lot of work, and if you don't do your job, somebody else has to pick up your slack! Sean *CAN'T DO THIS JOB! He* can't read! You have to advocate for Sean, and I have to advocate for my students."

I thought many things during this conversation but didn't let them leave my lips like—Really? Students that are AP, being recruited to several colleges, and they need advocacy? And what a real-world experience that would be if Sean couldn't do the job. I pick up the slack for coworkers all the time. If it's an AP class, then the GPA requirements should be 4.0 not 2.5. Instead of saying what I was thinking, however, I calmly addressed her concerns one by one. "He can read. He reads at a third-grade level."

"He can't plan luncheons!"

"I told him he would have to plan parties and asked him what you need. He said, 'You get pizza or Subway, sodas, water, napkins, tablecloths . . .'"

She broke in. "He can't order pizza. They wouldn't be able to understand him!"

"You know he has an aide. If they couldn't understand him (*like if they don't speak English*), what if he was to give her the phone and she finish the order for him? She'll be here to help him during the day; she will make sure no balls are dropped at school—I'll make sure no balls are dropped after school. You know I'm responsible since I was your volunteer coordinator. I assure you nobody will have to pick up the slack for Sean." I continued down the list of job requirements. "He can pass out balloons during the football games . . ."

She raised her voice and exclaimed, waving her arms, "There's so much more to the balloons than that! The balloons have to go into a *specific bag* or they come flying out of the bag—they have to be passed out at a *certain time*. If they are taken out too early, everybody just grabs them!"

I said, "Sean can tell time. He can even tell when it's the end of the first quarter." Then I just looked at her with an expression of disbelief. (*Really? She's going to talk about a specific bag and a specific time to pass out balloons? Sean follows instructions. It's not like he's going to say, "No, I'm going to use a different bag instead of the one you want me to use." All I could think was, "Thank you for another chapter of Who's the Slow Learner."*)

THEN she said, "Last year, the students couldn't celebrate when they won the election—they were so upset the newspaper article was all about Sean and none of them were mentioned."

I said, "The reporter called and left you several messages, but *you* never called him back. He wanted to interview all of the other candidates too." I could visibly see her realization that *she* was the reason that none of the other students were mentioned in the article—not Sean. I said, "I assure you there would be no media this year, and if I am contacted I will tell them to wait until *AFTER* the election is over to print anything. I've tried to talk Sean out of this, but he's determined to run. My biggest concern is NOT that he can't do this job, because he certainly can. My biggest concern is **putting him in a hostile situation**—he knows when people don't want him around, and he will act out and have behavior issues if he feels that he isn't welcomed. And now that you tell me that the *STUDENTS* created the requirements, I'm not just concerned that you will be hostile, but concerned the students will be hostile too, and Sean doesn't deserve that."

She said, "I will not be hostile to Sean, and I will not allow other students to be hostile if he's elected. I'll modify his materials, and his writing and reading samples will be modified, and he will graded based on his ability level." Her tone was very sarcastic and condescending, and I didn't believe for one moment that she would be nice to Sean if he were elected.

I continued to explain, "Sean has endured many discriminatory practices, including being put in the play at the last minute last year. Each incident sets him back, and it's not fair to him."

She said, "I heard about the play. That was terrible." (*And this ISN'T terrible?*)

I had to leave. I had to discontinue this conversation. I was at the end of my ability to stay calm. I had overwhelming feelings of inflicting bodily harm on her or getting in trouble for profanity again, so I said, "Thank you for your time. I have to get back to work."

To Run or Not to Run

Vengeance is for people who don't have the patience for karma.
—Carrie Fischer

Rick and I agonized over this situation, and we were certain we could not put Sean into another hostile situation. I had helped him create a campaign slogan, taking Obama's lead: "Yes, I Can" was his slogan and on his campaign handouts each job was listed:

YES, I CAN . . .

--Teach positive cheers on
  the announcements
--Pass out balloons at home
  football games
--Special recognition of all
  qualifying CIF teams
--Recruit/assign two mascots
--Attend school activities
--Recognize an athlete from
  every varsity sport
--Create a sports schedule
  for ASB members

VOTE FOR:
Sean McElwee
ASB Commissioner of
Boys and Girls Athletics

I had ordered custom-printed paper carnival bracelets. Sean's co-campaign managers, seniors now, had purchased the supplies to create posters for his campaign. Time had been invested, money had been spent. But we just couldn't do this to him, so we started working on him the weekend before the application packets were due to be turned in. We asked Sean if he really wanted so much work to do during his senior year, if he wanted to work during football games and not sit with his friends. Each time he would say, "I want to work! I want to do it! I can do it!" And finally on Sunday night he gave up. With a dejected tone, he said, "All right. I won't run." And my stomach turned. I had NEVER discouraged my son from anything he was interested in. I had never taken the easy way out because of him, but I truly felt it was in his best interest. I felt certain with his growing popularity he would win, and then have to spend his senior year with a teacher who was forced to accept him. Nightmares of intermediate school swirled in my head, and I could only imagine the nastiness that was to come. I also had a plan to take this negative situation and make it fair for ALL students with intellectual disabilities at the school. So I typed the following e-mail:

Dear ASB Director, Principal, Case Carrier, Special Educator, District Inclusion Specialist, District Director of Special Education, and Superintendent of Schools,

It is with a sick stomach and a sad heart I am e-mailing to report that we have succeeded in discouraging our son, Sean McElwee, from running for election for the ASB commissioner of Boys and Girls Athletics.

The word "can't" is the biggest four-letter-word in our household. And while we have every confidence that our son CAN fulfill the duties of the position with the supplementary aides and services provided by both the ADA and IDEA, we are also confident that, as it stands, he will encounter negativity and hostility in this classroom.

While inclusion has been successfully legislated, we know

firsthand that you cannot legislate attitudes.

Mrs. Dreier, after our conversation last week, I cannot allow my son to encounter and endure more hostility in situations where he is not welcome because he has Down syndrome. The damage done to his esteem and confidence by past placements and attempted placements, denied to him, are nothing anybody should endure.

When you told me that the students enacted the discriminatory academic requirements in this year's application for election, my heart broke. Students have been Sean's biggest advocates over the past 11 years he has been in school. Students called me at home when teachers were being mean to Sean in intermediate school and told me what was happening. Students wrote a letter and stood up for Sean when the baseball coach was going to remove him from his assistant position. Students went up against the drama teacher last year when he didn't cast Sean in the Drama I play. This is the first time students have discriminated against my son.

We believe that the opportunity to educate those students in ASB about discrimination and the law has not been lost. We also believe from firsthand experience that discrimination among the high school teaching staff, while improving under the new principal's direction, is still alive and strong. We would like to request the director of special education to provide an in-service to both the ASB classroom AND the entire teaching staff of the high school, educating them on IDEA and ADA and the rights of people with intellectual disabilities and that it is every teacher's responsibility to educate them, not just special educators.

Also, we would like to request that the new principal and the director of special education see that the ASB Application Packet be scrutinized and modified to specify the modifications and accommodations that are available for students with disabilities, should they choose to run for an elected position. We would like to request that this happen ASAP, and an announcement, both during the morning announcements AND in the daily written e-mail announcements, be distributed.

And finally, in the spirit of inclusion, we would like to request that two new appointed positions be added to ASB. We would like to request that these appointed positions be open for students with intellectual disabilities. With a written recommendation by a special education teacher, these students could embody the "Spirit Team" advertisement that is in the daily announcements for ASB candidates. These students CAN pass out balloons at the football games, attend school activities as ASB representatives, perhaps WEAR the mascot outfits, AND teach cheers on the morning announcements, sell hot chocolate, and ask for donations from local merchants. These students can work during the ASB classroom and demonstrate to the students of Trabuco Hills High School that they are ABLE.

Today's daily announcement starts with this statement: **"INTEGRITY" must be stronger than temptation.** We are confident that this statement can be modeled for the students by the staff at the high school.

Sincerely,

Rick and Sandra McElwee

Four days later: no response from anybody regarding this e-mailed letter. I called the inclusion specialist and asked her if anybody was working on my requests, and she said, "No. Nobody." She had always been my supporter in the past, and was always able to make things happen, but I got the impression this was past her pay grade, and she was not able to make a difference here, so I asked, "Do you think I should file a civil rights complaint?" Normally in the past when I asked a question like this she would have said, "Let me work on this." And she would have made it right—but this time, she said, "You've gotta do what you've gotta do." She was sending me the signal that she was all right with it.

But I needed to be sure. I contacted another educator at the school and asked the same question. The response, "It takes parents like you to make positive changes happen; go for it."

Not Sean's Safety

Tough times don't last. Tough people do. —*Trace Adkins*

A few weeks after the ASB election debacle, we attended Sean's IEP to plan his senior year. We asked, again, for him to be made an assistant to the football team. During Sean's junior year, the school psychologists had been shuffled, and we had a new female school psychologist, Mrs. Nolan. I was hoping she had not been relegated to the school's policy of excluding students with disabilities. But I was wrong. She was towing the company line.

Once again, the excuse of *safety* was the reason Sean couldn't be a football assistant. We were past asking for after-school hours; we were just simply requesting during seventh period and to be on the field during the games. We were paying attention earlier in the year and noticed two 12-year-old *BOYS* who were on the field running water out to the huddle. I guess their safety was nobody's concern. I asked specifically what they were concerned would happen to Sean to endanger him. Mrs. Nolan said, "What if Sean is running randomly around and a football player ran into him and hurt him?"

I responded, "I will sign a liability release—I will release liability to the school, the district, the coaches, the players, even the Astroturf manufacturer. Sean has more of a chance of being hit by a car in the school parking lot than he does being hurt by a football player. He is always aware of where the ball is, and as long as he is given duties and knows what his job is, he won't have a reason to randomly run around."

And she responded, "But what if the player is hurt?"

I had no control over my facial expression. I was flabbergasted as I said, "Really? You are concerned about a football player who is two to three times *BIGGER* than Sean, padded up, and participating in a sport where they run into each other *on purpose* and who might be hurt? I'm just going to call that exactly what it is—*STUPID."* I did go on a bit of a rant and continued, "Sean is treated like a criminal here. No, his behavior isn't perfect, but he is not the worst student on this campus. He's never cheated on an AP exam, he doesn't have a blanket in his locker so he can have sex with his girlfriend on campus. He doesn't do drugs or bring weapons to school. But he's criminalized and made to pay the price by being excluded for simply being disabled."

In the book of James (yes, from the Bible) James 1:19 NIV, says, "My dear brothers and sisters, take note of this: Everyone should be quick to listen, slow to speak and slow to become angry." I was slow to get angry. I had endured 4 years of *educators* refusing to educate my son and rejecting him on the basis of their prejudices. Now, once again, his opportunities for growth and education were limited by the *professionals* who simply were afraid of a 5 foot 1 inch, 110-pound teenager who happened to have Down syndrome. I was angry, and finally—I was done.

Civil Rights Complaint

And one day, some great opportunity stands before you and calls you to stand up for some great principle, some great issue, some great cause. And you refuse to do it because you are afraid . . . You refuse to do it because you want to live longer . . . You're afraid that you will lose your job, or you are afraid that you will be criticized or that you will lose your popularity, or you're afraid that somebody will stab you, or shoot at you or bomb your house, so you refuse to the take the stand. Well, you may go on and live until you are 90, but you're just as dead at 38 as you would be at 90. And the cessation of breathing in your life is but the belated announcement of an earlier death of the spirit. —Martin Luther King Jr.

I did it. I finally filed a Civil Rights Discrimination Complaint. I didn't just file on Sean's behalf. I included all of the 400 students who were disqualified from running for election because they could not read aloud from a tenth-grade text preselected by ASB—*FLUENTLY*.

The form and filing instructions were easy to find on the Internet on the U.S. Department of Education's Web site. The U.S. Department of Education Office for Civil Rights (OCR) in California is located in San Francisco, Item 6. On the form it states:

> Describe the discrimination. OCR enforces regulations that prohibit discrimination on the basis of race, color, national origin, sex, disability, and/or age. All that apply: "Disability."
>
> Why you believe the discrimination was because of race, sex, disability, or whatever bias you indicated above or why you believe the action was retaliatory.

I filled in the following:

> My son, Sean McElwee, competed in an election for the ASB commissioner of Boys and Girls Athletics last year, April 2009. He lost and was going to try again this year. This year, March 2012, they changed the requirements to run for elected office to add:
>
> Students must pass a writing sample (graded on a rubric standard).
>
> Students must be able to read fluently from an excerpt that ASB provides (grade 10 literature).
>
> FLUENTLY? Due to my son's disability, his speech is not perfectly fluent. Also, there are an additional 200+ students with learning disabilities at the school who could perform this job (as well as my son who has Down syndrome). Additionally, there are around 200 more students who are English language learners who also could perform the duties of ASB without reading fluently.
>
> I have last year's application form and this year's with the changes to demonstrate the differences. I will fax them with my consent form.
>
> I asked the principal and the ASB director, both in person and in writing, to remove the discriminatory requirements, to no avail.

I was told my son would receive an accommodation in grading the writing sample, but his was never provided to the student body via announcements or in writing, so any other student who may have been discouraged to run for election because of the requirement didn't have the opportunity.

I requested that the director of special education, in writing, review the document and add language regarding the ability to utilize modifications and accommodations and received no response.

Students with disabilities have been denied access to many electives at this high school, and my son has been discriminated against in several attempts to be in regular education classes including:

No-cut track and field

Drama—he was in a drama class and denied rehearsals for the class play and only put in the play 30 minutes before it occurred. He was denied retaking Drama I or other drama classes.

Read 180 special education reading class

Football team assistant

Many of his friends with disabilities have been denied choir, art, drama, and several other electives as well.

Resolutions

Try to think of everything as a blessing because you never know when you have a blessing in disguise. — Kate Nowak

OCR complaints must be filed within 180 days of the discriminatory act. The other infractions I listed were too old to be considered on this complaint. But the ASB election complaint was cut-and-dried. I had written proof of the before and after. The lack of oversight with the ASB director put the district in jeopardy. I filed Sean's complaint on March 20, 2010. There was a confirmation that it was received, and the district was notified that I had filed the complaint. The director of special education asked me to send her a copy of what I had filed.

NINE MONTHS LATER, I received a phone call from the OCR asking questions to clarify dates and specific people involved. On January 26, 2011, I received a seven-page response from the OCR and the school district which ended with this Resolution Agreement:

The district without admitting to any violation of law, agrees to implement this Resolution Agreement to resolve the issues investigated by the U.S. Department of Education, Office for Civil Rights (OCR), under Section 504 of the Rehabilitation Act of 1973 and Title II of the Americans with Disabilities Act of 1990 in the above referenced OCR case number.

I. Policies and Procedures for the Associated Student Body Eligibility Criteria

    A. The district will develop policies and procedures to ensure that eligibility criteria for the Associated Student Body (ASB) of all high schools in the district do not discriminate against students on the basis of disability or language status. The policies and procedures will include:

        1. A statement of nondiscrimination in the Associated Student Body. The statement will include, at a minimum, that the district is committed to providing an equal opportunity to participate in the ASB without regard to race, national origin, sex, or disability. The ASB is further committed to taking steps to ensure that the contributions and perspectives of all students are included in its programs and activities, including providing reasonable accommodations necessary to include students with disabilities.

        2. The district will review current and future changes to ASB eligibility criteria to ensure compliance with Section 504 of the Rehabilitation Act of 1973, Title II of the Americans with Disabilities Act of 1990, and/or Title VI of the Civil Rights Act of 1964

and their implementing regulations, including 34 C.F.R. section 104.4, 28 C.F.F. section 35.130, and 34 C.F.R section 100.3. Pursuant to these laws, no eligibility criteria will be retained or adopted that tend to screen out individuals with disabilities or English language learners unless such criteria are directly related to the essential responsibilities and functions of students on the ASB. Further, individuals with disabilities who can meet these criteria with the benefit of accommodations that do not fundamentally alter the nature of the program will be considered to have met the criteria in question. The district will ensure any eligibility criteria that do not comply with the above listed regulations will not be adopted or implemented unless they are revised as necessary to comply with these laws.

B. The district will develop specific procedures for students with disabilities to request modification to the ASB elections criteria and duties. The procedures will apply at all high schools in the district. The procedures will include:

1. Notice that disabled students who do not meet elections criteria may request the benefit of reasonable accommodations in determining whether the student is able to meet the criteria. The notice shall include the manner in which parents or legal guardians and/or students may request a reasonable accommodation. Notice that accommodations will be provided will be printed on all ASB elections applications.

2. Specific timelines for consideration of a modification request, including provision of a written determination prior to the ASB application deadline.

3. Convening an IEP of Section 504 team to evaluate the request and make an individualized determination of appropriate modifications.

4. Notice that parents or legal guardians of disabled students are not required to attend ASB meeting, activities, Leadership Class, or camp with their child as a condition of their child's participation, unless the same requirement is applied to the parents or legal guardians of nondisabled students.

5. Parents or legal guardians of disabled students will be provided with notice of procedural safeguards and district disability discrimination grievance procedures in the event that an accommodation request is denied and a student ruled ineligible to compete for membership.

C. By February 7, 2011, the district will provide a draft of the policies and procedures to OCR for approval. The district will rely on OCR to provide approval within a sufficiently reasonable amount of time such that the district can enact the approved policies and procedures by March 1, 2011.

II. Instruction and Outreach

A. By March 1, 2011, the district will provide instruction or some other form of learning opportunity for the Leadership Class at the high school regarding the district's duty to provide disabled and ELL (English Language Learner) students with equal opportunities for participation in ASB. The instruction will be provided by individuals with experience in providing educational and extracurricular services for disabled and ELL students.

B. By March 28, 2011, the district will take steps to reach out to students with disabilities and ELL students to encourage participation in the ASB at each high school in the district.

> These steps may include providing information on the ASB
> and the elections process to special education teachers,
> IEP, and Section 504 teams, Community Advisory
> Committee, and English Language Advisory Committees.

The resolution didn't cover every one of my remedy requests—it
left out in-servicing the entire teaching staff of the high school, educating them on IDEA and ADA and the rights of people with intellectual disabilities and that it is every teacher's responsibility to educate
them, not just special educators.

I was told there was a 2-hour in-service training for all four high
schools' ASB students and directors. They held it at the district office, and the students enjoyed learning disability history and learning
about ADA and what kind of accommodations they could make so
everybody could be involved. The last part of the in-service had the
students brainstorming ideas of how they could involve students with
disabilities at their schools.

Sean's case carrier, Mr. Ainsworth, told me that ASB students
came to all of the special education classes and did a presentation on
what ASB was and what they do, and encouraged the students to run
for election. I don't know if any special education students did take
them up on it. Sean was a senior so he was ineligible to try again.

I was able to score a copy of the ASB Election Packet the year
following the discriminatory events—and my heart dropped. On the
listed requirements for every single position it read, "Must be able to
read the daily bulletin from the video teleprompter." Mrs. Drier kept
that reading requirement. There was an ASB Officer Accommodation
Request page at the end of the packet, so I guess there could be a
requested accommodation to that requirement, if the students got
that far into the packet without being discouraged by the reading
requirement.

Real Independence Includes Transportation

Learning from experience, learning from people, learning from successes and failures, learning from leaders and followers: personality is formed in these reactions to stimuli in social environments.—James MacGregor Burns

I try to use natural supports as much as possible. Natural supports are peers, not educators. Sean was a sophomore and needed to learn how to get home from school on his own. Our school district didn't send a big bus to our neighborhood. The regular education students were required to ride the public bus, so Sean needed to ride the public bus like everyone else. The students in the special day class were learning to ride the bus as a life skill. Since Sean wasn't in that class I needed to arrange for him to learn this skill outside of school. My neighbor's daughter agreed to teach Sean to take the public bus home after school. We started 2 months before school ended his sophomore year. She would meet him on campus at a place she selected, teach him where to cross the street, and how to wait in line for the public bus.

I paid her $5 per day (she thought $25 a week was awesome—so did I), and I paid for her bus pass. She walked him through the steps for a month. For the next 2 weeks, I told her to have him talk her through the steps. THEN I told her to just follow behind him and make sure he was able to do it alone, with no reminders or prompting. Two months from the start, he was independent on the bus, knew where to get off, and *I thought* he knew how to walk the four blocks home! Then she confessed that they actually would go to Taco Bell as soon as they got off the bus and her mother picked them up and drove them home! *She* didn't want to walk the four blocks home! So, I had to add another $5 per day to entice the walking, her mother still picked up her heavy backpack for her, and she showed Sean how to walk home. *THEN* he was independent!

BUT the bad habit had started. So when school started his junior year, he took the bus home each day and went straight to Taco Bell. He would save enough money from lunch to get a soda and a bean burrito. He would eventually get home, but many days I would stop by on my way home from work and pick him up. I finally caught on to his after-school snacking when he wasn't hungry enough for a healthy dinner. So, I limited the amount of money that he could take—he didn't need that fourth meal (Taco Bell's current ad campaign) or the soda every day.

One day Rick was home sick and Sean was supposed to be on the bus home. Sean called, panicking and yelling into his cell phone, "Dad! They didn't wait! The bus left me! They didn't wait!"

Rick said, "Wait for what?"

"I was at McDonald's, and they didn't wait for me!" Ah another lesson in life: the public bus is not your private taxi service.

Another day he called Rick again. "Dad, I don't know where I am!"

"Why?"

"The bus didn't stop! I got off next, but I don't know where I am!"

Rick said, "Look around, is there a store?"

"Yes, but I don't know what it is!"

"Spell it for me."

"A-L-B-E-R-T-S-O-N-S!"

"OK, stay there, I'll be right there to get you." Rick picked him up on the corner one stop past his regular disembarking point. Rick asked Sean "Why didn't you get off at the right stop?"

"Because I was dancing!"

Oh yes, we have our priorities!

Proud AND Pissed

Nothing in the world can take the place of persistence. Talent will not; nothing is more common than unsuccessful men with talent. Genius will not; unrewarded genius is almost a proverb. Education alone will not; the world is full of educated derelicts. Persistence and determination alone are omnipotent. The slogan "press on" has solved and always will solve the problems of the human race. — John Calvin Coolidge

In Sean's junior year, he was becoming more and more independent. He had his cell phone and was supposed to call us every time he changed locations. One Friday afternoon, he decided to go the park across the street from our house to play basketball. My instructions were for him to come home at 5:00, shower, then we were all going to go to the high school football game. At 5:00, I called to remind him he needed to be heading home—but he didn't answer. That was a clue he was doing something he wasn't supposed to be doing. I walked across the street to the park to get him and discovered the basketball court had been resurfaced and he had not been able to play there. He was nowhere to be seen. I called, and called, went home, got in the car, and started looking for him. As I saw neighbors, I told them to call me if they saw him. They jumped in their cars and began searching too. It was almost 6:00, getting dark, and I was about to call the police when one neighbor called, "I just saw him get on the bus! I tried to get to him, but he was on it before I could reach him. It's the bus heading toward the high school."

He still was not answering his phone and the pending punishments were reeling in my head. I tried to catch up with the bus, to no avail. Rick had gone back home, and he called me. "Sean just called. He said, 'I'm at the school.' Then he just hung up on me." So I drove to the high school and sat at the entrance of the football stadium ready to snatch him up, ground him, and take him home—but he never entered—then a friend who came outside the stadium to meet somebody told me he saw Sean in the stands at the football game with his basketball. Rick and I went in to the game, and there he was sitting with a friend—and his basketball (doesn't everybody bring a basketball to a football game?) and we let him stew on what his consequence would be. I was SO PROUD that he had figured out how to get *to the* school, go to the game, and complete ALL those steps completely on his own. AND so PISSED that he didn't tell me where he was going. But alas, he has learned well from me—it's easier to gain forgiveness than permission.

Bleacher Therapy

A friend is one who walks in when the rest of the world walks out.
—*Walter Winchell*

Thankfully Sean was involved in many sports all of his life. Sitting with the parents in the bleachers—parents of kids with disabilities—I have my ready-made support group. If it had not been for the parents who were from three different school districts, each with their own battles, bouncing ideas off of one another and commiserating together about the slow learners known as "educators" that we were encountering in a variety of schools I would have dug a hole and climbed into it.

Sean inherited his father's athletic ability. He was coordinated and could hit a pitched ball at only 4 years old.

During the spring of his first (special ed) kindergarten year, we signed him up for Challenger Baseball through the Little League. He had been throwing things his whole life, so he was able to throw the baseball pretty accurately. He batted off a tee and ran to third base in the beginning. But over the next 13 years, he learned the game of baseball well. During his last year of Challenger Baseball, he was hitting home runs over the fence and out of the park. After he graduated from high school he became an assistant coach for a Senior Challenger Team.

We learned AYSO soccer sign-up through our regular education friends in elementary school and signed Sean up to play when he was turning 6. He was on a regular team, and there was another player who had autism on his team. This was true inclusion. At this age, soccer has no real rules, no real form—both teams of players simply chased the ball wherever it rolled. It looked more like a swarm of bees than a team with positions. Sean further learned to listen and follow directions, and he was on a team with kids he would be in regular education with for many years to come. He played on a regular soccer team for 3 years; then when they started keeping score we transitioned him to a VIP Soccer team of kids with disabilities.

Because regular AYSO soccer was so accepting, we signed Sean up for the Community Basketball League. The format of each session was to practice for the first half hour, then play a game the second half hour. Nobody loses, everybody wins. But Sean really struggled. Even though they had lowered the net to 8 feet, Sean could not even hit the bottom of the net with the ball. For 8 weeks he tried and tried to just get the ball high enough to reach the goal, much less make a basket. But he never got discouraged, and he never gave up. At the last practice he finally made ONE basket! All the other kids on the team gave him high fives over and over again. All the parents watching clapped and cheered, and the coach put him up on his shoulders and paraded him around the court. Sean was hooked on sports.

He also played volleyball in the Community League. This was helpful in him learning the game, and on vacations he rules the pool volleyball court.

One ambitious mom decided that there wasn't enough to do during summers, so she started a bowling league. Around 45 teens and adults with disabilities signed up every summer to bowl, and we continued our impromptu support group.

Sean was in seventh grade when our Down Syndrome Association started a weekly karate class. By the time he was a senior in high school, he had his green belt, and we, sitting with the other parents of teens with Down syndrome observing our kids, bonded every week. He was 19 when he took his black belt test and passed.

I had no idea what an amazing support network we were building. We had VIP Soccer in the fall, Challenger Baseball in the spring, and bowling in the summer. In high school, Pop Warner Challenger Flag Football in the fall and winter and Big Dippers Basketball in the winter and summer. Karate was all year-round. Sean also played Special Olympics Golf. We were covered with support in the stands all year-round by the time Sean was in high school. Sadly, I had a new story to share almost every week. I will always be thankful for the parents who were also encountering the same attitudes limiting the opportunities for their children as well. We had a built-in support group each week, and nobody else could ever understand what we were going through, but we were walking in the same shoes.

Senior Year

If there were no such thing as change there wouldn't be butterflies.
— Unknown

Senior Year IEP Goals

The decision was made to continue his goals from junior year, and only two new goals were added:

In a vocational and classroom setting on or off campus, Sean will perform a task through completion for 7 consecutive minutes independently per class period, once the task has been explained to him by a store manager or staff.

In a vocational and classroom setting, Sean will follow a two-step direction independently.

The first day of Sean's senior year he went off campus for lunch and discovered that the Taco Bell was closed for remodeling. Looking around, he saw the Claim Jumper Restaurant across the street and decided to go there for lunch. He was seated, ordered a pizza . . . and took a 2-hour lunch! The assistant principal called him on his cell phone and asked him where he was. He handed the phone to a waitress, and she told him where Sean was. The assistant principal walked over to the restaurant and brought Sean back to school. He had spent his entire week of lunch money on one meal! He didn't get suspended, thank goodness—they chalked it up to a case of senioritis.

Sean's first semester classes were MOD U.S. government taught by Mr. Ainsworth. He also had MOD math, MOD English, and vocational training with the SH class and traffic.

Traffic was the classroom driver's education class. The description read: The integration of both classroom and laboratory experiences. Students learn the safe operation of the vehicle, the effects of alcohol and other chemicals on driver performance, rules of the road, and positive attitudes when driving within the highway transportation system.

Sean had been bugging Rick and I about learning to drive. We told him he had to take two classes and pass two tests before he could drive. That didn't deter him. The traffic teacher had been his regular education PE teacher, and he accepted Sean into his class. The first 5 days they took all five of the state's beginning driving permit tests. Few students in the class passed the tests. I asked that they provide the same accommodations that the state allows, which included *READING* the questions to the test taker and allowing verbal answers. I didn't want Sean to pass the test. I don't think his reflexes are quick enough to drive and to react fast enough if somebody pulled in front of him or walked in front of his car. But I was not going to discourage him and tell him no. I wanted him to try to come to the same conclusion on his own. He worked hard in the class, but he couldn't pass any of the beginner's permit tests. When the class was over he said, "I don't need to drive, I can take the bus." We haven't heard much about driving from him since.

The educational consultant had encouraged me to put Sean in the SH-SDC class for one period per day so he could get "work experience." They had unpaid practice jobs at the drugstore across the street from the high school. They also worked at a clothing store and a bagel shop. Sean loved going to work for one period per day. He was able to stay on task and learned some valuable skills, like sorting underwear— men's underwear. The reason the consultant thought he should do this is that the evidence shows that students with a work experience in high school have more successful outcomes after high school than students who don't have any work experience. Students who work and get paid for it have an even higher rate of success. Since he was disqualified for the WET Workshop from the previous year we thought this was a good idea. The SH-SDC teacher invited Sean to go with them on their Friday community-based instruction (CBI) trips, and I let him make the decision each week if he wanted to go. For the fall, he chose to mostly stay at school and attend the pep rallies.

Ball Boy

The best way to guarantee a loss is to quit. — Morgan Freeman

Because Rick is a coach in the Pop Warner Football Challenger Division Flag Football league and he attends the coaches' meetings, he found out that we were to have a new varsity football coach starting Sean's senior year. Our district's e-mail is set up with the last name, first initial before the @ so Rick tried the e-mail address and sent the following:

My name is Rick McElwee, and my son Sean will be a senior next year at the high school. Sean would very much like to help out with the football team next year. Sean has Down syndrome and loves sports. He has been around and participated in sports since he was 5 years old. The last 3 years he has been an assistant for the varsity baseball team. He is going to help the baseball team again next year, but he keeps telling us he wants to help with football also.

We could bring him by the school for an interview if you are interested in having Sean as an assistant, carrying balls, water, equipment, or anything else you can come up with.

I know this is a busy time, but we hope you can get back to us since we are finalizing his schedule for next year.

Thanks,

Rick

HE REPLIED!

I did have a conversation with the principal regarding Sean becoming one of our ball boys for our football games during the 2010 season. He did approve my intentions to have Sean as one of our ball boys. I want to lay out my ball boy plans to you, and if you approve, then I would love to have Sean part of our ball boy staff:

1. All of our ball boys will get a complimentary football shirt from me.

2. All of our ball boys are required to get their own transportation to and from each football game.

3. I will designate a coach to watch over the ball boys during the game.

4. A parent must be in the stands to oversee their own child, and if we decide as a coaching staff that a ball boy is a distraction on the sideline or a safety concern, we will escort that ball boy back to the stands to be reunited with a parent or parents for the remainder of the game. It will be determined by our coaching staff if that ball boy will be able to return as a ball boy.

5. After the game and the team and coaches are walking off the field, each ball boy is required to meet their parent or parents either on the field or by the gate to transfer supervision.

6. Finally, all ball boys must have a written permission from a parent for their son to participate in our ball boy program and state in the note that the football program, the high school and the school district, is not responsible for any injury that occurs during a football game to the ball boy. A parent signature must be present on the written note.

I hope to see Sean out there for the 2010 season and, again, let me know if you agree with our terms and give me Sean's shirt size. Thank you.

Head Football Coach

We were thrilled, and Sean was on cloud nine. We went to a scrimmage before school started, but they didn't give Sean any direction or training. I didn't know what a ball boy's job entailed—and I didn't realize that the rest of the ball boys *were* boys. Two 12-year-old boys and Sean were the ball boys. The kids didn't know Sean, and nobody even introduced him to them. There were no duties during football practice. During the games they were just running up and down the sidelines holding footballs—and at first, one boy held two balls, and Sean held none. The second game Sean asked that boy if he could hold one of the balls. When the team was kicking field goals, the boys would run behind the goal posts to catch the kicks—Sean had been warned to not do anything wrong, and he didn't know that was part of the job, so he stayed on the sidelines and thought the boys were going to get in trouble, until *we* told him before the next game that it was OK to catch the field goals behind the posts. The other two boys were extremely competitive and were vying to catch the balls, hold as many balls as possible, and Sean just ran around following them like a puppy.

He was only there for Friday nights, so there was no opportunity to build a relationship with the team. After a few games, he became bored, and one of his friends who also has Down syndrome, ended up on the sidelines somehow and was distracting Sean. I could not get Sean's attention, and when I finally got him to come to the gate to talk to me, I asked him why he wasn't doing his job, and he said, "Mom, it's embarrassing. It's for babies." I told him if he didn't get out there right away and get to work then he was going to be fired. He continued messing around with his friend and hanging out with the cheerleaders. There was a disco dance after the game that night. I had Sean's disco clothes in the car and at half-time I took him out to the car to change clothes. After I got him into the car, I drove away and took him home—he missed the last disco dance of his high school years. This may seem like a harsh punishment, but we had fought and argued for 4 years to get him any sort of position on the football field, and he wasn't following through on his part of the bargain. He was not supervised by an assistant coach as the coach's requirements stated, and he never received training or direction. He was set up for failure.

I e-mailed the football coach and told him that I fired Sean, and thanked him for the opportunity. I didn't know it, but Sean started advocating for himself and went to the football coach's class one day and apologized and asked for another job that was for somebody in high school. He didn't get another chance, but he was learning to speak up for himself.

Glee Fan Club

Lack of something to feel important about is almost the greatest tragedy a man may have. —Arthur E. Morgan

Sean was obsessed with the TV show *Glee*. Since every opportunity for him to lead had been taken away from him, and he was dating an actress from the show, I suggested that he start a Glee Fan Club. Each fall they had Club Rush Day with a ton of club choices at the school. Sean loved the idea. He recruited some of his friends from the SH class to be officers, and a brother of one of the students was also a club member. Sean brought home the application packet and asked Mr. Ainsworth to sponsor the club. He made a poster to advertise his club and created flyers to hand out too.

Club Rush Day came, and I went to the school with the poster and the flyers. They advertised they had a limited number of tables for the clubs to use, so I went early and saved one for Sean. I had the tablecloth on it, and Sean had arrived and was putting out the sign-in sheets that ASB provided. He was putting out the TV show photos and flyers that announced the first club meeting, date, time, and location when the Mrs. Dreier arrived at our table in a huff. She commanded Sean to remove the items and said that the table was in the wrong place and was supposed to be for a vendor who was on campus that day. I could not believe this woman would not leave Sean alone! There were another 20 tables that she could have commandeered!

He rallied, though, and wasn't as shaken up as I was. Then all of a sudden, she was back and brought another table, and we scrambled to set everything up again.

As they started recruiting members I walked around to see what other clubs were forming. There was the Jersey Shore Club, The Key Club, and then I stopped dead in my tracks. There was a "Gleek Club!" All of the announcements said there would be no duplicate clubs, and if two submitted the same purpose or name they would be combined. But Sean's club had not been combined—it had a competitor!

The Glee Fan Club was able to one-up the Gleek Club, though— Sean's club invited his girlfriend to make an appearance during their lunch meeting one day! The announcement was made on the daily announcements for 3 days prior to the meeting that Becky Jackson the Cheerio played by Lauren Potter would be making an appearance during the weekly club meeting. They moved the meeting to the Multipurpose Room because they expected a larger turnout than average. Sean's girlfriend brought some autographed souvenirs from the show, and we raffled them off. It was a huge success! Sean's Glee Fan Club met every other week and watched DVDs of the previous season and sang along with the songs in the show. The Gleek Club fizzled—neener-neener.

Scrooge

People who soar are those who refuse to sit back, sigh, and wish things would change.
They neither complain of their lot nor passively dream of some distant ship coming in.
Rather, they visualize in their minds that they are not quitters; they will not allow life's circumstances to push them down and hold them under.—C. R. Swindoll

Because Sean was in the SDC-SH class one period per day they invited him to participate in their Christmas play, *Scrooge.* Sean was thrilled to have an opportunity to be back on stage! He was cast as

Jacob Marley. He rehearsed along with the class on the days that he wasn't working. The class was able to procure the school theatre and filled it with family members and Best Buddies Club members. The class performed a fantastic rendition of *Scrooge*, and Sean performed his role dramatically. We also were able to invite his friends to watch him, and that made the night complete.

Retalia-Shunned

A fool is quick-tempered, but a wise person stays calm when insulted.
—*Proverbs 12:16, NIV*

Near the end of the letter attached to the Resolution Agreement of my civil rights complaint there was a paragraph that stated:

Federal regulations prohibit the district from retaliating against you or from intimidating, threatening, coercing, or harassing you or anyone else because you filed a complaint with OCR or because you or anyone else take part in the complaint resolution process. Contact OCR if you believe such actions occur.

At the time I didn't think much about this paragraph . . . until the second half of Sean's senior year was beginning. I was organizing the Spread the Word Campaign again, and there had been talk about having it for 1 day this time, instead of an entire week. Our principal had not been at the previous two PTSA meetings, and I needed to get the dates that it was scheduled for so I could plan my work schedule. I e-mailed him repeatedly, and he simply was not responding. The OCR complaint was in the process of being resolved, and all I could think was that he was mad at me.

I finally got frustrated and sent him a nasty e-mail:

Dear Mr. Witherspoon,

I had great hopes when you were hired as the principal at our high school since you had a lot of experience with students with special educational needs at the high school you were assistant principal in being included in extracurricular activities at that school.

The nonresponse to the Spread the Word Campaign e-mail requests for dates has spoken volumes to me.

I filed the civil rights complaint after my son and his friends with disabilities were discriminated against repeatedly at our high school, and after bringing the discriminatory ASB requirements to your attention and the attention of the school district and nothing was done to announce accommodations to the student body, so I felt I had no choice.

I had hoped that the case would empower you. You could make *ME* the bad guy and explain to the staff that they can no longer discriminate against students with special educational needs—that this would be a precedent.

Instead, you have ignored my requests to simply provide a date or dates to continue the Spread the Word Campaign that was started last year.

Sean's girlfriend was interviewed on CNN earlier today. I ask that you take a minute to watch the interview and listen to the words of Timothy Schriver when he explains how the **adults condone** the bullying of students with special needs.

You see, the adults at this high school have been the only ones to discriminate against my son. [I then listed all of the ways he had been limited in participation at the school.] If Mrs. Dreier had not been afraid, he would win the election, then she would not have allowed her students to create the discriminatory policies. The fear I have is that the teachers' examples are being TAUGHT to the students, the students who will work side by side and even hire my son in the future.

Sean is in regular PE this, his last semester of high school because there are no other electives available for him to take. We are thankful that the baseball coach is allowing him to continue to be the assistant for the baseball team.

I hope that you are able to enact change at this school soon—Sean's elementary school became an inclusive school after he pioneered inclusion there. You have many, many students with intellectual disabilities coming up behind him from his elementary and intermediate schools. I was trying to continue to pave the way for them—to leave it a better place. I hope you are able to do a much better job than I have been able to do. The students—*all* of them—deserve it.

I hope the Spread the Word Campaign is allowed to occur. I will e-mail the PTSA president the pledge posters and the instructions and hope she has time to facilitate this event.

Sincerely,

Sandra McElwee

PTSA Special Education Chairperson

He replied:

Mrs. McElwee,

I have been trying to find a teacher to run the Spread the Word Campaign for the past 3 weeks. I have received pledges from three different teachers that they will be involved next year. The issue is not that they don't care or they don't want to help our special education students. They just don't want to be subjected to lawsuits.

If you think that your OCR complaint would have "empowered" me, it would have been nice for you to ask. The result was 180 degrees from what any of us could have wanted. I have not had a single staff meeting since I became principal here where I didn't talk about special education, the need for inclusion, or the role of general education to support special needs students. I have held meetings with the elective teachers on campus and given them options for how they can include special education students in their programs. Every teacher I have hired has been asked to address the placement of special education students in their classes and how they would modify their curriculum to allow access to special education students. To my knowledge, I am the only principal I know of who does this. I address the progress of special education students when I do evaluations on EVERY teacher I work with, not just the special education staff. Again, I am the only principal that I know of who does this.

The staff is very much aware of my advocacy for special needs students. In their eyes, they see that I am a supporter and advocate for special education, and yet, I got sued in your OCR complaint. Why would anyone volunteer to subject themselves to that? In their eyes, if you would do this to an obvious ally, what would you be willing to do to them? I can't look a single staff member in the eyes and assure them that they won't be named in the next complaint if they volunteer to help, and they have asked me that very question.

If your motivation was to move special education forward on this campus, you have only succeeded in holding us back another year. I can assure you, your disappointment cannot begin to compare with mine. It may take me years to overcome this setback, but I assure you, we will continue to move this school forward and improve special education on this campus.

I have met with the Best Buddies president, and we are moving forward on the Spread the Word Campaign in an abbreviated format that SHE requested. We will do the PSAs and the announcements with an offer to the students to go to the Web site to sign the pledge there. It is our hope to have a full program again next year.
Mr. Witherspoon

I was shocked. I was disappointed. Did I truly set the school back? Did everything I *thought* I was trying to accomplish get waylaid?

Then I remembered the retaliation paragraph. This was more evidence that the teachers didn't understand the *law*. And really, there is a law because people don't do the right thing in the first place!

I responded:

Dear Mr. Witherspoon,

I am extremely sorry that the OCR complaint had the opposite effect than I intended. I truly believe it is sad that we need laws at all, but history shows people simply do not do the right thing because it is the right thing. It's even sadder that I tried to be nice. I asked nicely. I used every one of my sales skills to positively present Sean's abilities . . . and still was met with a slammed door. The teachers who think becoming involved will subject them to lawsuits are way off base—NOT becoming involved, *denying access*, is why complaints and suits occur. Even when teachers try and get it wrong, it's appreciated that they tried at all.

I have complete confidence that you "**can**" turn the teachers around at the school. I simply ran out of patience as my son was running out of time, and he has missed so many opportunities that could have benefited him in his application to the UCLA Pathways program.

The OCR complaint was not directed at you. It was a district complaint since I had gone to the district asking for the accommodations and modifications to be published and they did nothing. I don't know if you are aware (because you were not there the year before), but when Sean ran for ASB the year before, Mrs. Dreier had met with a district special education administrator and asked if she could create the prejudicial requirements that she indeed did put in place—she was told "no" by the special education administrator, and did it anyway . . . Actually, she had her students do her dirty work, and that was the most heartbreaking to me—students who had supported and been advocates of Sean since he was in kindergarten were turned against him.

I feel the remedies of the OCR complaint are positive. The training with the ASB students from every school on Tuesday, February 22nd, was well received. Over 80 students were educated in the abilities and rights of people with disabilities and brainstormed ways to include students with disabilities—and that is very positive. The ASB students will one day work side-by-side with my son and will be in positions to even hire him. Now they know that he will not be an extra burden and create more work with his presence as they were taught by the ASB director.

I am sorry that I lost it when you didn't reply to my e-mails. I didn't know that you were seeking a teacher. I would have been able to help with a few teachers there if I had known that.

I have forgiven everyone involved in this issue. I only hope you can forgive me.

Sandra McElwee

During Sean's FINAL semester of high school, he should have had three electives. Instead, his schedule ended up with MOD English, MOD economics, baseball assistant, and *THREE* periods in the severely handicapped special day class. (He didn't like being in the PE class with freshman so that class was changed.)

We asked for dance class again—and were told it was full. Sean wanted to take TV-Video Production again—and it was not available. We inquired about the weight lifting class. We were told each elective we were requesting was not available, and I felt I had failed Sean. If we had put any goals on his IEP for these classes, then they would have had to make room for him. I thought it was my fault for not planning better. I didn't even consider it was retaliation . . . until Sean tried out to give a speech at graduation.

Graduation Speech

Failure is not disqualification. Everyone fails. — *Rick Warren*

Before spring break, the daily announcements had been advertising for seniors to try out to give a 1-minute speech at graduation. Over spring break, while we were in Hawaii, Sean told me he wanted to try out. He met the requirements, the GPA minimum of 2.5, he had not been suspended for 2 years so that requirement was met, but the person in charge of the tryouts was Mrs. Dreier. I told Sean, "You can try out, but you won't get it." He was not discouraged. He wanted to be a teacher, and public speaking is the first step.

While we were on vacation I prompted him to be thinking about what he would want to say. He thought and thought, then one morning, said, "I want to tell them important things."

So, we started making a list of what Sean thought was important. And the final outcome was:

Sean's Senior Speech:

Lessons to Live By:

Never give up, never be afraid, and never accept NO as the answer.

Never be afraid to try anything that's legal.

Everyone makes mistakes. Don't give up—keep going.

Stop using the R-word.

Don't hate.

Get a job anywhere and hire people with disabilities.

Give it your all, even if others don't think your all is good enough.

Tell your parents you love them all the time.

Worry about nothing. Pray about everything.

Choose to be happy—it's a choice, and it always rubs off on other people.

Seniors—Rock the house!

You're amazing, YO!

He practiced and practiced, and he was easily under 1 minute on the day he tried out. When he got home from school that day he told me it went well. His aide had gone with him to the tryout, and she wrote in his communication notebook that he did a great job. I asked him who else tried out. There was one other boy and the class president. I was a little shocked; I thought the class president would speak without having to try out at all. The tryouts were on a Thursday.

The following Tuesday, Sean was suspended. I was unavailable when the school called, so they called Rick who went to pick him up.

The principal told Rick that he witnessed Sean throw an empty plastic water bottle at another special education student after she called him a loser. The bottle didn't hit her. Rick was amazed that the principal had seen this with his own eyes, because Sean was hanging out in an obscure area of the campus that day, not in the quad or where most of the students would be found.

When I found out he had been suspended I freaked out—suspension doesn't just disqualify you for speaking at graduation, it also disqualifies you from going to the prom! Prom was 11 days away. We had already rented a tux, and a group of his friends was arranging a limousine to ride in. I was so upset. I couldn't talk to the principal without losing it. So it was up to Rick to advocate for Sean, and he called the principal to ask about prom. The principal said he would think about it and get back to us.

That night I couldn't sleep. Lying in bed it suddenly came to me. This was *retaliation*. Sean tried out to do the speech at graduation. Instead of just not selecting him, he was suspended for something obscure. Then it dawned on me that was why he didn't have any electives this semester. I had already realized the Spread the Word campaign was retaliation, and I could handle *me* being retaliated against, but not *my son*.

I was afraid they would find more insignificant infractions since it was apparent they were watching him, so I decided to keep him home the rest of the week.

On Friday, 8 days before prom, there was still no response from the principal. Rick e-mailed him, and he responded that he would let us know on Tuesday (it was Memorial Day weekend, so school was off on Monday).

Tuesday came and went. We had to decline chipping in on the limousine with Sean's friends. We would be out $125 for the tuxedo rental. Thank goodness his girlfriend was out of town and we didn't have to worry about her disappointment or ordering her corsage in time. Rick called, and he e-mailed the principal; still no response, so he called the superintendent and reported that the principal was not responding. Wednesday evening, Rick, Sean, and I were entering the Multipurpose Room at the high school for the baseball banquet. Rick's cell phone rang. It was the principal. Rick suggested that he come into his office since he was standing right outside of it. During this meeting, the principal was suggesting another punishment for Sean. He suggested that he not attend the senior cruise.

Rick replied, "Sean's Positive Behavior Plan says the consequences have to be immediate. If you punish him 2 weeks from the infraction, he won't know why he's being punished. And isn't being suspended punishment enough? Why does he have to lose his senior activities for throwing an empty water bottle?"

Sean was granted permission to go to the prom, and no additional punishment was given.

Diploma or Certificate of Completion?

Some quit due to slow progress, never grasping the fact that slow progress is progress. — Unknown

We weighed the pros and cons of getting a diploma for quite a while. Finally we decided not to pursue a diploma for three reasons. Number one, Sean was not that interested in achieving one, and it would have taken a lot of hard work for him to complete all the credits he needed to graduate. Number two was the State CAHSEE California High School Exit Examination. He could have probably passed the math portion with hard work but would have never been able to write the essay portion of the English exam. Number three, we were told repeatedly that he would be exited from the school district if he achieved a diploma and would not be able to attend the district's transition program. And I was told repeatedly by every person I asked, from the regional center, the school district, advocates—everybody—that he would not have any support between graduation and age 22 if he received a diploma.

One year after Sean completed high school, the state of California suspended the CAHSEE for students with special educational needs. They accepted the required class credits toward a diploma. Then another year later, I found out if Sean *had* received a diploma, that he could have accessed the regional center's (Department of Developmental Disabilities) funding for a day program, allowing him to have community college support, a real paying job with a job coach and more. Check your state's rules and know they can, and do, change. In hindsight, we should have continued pursing the diploma and the decision could have been made a week before school ended whether Sean would have received a certificate or diploma.

Graduation—Not the End, but the Beginning

Things don't go wrong and break your heart so you can become bitter and give up. They happen to break you down and build you up so you can be all you were intended to be.—Charlie T. Jones

Sean didn't know a lot of what was going on behind the scenes through high school. He didn't know I filed an OCR complaint. He didn't know about the conversations I had with the drama teacher, ASB director, and others. I was truly afraid if he knew what had gone on he would have reacted negatively toward those people and his reactions would not have been accepted as a normal response to prejudice. It would have been seen as simply bad behavior.

The night of graduation, I dropped Sean off at the staging area and confirmed he would be walking alphabetically. At another high school, a friend's son had been grouped with the special education class, and they walked together. Each family received four tickets to graduation. The stands were packed. Two of Sean's grandmothers were present. I stood in line for 2 hours and held seats for them, and they arrived 30 minutes before the ceremony started. It was sizzling hot out, and we had umbrellas to shade us until the ceremony began.

The students entered the stadium and filed past a photographer who photographed each one. Then they walked through the center aisle to receive their diploma. Sean's aide had drawn me a diagram in his communication notebook where Sean would be sitting so we were on the correct side of the stadium. He was so excited, along with his fellow students, to get his diploma cover. The daughter of one of my friends—who had conspired in elementary school to add the inclusion facilitator who modified curriculum—was escorted on either side by the special day class teacher and an aide from that class. Rick and I both looked at each other with disgust that they would do that to her. She had been successfully fully included in elementary school. Then her parents decided to stop fighting the system and allowed the intermediate school and high school to put her in the segregated severely handicapped special day classes. She had acted out for the last 6 years, bored with the curriculum, and challenging the educators who refused to challenge her academically.

In comparison to the sixth-grade promotion I felt no sadness; I felt relieved! I had a poster made and hung it at Sean's graduation party: FREE AT LAST! FREE AT LAST!

Grad Night Accommodations

I don't know what your destiny will be, but one thing I do know: the only ones among you who will be really happy are those who sought and found how to serve.—Albert Schweitzer

The grad night trend began about 2 decades ago when parents around the country were concerned with the number of teens who were killed in drinking and driving accidents on the night they graduated from high school. Grad night preparations begin before school even begins in the fall and are huge events that require significant preparation. Traditionally held immediately after graduation, these events last all night and parents pick their teens up at the high school at 6:30 A.M. Our school had previously gone to Disneyland as a grad night event, but Sean's senior year Disneyland wasn't going to be open the night they graduated. Being the PTSA special education chairperson, I was concerned whether any of the special education students had attended grad nights in the past. I asked all of the special educators and could not find one student who had ever attended.

Sean was very attuned to the extracurricular activities at the school, and I knew he would want to attend grad night, and I also knew he would want to go with one of his friends from the special day class. I wrote an accommodation and submitted it for approval. This accommodation was printed on the grad night flyers and on the daily announcements that students with special educational needs would be allowed to leave grad night early if they were accompanied by a chaperone provided by their families who drove to the grad night and drove the students home.

So I chaperoned Sean to grad night and two of his friends from the special day class also went and were chaperoned by adult siblings. We stood back and just kept an eye on them, making sure to not interfere with their fun.

Grad night was held at a summer campground that had six carnival rides, a zip line, two large buffet lines, a DJ, and dancing, and then around 2 A.M., a hypnotist took the microphone and hypnotized several grads. It was highly entertaining. Sean was mesmerized and concerned that the hypnotist was hurting his fellow graduates. I assured him they would be fine. I was impressed that the hypnotist left the students with subliminal messages of "Don't do drugs and don't text and drive."

As usual, Sean surprised me. I thought he would make it to around 2 A.M., but the sun was rising around 5 A.M. when he finally announced he was pooped out. We both slept the entire day when we got home.

Social Life

We all need a rich social life. As Sean gets older I see more and more of his friends who hit their early 20s and become depressed. They aren't able to verbalize that they feel sad, and they may not even know why they feel sad, but the regression that comes with the depression is devastating. I can't stress enough how critical it is to facilitate friendships and activities for our kids to keep them happy and active.

When Inclusion Becomes Exclusion

The most imperfect model is the pursuit of perfection. — *Byrd Baggett*

It was a journey to Sean's senior year of high school—some of it amazing, and some, sadly, less than amazing.

Even though the law provides for inclusive education, you cannot legislate attitudes, and that includes not just the educators but also other parents' attitudes.

One issue that reared its ugly head in the last 2 years of high school is *disability prejudice* WITHIN *the disability community!*

Parents who chose not to include their children in regular education, for a host of reasons, have found themselves in a happy community of people who have created their friendships apart from those who elected inclusive education—to the point of EXCLUDING the (now) teens that have been fully included all these years.

And the sad reality has occurred where the *typical* students who so readily accepted our kids in elementary school—I almost went broke buying gifts for all the birthday parties Sean was invited to—now have their own lives and are very nice, but rarely call and invite or take Sean to any parties, sports events . . . well—any place at all.

And then there's my son's *attitude* toward other people who have disabilities! One of the ulterior motives behind inclusion (other than an education and appropriate social skills) is to sensitize typical students to not be afraid of people with disabilities. To teach them, by daily exposure, that we are all more alike than different. But to that end, our students who HAVE the disabilities also are not exposed to other people with disabilities—when other parents chose a segregated education for their children. Thus, this conversation that occurred with my son on the way to his First Red Carpet Ball—the formal dance that the Down Syndrome Association of Orange County holds each February:

"Mom, is everybody there going to have Down syndrome?"

"Well, most everybody. They can bring a date who has a different disability or no disability, but you have to have Down syndrome to even buy a ticket. Why?"

He thought for a minute, then said, "Because my Down syndrome is different than theirs." He was unable to verbalize *what* was different between *his* and *their* Down syndrome—but it's probably a lot like me—when I see someone my same age and I think, *My wrinkles aren't THAT bad. Are they?* Denial is a lovely thing.

Sean was 15 when that conversation happened, and I recognized then that I needed to do some *disability immersion* or he was going to be one lonely boy. Or worse, become a fearful jerk like so many we have encountered over the years!

So, we attended every disability event possible, went to movies, and did fun things with friends who were disabled and even started a social club named Cool Club, with 16 teens that have disabilities!

I realized this was not an isolated issue when Sean began dating another young woman who has also been fully included. She would pull me aside and tell me about another boy she liked *better* than

Sean on almost every date—this boy did not have Down syndrome, and also had no interest in her. But just like Sean, she saw her Down syndrome as *different,* and she ultimately decided she did not want a boyfriend with Down syndrome and broke up with Sean.

Sean especially had a strong aversion to people in wheelchairs. He needed a volunteer job, so we approached the person in charge of our disabilities ministry at our church and she agreed to allow Sean to volunteer in the 6- and 7-year-old Special Sunday School Class. The first Sunday there were four boys in wheelchairs. After church I was quizzing Sean how the morning went. He said, "Mom, they creep me out." So we had an opportunity to talk about how they were just like him, but they used wheels instead of feet.

It took a few months, but the proof that he was desensitized came during a day at a local lake where a nonprofit was teaching water skiing and jet skiing to people with both intellectual and physical disabilities. There was a woman in a wheelchair with her ambulatory husband. Sean was fascinated by them. He sat on the ground in front of her wheelchair for about 30 minutes having a great conversation—till I heard him start getting too personal. He asked, "Are you two married? For how long? How did you meet?" I was getting concerned that he was about to ask them if they had sex! So, I joined in the conversation and redirected the trajectory. But he was completely comfortable, probably *too* comfortable, and I realized the disability immersion program I had instituted a year earlier was effective.

So, heads-up, when you fully include your kids and nobody else does. Remember to supplement with outside activities involving peers who also have disabilities! And for those of you who did not choose inclusion? Can we play?

Cool Club

I wrote the following article for the National Down Syndrome Congress newsletter. I presented Cool Club to two conferences, encouraging parents to start one in their area.

Teens and Adults with Intellectual Disabilities Don't Need to Be Socially Isolated

By Sandra McElwee, Rancho Santa Margarita, California

With no social activities on the calendar and a long summer looming ahead, an idea was hatched. Dreading the inevitable boredom, 16 teens and their parents banded together to create something new—Cool Club. The Cool Club's mission is to provide a safe, fun environment where members are encouraged to develop trusting friendships, learn appropriate social and communication skills, and promote tolerance and patience between members and their families. One year later, Cool Club is a great success.

How it works

The concept is pretty simple. Most teenagers like to socialize with friends, and teens with intellectual disabilities (ID) are no different. But teens with ID may have less opportunity to hang out with peers without some assistance in planning and executing social gatherings. With Cool Club, families take 1 weekend to plan an evening activity for a group of teens. Being responsible for 1 weekend means 15 more weeks of fun planned by other parents. Even the busiest parents could muster up three times a year! So, two moms quickly set up a calendar and each family picked a weekend to host the group.

The moms also put together some rules about communication, supervision, and basic requirements that all families agreed to follow.

Since it was summer, there were a lot of pool parties and bowling was a hit, too. We quickly learned our group didn't like to sit quietly and watch a movie at the theater. They want to socialize with each other, laugh loudly, and high-five each other without disturbing other moviegoers. So, a movie in someone's home is better. Our teens like to do anything that other teens do—play miniature golf, hang out at the mall, eat at Benihana and other restaurants with an entertaining theme, and watch plays and sporting events!

Each week, the host family e-mails all club members with the day and date of the event (Friday or Saturday), location, including address and pertinent phone number, time to arrive and pick up, what the event will entail (bowling, party, swimming, etc.), and any special instructions, such as the amount of money needed, food for potlucks, etc. There must be a minimum of one man and one woman at every event, so the single moms and dads request another parent to help when it's their turn to host.

While their teens are at Cool Club, parents enjoy date nights or just have weekend time alone. This isn't a "babysitting" co-op, however. Parents can't leave siblings to potentially double the number of teens. The hosts, though, can have all of their other children there to help out. If a planned activity needs additional supervision, that information is included in the e-mail and another set of parents volunteer to help.

The format has been very manageable. Out of 16 teens, attendance averages eight to 10 per activity. Attendance is not required for every activity and several members have single parents and are not available every weekend. Our teens attend five different high schools. Many have participated on the same sports teams since they were children and some know each other from school. Several have a common friend in the group, but most are new friends. None had frequent social opportunities before Cool Club was founded and new friendships have bloomed.

All are welcome

We do not tolerate intolerance. Every teen in Cool Club has had an issue at some point in their lives. To accept everybody, no matter what, is what we look for in our communities, so we want to be the models of that acceptance. *Everybody* deserves the opportunity to have friends and fun, so everyone is welcome and accepted. We have a few members with behavioral issues, such as eloping or hitting. Parents know if their teen fits that description. If so, the teen is welcome to come with a parent in attendance. One young woman used to need her parents' presence. But now that she knows what is expected of her, she rises to the occasion and is able to come solo.

She is awesome!

What is the hardest part of Cool Club? Well, the original group had a couple of unreliable parents. When it was their week to host, they dropped their teens out of the group in lieu of hosting. All of the teens were bummed to have a weekend with nothing planned for them to do. For the rest of the parents, it was a reminder of what life was like *before* Cool Club. We are more dedicated than ever to continue!

Building on success

It's time for some new Cool Clubs to form. As other parents have found out about our Cool Club they've begged to have their teens join. We are committed to keeping the group size manageable, so we're helping other parents to start their own Cool Clubs.

The most difficult part of forming a new Cool Club is finding potential members who are interested in social activities. While everyone knows at least one other person with a disability, word of mouth only works to a certain extent. To find a larger group of prospective members I approached a local organization that serves clients with a range of disabilities, which allowed me to do a Cool Club presentation to clients and families. They advertised the event through e-mail blasts, forwarded around the county. I shared how our club started, and then I split them into groups by age—high school, transition age—and adult—and more Cool Clubs were formed! Ask your local DS association, school district's special education department, transition programs, Parent to Parent, or other organizations who serve clients with ID to help spread the word, too.

Because adults with ID also need the same social opportunities, I plan on starting some adult groups. I'd suggest limiting the group to about 12 since adults may have fewer social opportunities than teens and will attend every week.

It's been almost a year now, and I've planned three (manageable) events. My son hates to miss a Cool Club activity, and every Friday his questions start—*When is Cool Club? Who is doing it? What are we doing?* Parents find the teens are starting to plan (okay, dictate) their own activities and now our job is to follow through with the details!

As I finalize this book, Cool Club has been going on for 4 years, and there is no end in sight. Teens and adults with no social opportunities become depressed, and depression creates behaviors that nobody should have to endure.

Afterward

Success in the affairs of life often serves to hide one's abilities, whereas adversity frequently gives one an opportunity to discover them.
—Horace

As I finish this book and remember how I always told the educators that they just had to be smarter than Sean, I realize none of us were smarter than he. He always outsmarted us all, and today, he is extremely independent and still outsmarting Rick and me.

There is life after high school. As I finish this book, Sean is living a full and rich life. His week includes volunteering at our church's children's ministry—as a Sunday school teacher's assistant in the class for 6- and 7-year-olds with disabilities. He is a huge inspiration to the parents there. He takes classes at our local community college. He has no interest in academic classes and has enjoyed golf, bowling, dance, physical fitness, stretching, outdoor recreation, and acting classes. Monday through Friday he attends our district's transition program. They have taught him all of the bus routes. He now knows how to get around our community and the surrounding communities. The transition program also includes work experience. His work experience has put him in a few positions. He enjoyed working at our church's food bank—where he also volunteered to say the prayer when the volunteers finish their morning meeting. He has cleaned gym equipment, worked at a school preparing lunch for the students, and assisting a PE teacher, and on one day, he rolled silverware into napkins at Chili's. I say 1 day, because he quit and said he never wanted to do that again!

Sean also has had a personal trainer and regularly works out at the local 24-Hour Fitness. He completed his karate class by earning his black belt. The test was grueling. He had to spar with two black belts at once, and they didn't let him off easy. For a year he took an acting class at the Down Syndrome Association of Orange County. It was in that class that he finally began answering *"why"* questions— the one item on his IEP the entire time he was in school that he never achieved. Just proof to never give up on a goal!

He attends Young Life's Capernaum Club on Wednesday nights. Friday afternoon practices and Saturday he plays either Pop Warner Challenger Flag Football, or Little League's Challenger Baseball depending on the season. And he attends Cool Club either Friday or Saturday nights. There's a basketball league that he also plays in on Sunday afternoons. In his free time, Sean plays video games, watches TV, or by himself walks to the bus and goes wherever he wants to. I had to install an app on his iPhone to track his location without being too nosey and calling to ask him where he is.

One day during Christmas break he had quite the busy day. First, he went to the local grocery store to buy a new bus pass. Then he went to a fast-food restaurant for breakfast. His next stop after changing buses was the movie theatre where he saw a movie and bought lunch. After enjoying a movie, he took a bus to the bowling alley and threw a few frames. A couple of times he has taken the bus to his girlfriend's house, which took him 3½ hours and four bus changes. I'm thankful we live in a safe area.

He has survived all of the negativity from his high school and intermediate school years but is still cautious with new experiences until he knows the person in charge is nice and wants him there. He is preparing to move to Glennwood House of Laguna Beach, a new supported independent living facility that will house 50 adults with disabilities in 42 apartments.

Hindsight Is 20/20

*I can choose to let it define me, confine me, refine me, outshine me,
or I can choose to move on and leave it behind me. — Unknown*

After looking back on intermediate school and high school I can
either see a rosebush with thorns, or I can see a thornbush with roses.
I choose to see the roses first.

- ♥ The baseball team that embraced Sean for the whole 4 years.
- ♥ The incredible students who embraced Sean and literally
  went to bat for him in both baseball and drama, and in his
  bid for election.
- ♥ The hoards of students who hugged him as he arrived at any
  sporting event.
- ♥ The second case carrier who worked hard within the school
  to gain new opportunities for Sean

I saw so much character in the regular education students, and
really, they are the ones holding Sean's future in their hands. One day
they will be his coworkers and his managers.

Our school district has four high schools. For many years only
one of the high schools had housed all of the high school special day
classes on its campus. The elective teachers at that school were used
to including students with disabilities in their classes, and they had
seen the positive impact on the regular education students. Their Best
Buddies Club is SO HUGE they have a ratio of four buddies to one
special education student.

Sean did attend his neighborhood high school in the MOD classes that had around 12 students in each class. Most of those students
had mild learning disabilities. They did not want to be associated with
somebody who was truly *intellectually disabled*. Plus, Sean had never
been in class with these students in prior grades; consequently, he
had no friends in his core classes.

I was trying to change a school that didn't want to be changed.
I felt responsible for all of those students that were following Sean's

path from elementary school inclusion on to the high school. I wanted to pave the way, so their parents wouldn't have to fight or argue about anything, and I was concerned about what would happen when they were told "No" for the first time. Would they know where to turn? Would they acquiesce? Or would they seek out the resources to support continuing inclusion for their children?

I placed such a high importance on Sean's elementary school friends that I sacrificed his elective class potential (unknowingly) to attempt to nurture those relationships. Sadly, unless Sean simply *showed up* at a school activity, there were no true friendships. They were *nice* and allowed him to hang with them, but nobody ever called and invited him to do things—and when our Best Buddies began, his Best Buddy never called him, never came to our house to hang out, and never took him out anywhere. I was later told by a few of Sean's friends from elementary school that they had wondered where he went in eighth grade. Then they saw him here and there in high school, but never had classes with him again. They didn't think much about it, because the school was so huge, but they didn't realize that it was because the teachers didn't want him in their classes. Even though he was on campus, he may as well have been invisible because of his segregation.

If I would have sent him to the other high school he would have only known TWO people on that entire campus (from our church), but the elective teachers would have welcomed him into their classes. His horizons would have been broadened, and he would have had more educational experiences and sports team and extracurricular opportunities. He wouldn't have felt the rejection of the teachers. The Best Buddies Club would have made sure he met more students and had more friends. And I would have been able to enjoy his high school experience, instead of turning into a Mother From Hell.

But I couldn't see the options for the anger. I couldn't think about alternatives like switching schools, because *I was DETERMINED to CHANGE this school.*

So, even though inclusion *SHOULD BE* in your neighborhood

school, don't ignore the possibility to transfer to a school where you do not have to reinvent the wheel for your child if it's a better placement for his or her needs.

Positive vs. Punitive

Save us from those who walk in darkness and think it is light. Save us from those who are mean and think they are kind. Save us from those who destroy us as they claim to protect us. We desire to reason with our captors, who are physicians who do not heal, teachers who do not teach, caretakers who do not care, reasonable men who do not reason.—Burton Blatt

You can't legislate attitudes. And unlike the Wizard of Oz, you can't give someone a heart, courage, or a brain. I did learn that just like punitive didn't work for Sean, it also didn't work for the educators. Positive worked the best for both Sean and the educators—positive reinforcement of the good behaviors, ignoring the bad behaviors.

A big lesson I learned is that people can be jerks, and you can't make them be nice. There's no do-overs. But you can choose whether or not to let the jerks affect you. Shadows cannot exist without the light, and finding the light, seeking out the people who appreciate your child's gifts makes it much better. Good people in this world still find Sean, and I am blessed through osmosis.

The principal in Sean's high school was a good guy and was trying hard to change the school. I should have discussed my idea of filing the civil rights complaint with him, but I reacted to the constant injustices toward Sean and did it without consulting him. The last thing I wanted to do was make it harder for him to convert the school. I also didn't want to give the impression that parents of students with IEPs were going to be looking for every opportunity to file a suit. The IEP is a legal document for a reason. People don't just do the right thing without supporting laws. But I let my emotions and my negative thoughts and the growing paranoia win my head by filing the civil rights complaint and then the retaliation complaint. I felt that I needed to use the tools that the law provided for, but deep down, I knew that kindness and cooperation would have created better outcomes for all concerned.

Finally, I am ready to forgive—and you only have to forgive once. To resent you have to do it all day every day. You have to keep remembering the bad things. I'm making the choice to forgive and be happy again.

Hope for the Future

Among the things you can give and still keep are your word, a smile, and a grateful heart. —*Zig Ziglar*

I mentioned at the end of sixth grade that people who had children with special educational needs were moving to our neighborhood to send their children to the elementary school that Sean attended. Now there is a mass exodus. The incredible principal retired, and the psychologist was transferred to another school. Their amazing leadership was lost, and the new principal and the new psychologist actually started telling parents at their IEPs, "There are classes where your child belongs at another school." They completely undid everything that was accomplished. I ran into the speech therapist at the grocery store, and she lamented that the only students she was working with had lisps. The challenge was gone, the students at the school are losing out on inclusion and she told me the teachers were disappointed as well. Another parent told me the bullying there is unbearable.

But all hope is not lost! There is a new superintendent and a new director of special education. I met with the new director of special education, and he has a 3-year plan to bring our district into the world of inclusion at *every* school at *every* level! I have high hopes that he can accomplish this for the students coming up behind Sean and that no student and no parent has to endure what the parents of our time had to endure to simply gain an appropriate education for our children.

Will You Carry the Torch?

Faith is being sure of what we hope for and certain of what we do not see.—Hebrews 11:1NIV

There are times in your life that God gives you what seems like an impossible task. Have faith He will give you the strength to accomplish the task.

We first have been entrusted with our children who have disabilities. When your baby was born, you probably felt that raising this child would be an impossible task.

Now it's time for the inclusive education revolution to be completed. School districts have gotten away with immoral exclusion long enough. It is time for the change to be consistent throughout the country. But it is going to take parents of all children with disabilities to believe the evidence that their children and all their typical classmates will benefit from their presence.

The value of our children's lives hang in the balance. Babies diagnosed with Down syndrome by prenatal tests are at the most risk for being killed. The reason is that their potential parents know nobody with Down syndrome and have no knowledge of the potential that people with Down syndrome's lives hold. Without inclusion—in schools, in work, in communities, in activities, in life—our children become the best-kept secret, a secret that will die with our generation if we don't stand and require the law to be upheld.

Pastor Rick Warren encouraged our congregation during a sermon, "Faith is obeying when I don't understand it. Trust that God has a plan and can see what you cannot see."

If everything had been as easy as it was during elementary school, I probably would have never written this book. In a daily devotional, Pastor Rick wrote, "Your pain often reveals God's purpose for you. God never wastes a hurt! If you've gone through a hurt, he wants you to help other people going through that same hurt. He wants you to share it. God can use the problems in your life to give you a ministry to others. In fact, the very thing you're most ashamed of in your life and resent the most could become your greatest ministry in helping other people."

I pray the information in this book provides a catalyst for change in districts across the country. I pray that it encourages *you* as a parent of a child with a disability to step out in faith and give your child the best opportunity for independence. And I pray that this inspires *teachers* to see the true mantle of their power and ability to change lives for the better and learn how *not* to behave by the example of the negative secondary educators.

Moses went through many tests. You can be tested by prolonged pain. Our culture wants us to base everything on our feelings. It may not be easy, and I certainly didn't feel good when I was fighting for Sean—but even through the pain of hearing the discriminatory comments from people who are supposed to cherish and love teaching children, I kept up the good fight for not just my son but for your sons and daughters too. Keep up the fight—for the sake of your son or daughter and for those who will be allowed to be born in the future. A better world is in our hands.

Coming Summer 2014

WHO'S THE
Slow Learner?
ADVENTURES IN INDEPENDENCE

Sean McElwee lived a rich extracurricular life outside of his school day. *Adventures in Independence* is the sequel to *A Chronicle of Inclusion and Exclusion*. Additional stories backtrack to Sean's early years and the ways his parents supported and facilitated his life skills education to achieve the long term goal of independence.

- Hold on for the twists and turns as Sean's parents learned that he was adept at navigating bus routes.
- Ride the emotional roller coaster of courtship with an extra chromosome.
- Educational challenges continue as Sean's transition program refuses to individualize his program.
- The story culminates with Sean achieving his long term goal of moving into his own supported living apartment in a beach city in Southern California at only 19 years old.

CPSIA information can be obtained at www.ICGtesting.com
Printed in the USA
LVOW01s2139250615

443958LV00011B/118/P